"We all go to work with a relationship résumé that shapes how we feel about ourselves, how we trust, how we communicate, and how we manage conflict. *Getting Along* offers a clear guide to navigating the murky waters of relationships at work."

—**ESTHER PEREL,** psychotherapist; *New York Times* bestselling author; and host, *Where Should We Begin?* and *How's Work?* podcasts

"Amy Gallo is that rare combination of a first-class thinker and a wonderful writer. *Getting Along* tells us how to work well, even with that jerk we wish would get another job. Highly recommend."

—**DANIEL GOLEMAN,** bestselling author, *Emotional Intelligence* and *Social Intelligence*

"*Getting Along* is both practical and wise. And Amy Gallo is exactly the person you want by your side for the next step of your professional journey. If you're just looking to win your next argument or convince people to see things your way, this book is not for you. To put its wise advice to work, you have to actually care about what others think. You have to want to learn."

—**AMY C. EDMONDSON,** Novartis Professor of Leadership and Management, Harvard Business School; author, *The Fearless Organization*

"An accessible, actionable book about how to navigate your toughest collaborations—and turn them into some of your most rewarding work relationships."

—**ADAM GRANT,** #1 *New York Times* bestselling author, *Think Again*; host, TED *WorkLife* podcast

"A must-have for everyone in the workforce. Amy Gallo's handbook is a treasure chest of practical, evidence-based tips. I will be referring to and recommending this essential guide for years to come!"

—**DOLLY CHUGH,** author, *The Person You Mean to Be* and *A More Just Future*

"If you've ever lost sleep over a relationship at work, this book is for you. Amy Gallo has written a research-backed guide filled with relatable stories to help you turn the most complicated interactions into something to learn from."

—**LINDA A. HILL,** Wallace Brett Donham Professor of Business Administration, Harvard Business School; coauthor, *Collective Genius* and *Being the Boss*

"In this wise and deeply researched book, Amy Gallo has presented a powerful and actionable framework for dealing with difficult coworkers. No matter your situation, better working relationships start here."

—**DANIEL H. PINK,** #1 *New York Times* bestselling author, *The Power of Regret, WHEN*, and *DRIVE*

"*Getting Along* is the most useful and engaging book I've ever read about how to deal with the difficult relationships we all face at work. Amy Gallo identifies eight troubling characters that are found in every organization—such as the insecure boss, the know-it-all, and the tormentor—and blends research, wonderful stories, and her compelling voice to show how to make your relationships with difficult coworkers healthier and change them for the better. And she shows why doing all that work is worth your trouble."

—**ROBERT I. SUTTON,** bestselling author, *The No Asshole Rule, Good Boss, Bad Boss*, and coauthor, *Scaling Up Excellence*

"Amy Gallo has written a deeply thoughtful and very practical book about our humanity at work. It guides us wisely and compassionately in how to live and work with 'difficult people'—including those difficulties we create in our own minds."

—**MATTHIAS BIRK,** Adjunct Associate Professor for Leadership, NYU Wagner Graduate School of Public Service; Global Director, Partner Development, White & Case

"Finally, a no-nonsense, data-driven, practical guide for improving our ability to deal with difficult colleagues and bosses, no matter how challenging they are. Amy Gallo is just brilliant!"

—**TOMAS CHAMORRO-PREMUZIC,** Chief Innovation Officer, Manpower Group; professor, Business Psychology, University College London and

Columbia University; and author, *Why Do So Many Incompetent Men Become Leaders?*

"*Getting Along* is a nuanced, practical, and much-needed guide for how to handle your most difficult colleagues. Filled with actionable strategies and all-too-relatable examples, this book will transform the way you navigate relationships at work."

—**LIZ FOSSLIEN AND MOLLIE WEST DUFFY,** *Wall Street Journal* bestselling coauthors, *No Hard Feelings* and *Big Feelings*

"Amy Gallo provides incredibly valuable insight into how to navigate challenging relationships in the workplace. The practical, evidence-based approach will be a big help for people at all career stages."

—**KARYN TWARONITE,** a global leader in Diversity, Equity, and Inclusiveness

"*Getting Along* offers keen insight, compassion, and a practical road map to making the most of challenging work relationships. You won't just learn how to deal with difficult people, you'll learn how you can be a better coworker."

—**DORIE CLARK,** *Wall Street Journal* bestselling author, *The Long Game*; Adjunct Professor of Business Administration, Duke University Fuqua School of Business

"A must-read for anyone looking to level-up the quality of their work relationships—and their work lives. Gallo not only delivers actionable strategies for dealing with the most challenging work personalities (yes, even *that* one!), she drills home *why* navigating these relationships effectively is critical to your professional success."

—**HEIDI CHO,** digital media executive and builder of high-performing teams

"People are both the best and worst thing about work, and [this book] helps navigate that reality. It's an overdue and important discussion, because you can't have a good quality of life without a good quality of work life."

—**JIM MCCARTHY,** cofounder and CEO, Stellar Live; cofounder and former CEO, Goldstar; and cofounder, TEDxBroadway

GETTING ALONG

GETTING ALONG

HOW TO WORK WITH ANYONE
(*EVEN DIFFICULT PEOPLE*)

AMY GALLO

Harvard Business Review Press

Boston, Massachusetts

Library of Congress Cataloging-in-Publication Data

Names: Gallo, Amy (Business writer), author.
  Title: Getting along : how to work with anyone (even difficult people) / Amy Gallo.
  Description: Boston, Massachusetts : Harvard Business Review Press, [2022] | Includes index.
  Identifiers: LCCN 2022020652 (print) | LCCN 2022020653 (ebook) | ISBN 9781647821067 (hardcover) | ISBN 9781647821074 (epub)
  Subjects: LCSH: Conflict management. | Interpersonal conflict. | Problem employees—Psychology. | Psychology, Industrial.
  Classification: LCC HD42 .G256 2022 (print) | LCC HD42 (ebook) | DDC 658.4/053—dc23/eng/20220609
  LC record available at https://lccn.loc.gov/2022020652
  LC ebook record available at https://lccn.loc.gov/2022020653

ISBN: 978-1-64782-106-7
eISBN: 978-1-64782-107-4

To D & H

CONTENTS

Introduction   1
Can't We All Just Get Along?

PART ONE

LAYING THE GROUNDWORK
FOR GETTING ALONG

1 Why Work Relationships Are Worth the Trouble   19
Good or bad, they matter.

2 Your Brain on Conflict   31
How our minds often work against us.

PART TWO

THE ARCHETYPES

3 The Insecure Boss   49
"I'm great at my job . . . right?"

4 The Pessimist   67
"This will never work."

5 The Victim   87
"Why does this always happen to me?"

6 The Passive-Aggressive Peer   99
"Fine. Whatever."

7 The Know-It-All   117
   "Well, actually . . ."

8 The Tormentor   137
   "I suffered and you should too."

9 The Biased Coworker   157
   "Why are you so sensitive?"

10 The Political Operator   183
   "If you aren't moving up, you're falling behind."

11 Nine Principles for Getting Along with *Anyone*   203
   Change is possible.

PART THREE

PROTECTING YOURSELF

12 When All Else Fails   223
   Don't give up—yet.

13 Approaches That Rarely Work   233
   They'll only make things worse.

14 Taking Care   241
   Your well-being is priority number one.

Appendix: Who Am I Dealing With?   253
Figuring out which archetype(s) your coworker fits into.

Notes   257
Index   273
Acknowledgments   279
About the Author   283

GETTING ALONG

INTRODUCTION

Can't We All Just Get Along?

Early in my career, I took a job reporting to someone who had a reputation for being difficult. I'll call her Elise. Plenty of people warned me that Elise would be hard to work with, and I believed them—I just thought I could handle it. I prided myself on being able to get along with anyone. I didn't let people get under my skin. I could see the best in everyone.

I was in the job for less than two months before I was ready to quit.

Elise was even worse than I expected. She worked long days and on weekends. While she didn't explicitly ask her team to do the same, she often followed up at 8:30 a.m. on a request she'd made at 6:00 p.m. the night before. Her expectations for what I could get done in a day were wildly unreasonable. Each time she asked me to take on something new, I would explain that doing so would displace another "high priority" project that she'd assigned and labeled urgent the week before. She would say, "Why are you even spending time on that?"

The part I struggled with most was her tendency to talk badly about my teammates, questioning their work ethic and commitment to the company. She would regularly scroll colleagues' calendars and point out how little they'd gotten done when they'd had a meeting-free day. I had to assume that Elise was criticizing me behind my back as well.

The last straw came on a Sunday evening, three months after I started working for her, when I was lamenting how quickly the weekend had gone by. I had purposely stayed away from work, not even peeking at my email, but it didn't feel like I had taken a break. Instead, I had spent an inordinate amount of time *thinking* about Elise—while walking my dog, during a birthday party I'd taken my daughter to, and when I woke up in the middle of the night worried about what Monday might bring.

My relationship with my boss had invaded my psyche and, slowly, over time, had become more important—or at least more time-consuming—than my relationships with the people I cared about most.

Of course, it's not uncommon to think about our jobs outside of work hours, especially as the boundaries between our home lives and work lives continue to blur. We worry over decisions made (and not made), an overflowing inbox, and whether our work has enough meaning. But the thing that I agonize about most is my interactions with my colleagues, especially those who push my buttons.

I know I'm not alone. An overwhelming majority of people report working with someone they find difficult. One study found that 94 percent of people reported working with a toxic person in the last five years, and 87 percent said that team culture had suffered as a result.[1] In a survey of two thousand American workers, other researchers found that one in three people had left a job "due to an annoying or arrogant coworker."[2] In that same study, respondents reported that their number one source of tension at work was interpersonal relationships.

It's All about Our Relationships

When it comes to what makes people happy at work, experts often talk about meaningful work, a sense of accomplishment, knowing we're having an impact on others. But, for me, it's always been about the people—the connections I have with my coworkers, the regard for the leaders I've worked for, the rapport with the people I've managed, and the mutual respect with my clients. Whether I have a good day or a bad day often depends on who I interacted with and how it went.

Esther Perel, the psychotherapist and relationship expert, says that there are two pillars of our lives: *love* and *work*.[3] In each, we seek belonging, meaning, and fulfillment. And our relationships in these realms matter. Our jobs are where we spend our days—as a result, they're also where we have some of our most intense and complicated relationships.

Of course, it would be great if we got along with everyone we worked with. And I have had some amazing friendships with co-workers. Take my former consulting firm colleague who became a lifelong friend after we got stuck sharing a hotel room and stayed up talking late into the night discovering surprising connections before a client meeting. She was one of the first people to visit after my daughter was born, and I gave a toast at her wedding. Or when I reported to a college friend at *Harvard Business Review*—a setup that we both approached with some trepidation. We established rules to help us make sure that work wouldn't impact our friendship, and that she wouldn't be perceived as playing favorites. Some of these rules we followed with discipline; others, in retrospect, seemed naive. But that discussion about boundaries was enormously important. Over the seven years that we worked together, we encountered a few hiccups, and we worked through them. But overall, there was mostly upside. Our relationship is now stronger for all of the time we have spent together—a rarity in adulthood. And we have a new pillar of shared interest: our work.

These relationships made work more interesting, engaging, and joyful. I also believe they made me better at my job. Endless research backs me up. In her book, *The Business of Friendship*, Shasta Nelson says that "all the studies show that liking whom we work with is one of the most significant predictors for our engagement, retention, safety, and productivity. . . . There isn't a single study that shows we perform better, or are happier, without friends at work."[4]

Being besties with our coworkers isn't always possible, or even preferable. When I accepted the job reporting to Elise, I wanted to work with someone I respected and looked up to, someone who could mentor me. I wasn't hoping we'd be friends, but I also didn't want to cringe whenever I saw her name pop up on my phone.

Unfortunately, that's what I got. As the months wore on, each week came to feel like the same story, played out over and over again. I would vow to care less about how she treated me, or to shower her with kindness in an effort to smooth out her sharp edges. On a good week, I could hold on to that intention. But the minute she insinuated I wasn't working hard enough, all those good intentions flew out the window. I would behave passive-aggressively, agreeing to do something but not getting it done on time, or complain about her to my teammates.

Too often, we just put up with difficult people like Elise. This is true whether we're in our first job or our tenth. We figure that since we don't get to choose our coworkers, we have no option other than to endure less-than-ideal or even toxic relationships. But feeling trapped in a negative dynamic makes it hard to be our best selves. We roll our eyes. We make a scathing remark we can't take back. We react in regrettable ways that violate our values, degrade the quality of our work, and make the situation worse. The resulting stress can be hard to escape.

Remote work—which more of us are doing than ever before—can exacerbate tricky interactions. We feel disconnected from our colleagues, only seeing them in tiny squares on screens. Text-based communications breed misunderstanding. Even simple disagreements get blown out of proportion. It's far too easy, in the heat of the moment, to type out a retort that you wouldn't say if you were looking someone in the eye. And it's harder to repair a situation gone awry. We can't rely on a serendipitous hallway conversation or a laugh by the coffee machine to smooth things over. Instead, in virtual meetings, most people stay on mute or even turn off their camera, making our interactions feel transactional and less human.

Can We Trust Our Instincts?

When we start a new job or take on a more challenging role, we give ourselves time to learn the ropes. We don't expect to know everything right out of the gate, especially when the new job requires skills that we don't yet have.

For some reason, we don't cut ourselves the same slack when it comes to getting along with difficult people. We think we should know how to do it—instinctively. After all, we've been interacting with people our whole lives, many of whom have challenged us (think of that relative who drives you up the wall or your frenemy from high school). I don't know about you, but no one ever sat me down and said, "Here's how you push back on an aggressive know-it-all," or "Try this approach for dealing with an incessant naysayer." I never took a class on handling the political operator in my office, and no mentor shared advice on what to do if I found myself working for an incompetent boss.

As my story about reporting to Elise makes plain, our natural instincts don't always help us deal with these more challenging encounters constructively. In retrospect, I can see how my mind was getting in the way. My identity as a competent, well-liked person was threatened, and in response, my brain formed a narrative: that I was an innocent victim and Elise was completely unreasonable. And then, I saw every interaction as evidence that this story was true.

Research shows that my reaction was neither unusual nor entirely voluntary. Conflict has a number of documented physiological and emotional effects that make it tough to remain calm and clear-eyed in the moment. That obnoxious boss might remind us of a previous manager who made our lives miserable, or a hypercritical parent, or how we had to fight for attention as a kid. So we feel threatened. Research demonstrates that even mild instances of stress can cause a rapid and dramatic loss of prefrontal cognitive abilities. We have less access to higher-order thinking, which governs our thoughts, attention, behavior, emotions, and our decision-making. Put simply, we don't think very clearly, and we lose our ability to make sound judgments, which is not a recipe for productive action.

Instead of taking constructive steps, we get caught up in our heads. We spend time worrying, trying to avoid the instigator, and even withdrawing from work. We're less creative and make slower, poorer decisions.[5] And we're more likely to make errors, even deadly mistakes. A survey of 4,500 doctors, nurses, and other hospital personnel found that 71 percent of respondents linked negative behavior, such as abusive, condescending, or insulting conduct, to medical errors, and 27 percent tied such behavior to patient deaths.[6]

We're not the only ones who suffer when we don't have positive relationships with coworkers. Our organizations do, too. It's overwhelming to think about the amount of time, money, and resources spent on dealing with interpersonal conflict at work—the wasted energy and the impact on performance. A study of thousands of teams across industries, sectors, and geographies found that 70 percent of the variance between the lowest-performing teams and the highest-performing teams correlates to the quality of team relationships.[7] I've seen real-life examples of the findings from this research, and you probably have too.

"You Won't Believe My Coworker"

Some years ago, I wrote a book about conflict at work. Since then, I've been lucky to speak to thousands of people, in virtual environments, conference halls, and in-person workshops about strategies for managing tension and difficult conversations in the workplace. I've noticed that the same thing tends to happen after every event. In the public Q&A— or more often, by the elevator or in the private chat on the side of the screen— someone will ask for help, often sheepishly. They will say . . .

"I have this one coworker . . ."

"I'm struggling with my manager . . ."

"You won't believe what my direct report did . . ."

I've heard some unbelievable stories: there was the founder who screamed every time someone used a phrase he hated; the man who co-opted his colleague's desk during his vacation; the colleague who stopped speaking to her officemate for three months because he'd accidentally left her off a meeting invite; the manager who sent one of her direct reports fifty emails (with the read receipt turned on) before 9:00 a.m. and then called her at 9:15 a.m. to ask why she hadn't responded to all of them; the CEO who expected one of her charges to work on her honeymoon and asked another to reschedule his wedding so it wouldn't conflict with an important trade show.

Some of these examples may sound familiar to you. The ugly truth is that there are people in every workplace—many of whom have earned respect and positions of power—who behave in ways that are thoughtless, ambiguous, irrational, even sometimes downright malicious. And yet the good-faith efforts of many of my post-event lingerers to turn dysfunctional relationships around have repeatedly failed: attempts to play nice were met with derision, endeavors to involve higher-ups backfired, or boundaries that were clearly set were violated anyway. Why?

Through my own experience with difficult coworkers, as well as the extensive research I've done on the topic of conflict, I've come to believe that much of the advice about navigating friction—including some of the principles I outlined in my previous book—is based on several faulty assumptions: that one set of tactics will work regardless of the type of difficult behavior you're dealing with; that everyone experiences and perceives challenging interpersonal dynamics in the same way, regardless of race, gender, or other facets of their identity; and that readers will be able to take generalized, high-level theory about conflict and apply it successfully to their own unique situations. Proposed solutions are often neat and tidy, one-dimensional, oversimplified, whereas real life is messy and complicated.

That's why I wanted to write this book: to provide a more nuanced, practical, evidence-based approach, one that acknowledges the complexity of unhealthy relationships at work and the immense discomfort they can create. I want to help people who feel trapped, aren't sure what to do, and have perhaps tried some of the usual advice and found that it didn't work for them.

A New Approach to Challenging Relationships

One of the fundamental flaws I've encountered in my personal and professional experience (not to mention in much of the literature on conflict resolution) is the assumption that all difficult people can be lumped together into one broad category of "jerks" and treated as a monolith. But let's face it: there are many, many forms of bad behavior, and the strategies you need to effectively collaborate with challenging coworkers will depend on the specific behaviors you're dealing with. That's why this book identifies eight common archetypes of difficult coworkers (more on that later) and provides advice tailored to dealing with each one. At the same time, it's important to acknowledge that some people defy categorization, so I also offer principles that will work no matter what type of bad behavior you're dealing with.

Throughout the book, I've tried to attend to issues of race, gender, and other identity categories. Many books ignore how bias plays into and complicates dynamics between colleagues. This book doesn't shy away from these issues. Not everyone experiences the workplace in the same way—and particular groups are often the targets of incivility to a disproportionate degree. I try to note places where the research shows inequities in the ways people are treated and variability in the effectiveness of deploying certain tactics among different groups. For example, calling out a passive-aggressive peer might be an approach that would work better for a white man than it would for a Latinx woman because of the narrow range of behaviors that are considered "appropriate" for women of color in the workplace.

I am a white woman with plenty of privilege, and I see the complexities of discrimination from my own biased perspective. Inevitably, I will get some things wrong. But if we hope to make progress, I believe we have to make identity part of the conversation around relationships at work, even at the risk of doing an imperfect job.

Another shortcoming of much of the advice out there is that it isn't practical enough—it's too high-level, too abstract, too general. My goal with this book is for you to be able to act *now*. You shouldn't have to do the work of trying to figure out how theoretical concepts can be put into practice. I've done that for you, drawing both on what I've seen work in my experience and also on academic research. I've integrated findings and advice from a variety of fields—neuroscience, emotional intelligence, negotiation, management science—to help you navigate these problem relationships in a productive and nuanced way.

My final and overarching wish is that this book will help you build interpersonal resilience, the ability to bounce back more quickly from negative interactions and feel less stress when you are deep in them. Conflict at work is inevitable—it's part of being human, but I think we can do better than simply put up with it or survive. The strategies presented in the eight archetype chapters, along with the nine principles outlined in chapter 11, are designed to help you work with just about anyone. And in the process of learning how to transform your most difficult relationships, you'll develop the skills and confidence you need to improve the quality of *all* of your relationships. As a bonus, the higher levels of self-awareness and enhanced emotional intelligence that you will gain will also make you a better leader. To be successful at any level in any industry, these are necessary skills, so being able to resolve conflicts and get along with anyone will boost your career prospects, too.

There is no denying that the stress caused by negative interactions with coworkers can affect our productivity, make work miserable, and even bleed into other aspects of our lives. But we don't have to throw up our hands or hope that a higher-up will take note and intervene. We can learn why problem colleagues behave the way they do, master tactics for dealing with their most difficult traits, and ultimately decide when to persist in our efforts or to walk away. With the advice in this book, you'll be able to put work conflict in its place, freeing up valuable time and mental capacity for the things that really matter to you.

The insights, tools, and techniques I offer are based on interviews I've done with academics, social psychologists, management experts, and neuroscientists over the past fourteen years. I also spoke to people who have been in your shoes, facing tough work relationships. These people shared their sometimes painful experiences with me via email or filled-out surveys. These stories appear throughout the book, with names and details changed for privacy. Through these personal stories, you will meet many individuals who were able to transform their relationships, turning enemies into allies. Others developed coping mechanisms to make the situation more tolerable, and still others made the tough call to leave their jobs to preserve their mental health.

The Archetypes

This book is structured around eight archetypes, each representing a common type of difficult person:

- The insecure boss

- The pessimist

- The victim

- The passive-aggressive peer

- The know-it-all

- The tormentor (*who you'd hoped would be a mentor*)

- The biased coworker

- The political operator

While these archetypes are likely to feel familiar and I'm sure that coworkers immediately come to mind who fit them, I also want to stress that these labels have limits. It can be helpful to identify the type of behavior you're dealing with—passive-aggression, for example—but it's rarely useful to pigeonhole a colleague as, say, a "passive-aggressive jerk." That kind of attitude will just cement the negative dynamic between you, rather than giving it a chance to improve. Archetypes can help you assess the situation, but the real work comes when you move beyond them to a productive frame of mind, allowing room for the possibility that the person can change their ways and perhaps that you've even misinterpreted their behavior or misassigned meaning to their actions.

It's also important that we don't diagnose people who fall into certain archetypes with psychological disorders. I've heard people throw around terms like "narcissistic personality disorder" and even "psychopath" when talking about their difficult coworkers. But resist the urge to play armchair psychologist. As Kelly Greenwood, the founder and CEO of Mind Share Partners, a nonprofit focused on changing the culture of workplace, told me, "You never know what's going on with people or what's causing their behavior. Folks with mental health conditions are sometimes defined as 'difficult' but that only furthers the stigma against them and often isn't the case."[8]

Which leads me to my final and, in many ways, most important point: I am going to challenge you, throughout this book, to see your own actions and behaviors through the lens of these archetypes as well. Who hasn't acted like a know-it-all on occasion? Or fallen into the victim role at times? Admitting that our coworkers are flawed, but probably aren't evil, and that we aren't infallible ourselves is essential to getting along. Advice that encourages self-awareness and leaning toward empathy and understanding will show up again and again in the pages to come. In fact, I'm going to share stories in which I realized that *I* was the jerk!

A Road Map for Better Relationships at Work

In this book, I'll walk you through how to find your own ways of getting along, whether you're just starting out in your career or you've already encountered your fair share of tricky coworkers. It's tempting to think you can just ignore your difficult colleague or not let their behavior bother you, but that rarely works. In chapter 1, I'll talk about the research on the importance of relationships at work and why it's worth your time and effort to try to make them better, even when they seem irredeemable.

The next step is to turn inward and better understand your own reactions to your problem coworker. Why is this relationship looming so large in your mind? Why can't you just let it go? In chapter 2, I'll talk about what's going on in your brain when you're embroiled in conflict. By understanding the chemical processes at work, you can learn to recognize and overcome your brain's fight-or-flight instinct and find a productive way forward with a clearer head. This process includes adopting the right mindset, raising your self-awareness, and managing your reactions so you don't escalate the situation instead of defusing it.

Then, in chapters 3 through 10, I introduce the eight archetypes. I delve into the research, including the psychological underpinnings of each brand of bad behavior and the motivation behind it. Why does your difficult coworker behave the way they do? What do they gain from acting out? Understanding the root causes of their behavior will make it easier to come up with a plan of action. I share tactics that have been shown to work in studies, in experiments, and in practice. And because it's often hard to know what to say when tensions are running high, I've included sample language that will help you find the right words to put the odds in your favor.

The eight archetypes are not meant to be an exhaustive list of the types of people you might struggle with in your workplace. It's possible that you have a coworker who doesn't fit into any of these categories or perhaps spans several of them. Pick the archetype that fits your colleague most closely or read a few of the chapters and choose a handful of tactics you want to experiment with. And, if you're not sure which of the archetypes you're dealing with, you can use the table in the appendix to identify their behaviors and see which category they might fall in.

Since some colleagues do defy categorization, in chapter 11 I'll share nine principles that will help you navigate conflict with any coworker, regardless of whether they fit neatly into one of the eight archetypes or not. In fact, these principles form the foundation for responding productively to difficult colleagues, establishing appropriate boundaries, and building stronger, more fulfilling relationships at work. These are the concepts that I return to over and over no matter the interpersonal issue I'm facing.

I don't pretend that these strategies will work 100 percent of the time. When your efforts at thoughtful self-examination and conflict resolution fail, it's time to batten down the hatches and focus on protecting yourself. In chapter 12, I'll talk about how to safeguard your career, your reputation, and your ability to do your job without losing your mind. Chapter 13 is focused on avoiding certain tactics that are tempting to try but rarely work. And, because dealing with a colleague you find difficult can be exhausting, demoralizing, and stressful—and taking the high road is even more taxing—the last chapter is dedicated to strategies that prioritize your well-being.

Will Your Colleague Change?

Much of the advice I give throughout the book requires you to be "the adult in the room." If you're looking to win a years- or months-long battle with your colleague, this isn't the book for you. The suggestions here are aimed at addressing problematic relationships in a nuanced, empathy-driven way. It's not about beating them at their own game or even outstrategizing them—it's about experimenting with different tactics to find solutions for your particular situation *and* that feel right for you. Sometimes trying something new, even something small, can shift the dynamic between you and a coworker who gets under your skin. The key is to recognize that your colleague is unlikely to transform into a different person. Ultimately, you have little say over whether and how much someone else is willing to change.

Of course, there will be times that your efforts won't be rewarded. In those cases, you don't need to be passive and accept the mistreatment. Take a proactive approach to protecting yourself by using some of the tactics I outline in chapters 12 and 14.

My relationship with Elise all those years ago never was as rewarding as I hoped it would be. But I didn't walk away—not immediately. I stayed in the job for several years. I worked hard at finding compassion for her and even recognized aspects of her in myself. Once I established boundaries about when and how I would interact with her and stopped thinking of her as the enemy and saw her as a flawed human instead, my job no longer felt like a daily slog. I spent less time ruminating about her. Elise didn't turn into the boss I wanted, but I found a way to get along with her until I was ready to move on to my next opportunity. And through that experience I learned what I could control: my own attitude, reactions, and approach.

These are contentious times. Certainly on a societal level, but inside workplaces, too. People take impassioned stands on issues that pertain to work and those that don't. Employees from different generations are working side by side and making lots of unpleasant assumptions about one another. There are more initiatives than ever before aimed at leveling the playing field for women, people of color, and other underestimated groups at work—and some people feel alienated or left behind by these efforts.

At the same time, I am heartened that we're talking more openly about relationships and emotions at work. We have "work spouses" and "office BFFs." We're acknowledging that we have deep and meaningful relationships with our colleagues, and that we don't leave our emotional selves behind when we walk into an office or log on to our laptop. Work is no longer a place we clock in and out of, but it's where we find and forge connections.

Now is the perfect moment to focus on the skills we need to navigate the often-tricky terrain of getting along with others. If you're reading these pages, you've taken an important first step: you're willing to give understanding and reconciliation a shot. I cannot promise that you will always get what you want. You may need to find ways to coexist, or bide your time until you can move teams, departments, or even jobs. My hope though is that the advice in this book will help you to act with authenticity, in line with your values to improve your work life. I believe that with commitment, self-awareness, and empathy, you can learn to get along with anyone, even the people who irritate and provoke you.

We can all have stronger and healthier relationships at work. Let's begin.

PART ONE

LAYING THE GROUNDWORK FOR GETTING ALONG

1

Why Work Relationships Are Worth the Trouble

Good or bad, they matter.

"It's just work."

I cringe recalling how many times I said that to my friends—or myself—during my first decade in the workforce. It was always a well-intended piece of advice, aimed at getting the other person (or me) to care less, detach a bit from what was bothering them, or walk away from a conflict before things got really heated.

But what I eventually learned is that work is rarely "just work." For better or worse, it's where we form our identities, feed our egos (or take hits to them), derive self-worth, seek community, and ideally, find meaning and fulfillment. And we do all of that alongside our colleagues.

When our relationships with people at work are strong, they are a source of energy, support, joy, and growth. But when they fracture, they cause us anguish, frustration, and even grief. Unhealthy dynamics with colleagues undermine our sense of trust and safety and our ability to do our jobs. They can even make us question our talents, competence, and sanity.

Take this story, shared by a friend about her father, who has since passed away. He was a scientist who loved his job at a pharmaceutical lab. He was devoted to his family and, as an introvert, valued his time alone. After work and on the weekends, he'd spend hours tinkering, mostly with old clocks, in his garage workshop. He told his kids that he cared about his work deeply, but he wasn't there to make friends. "Keep your head down and focus on what you're meant to do" was his advice.

Then, twelve years before he retired, he got a new boss who was incredibly passive-aggressive and drove him up a wall. Their relationship became a huge source of stress for him. At night, he'd come home frustrated by his interactions with this manager, eaten up by things she said and did, and worried about whether he'd reacted appropriately. My friend said that her father's preoccupation with his boss colored the last decade of his career, and the resulting stress probably took years off his life.

Could this man have been friends with his manager rather than constantly at odds? I doubt it. Remember, he was an introvert who wasn't interested in making friends. But his experience is a good reminder that we have no choice: we *do* have relationships at work, and they impact our happiness and our performance. That's why it's important that we tend to not only the relationships that energize us and make it fun to go to work, but the ones that push our buttons—or worse.

Work Relationships Loom Large in Our Lives

The irony is that in the early part of my career, while I was trying very hard to tell myself that my relationships with coworkers weren't that important, I was also meeting up with colleagues outside work, going to their houses for dinner parties, and forming what would become decades-long friendships.

Like my friend's father, the scientist, I couldn't avoid becoming entangled with my coworkers, and neither can you. Why is that exactly?

For one, because we work *a lot*. Most employed adults spend more hours, either virtually or in person, with coworkers than with family or nonwork friends.

In the United States, the average workweek has gotten longer over the past few decades, and we're working more weeks per year (an average of 46.8 weeks in 2015, up from 43 in 1980). These increases add up to an additional month of work in a year.[1] We even work when we're not supposed to. Data from the 2018 American Time Use survey shows that 30 percent of full-time employees report working on weekends and holidays.[2] Companies that study email traffic confirm that while people send fewer emails on holidays than on workdays, they're still sending a lot.[3]

Technology has compounded the problem, making it not only possible but often standard procedure to work anytime of day, wherever we are. Soon after I got my first smartphone, I was emailing my boss while walking my dog, and I was convinced I'd achieved multitasking nirvana. It no longer mattered if I was at my desk in my home office or at the dog park or at a coffee shop down the street. I could work from anywhere. Of course, by now (and thanks to a global pandemic), we're all familiar with the downsides of this phenomenon: chiefly, that we're always "on."

This constant availability means we're thinking about our jobs and the people associated with them, including peers, direct reports, clients, bosses, and senior leaders, more of the time. We might be anxious about our friends and colleagues who are at risk of losing their jobs in a reorganization, for instance, or about the fact that a pessimistic coworker is trying to torpedo our new initiative, or whether a client is going to come through with a contract. These are big, consuming concerns, and when we shut off our computers at 5:00 p.m. (or 6:00 p.m. or 7:00 p.m. or later), we typically don't put these worries away.

Over the past several decades, work-related stress has increased dramatically. Emily Heaphy, a professor at the University of Massachusetts, Amherst, who studies work relationships, told me, "There has been an increase in economic insecurity that makes people nervous and anxious about their work, so they are more attentive to it than people have been in the past."[4]

When you're struggling with a difficult coworker, it's tempting to write off the importance of relationships at work, to think, or even hope, that you can avoid them. But you can't. Professional connections make or break your experience on the job. And success in almost every role depends on getting along with others. The research on this is clear: if you want to thrive at work—perform your best, be engaged and productive, and think creatively and expansively—pay attention to your relationships.

The Case for Having Friends at Work

Am I advocating for making friends at work? In a book about dealing with difficult colleagues? Hear me out. It's not because I think your insecure manager or your passive-aggressive peer is going to become your BFF. But if you, like the younger me, don't believe that work is an appropriate place to make friends, I hope the research will convince you otherwise.

As Vivek Murthy, the US surgeon general, says in his book, *Together*, friendships are fundamentally connected to professional success and "it's in our relationships that we find the emotional sustenance and power we need to thrive."[5]

Social connections are a predictor of cognitive functioning, resilience, and engagement. We know that teams of friends perform better, that people with supportive coworkers report less stress, that being close with colleagues increases information- and idea-sharing, self-confidence, and learning, and that workers in mundane jobs are just as likely to feel satisfied and fulfilled as those with inspiring jobs if they invest in social connections.[6]

When you're working virtually, relationships may feel more expendable. If I'm sitting with my laptop at my kitchen table, does it matter if I feel connected to my colleagues? But research shows that connections to colleagues are just as critical in remote work environments. A survey of over twelve thousand people in the United States, Germany, and India, during the coronavirus shutdowns, found that respondents who were working at home during the pandemic reported that they were less productive on things like working in teams and interacting with clients—tasks that required collaboration with others. And there was a link between that productivity loss and work relationships. Of those who reported feeling less connected to their colleagues while working remotely, 80 percent said they were also less productive.[7]

Here are just a few of my other favorite findings about the benefits of friendship at work:

- Gallup, one of the leading researchers of workplace culture, has been asking about friendship in its studies for decades and has long been reporting a relationship between having a "best friend at work" and employee engagement. Its recent data shows that just 30 percent of employees reported having a "best friend" at work. But those who did were seven times more likely to "be engaged in their jobs, be better at engaging customers, produce higher quality work, have higher well-being." Also, they "are less likely to get injured on the job." In contrast, those who said they don't have a best friend in the workplace had just a one-in-twelve chance of being engaged.[8]

- Friendships are often good for your career, too. A research team at Rutgers University found that groups of colleagues who thought of one another as friends got higher scores on their performance reviews.[9]

- Having friends at work can also guard against burnout and make you more resilient. A group of researchers asked students wearing heavy backpacks at the base of a hill to guess how steep it was. Participants who were with a friend gave lower estimates than those who were alone.[10] One of the researchers explained in *Virginia Magazine*: "What we are finding is that things that we have always thought of as having metaphorical value, like friendship, actually affect our physiology. Social support changes how we perceive the world and how our bodies work."[11] In other words, we're better able to deal with stress and setbacks when we have positive relationships at work.

This last finding resonates deeply with me. At the beginning of the Covid-19 pandemic, my colleague Gretchen sent me a candle. I'll admit that I never really understood why people bothered with scented candles—do I really want my house to smell like a pine tree? But Gretchen was a fan, and I was touched. And I started lighting it every day before I sat down to work. I quickly came around. It was less about the candle itself and more about the ritual of lighting it and remembering that Gretchen has my back. Through the past few years, whenever I've struggled to stay focused, productive, and optimistic, my friends and family have, of course, been a source of comfort. But it's often my work friends who have helped me get through a tough day because we have a shared understanding of the challenges we're up against.

Of course, all of the benefits I've described—increased productivity and creativity, greater resilience, less stress, better performance reviews—are only realized if your relationships with your coworkers are positive and not corrosive. Challenging work relationships can have grave consequences for your performance and well-being.

The Consequences of Unhealthy Relationships

Research backs up what we know firsthand: that unhealthy relationships cause damage, sometimes more than we realize.

Negative relationships hinder performance and hurt creativity

Christine Porath, author of *Mastering Civility: A Manifesto for the Workplace*, has been studying the phenomenon of incivility at work for decades. Over the past twenty years, 98 percent of the people she's surveyed have experienced rude behavior at work and 99 percent have witnessed it.[12]

Her research shows the impact of this uncivil behavior is intense and far-reaching, particularly on our performance. Of those who were on the receiving end of mistreatment, Porath found (across seventeen industries):

- Forty-eight percent intentionally decreased their work effort

- Forty-seven percent intentionally decreased the time spent at work

- Thirty-eight percent intentionally decreased the quality of their work

- Sixty-six percent said that their performance declined

- Seventy-eight percent said that their commitment to the organization declined

- Twenty-five percent admitted to taking their frustration out on customers

- Twelve percent said that they left their job because of uncivil treatment[13]

Completing tasks, staying focused, and producing quality work are much harder when we are struggling with a rude or negative colleague. One experiment done with teams of doctors and nurses in newborn intensive care units in Israel showed just how costly being insulted can be. In the study, some teams were told by a visiting expert that he didn't respect the quality of the work they were doing. In the wake of this criticism, the teams who were berated made diagnoses that were 20 percent less accurate, and the procedures they conducted were 15 percent less effective.[14]

Being treated rudely also dampens creative thinking, because it results in "cognitive disruption."[15] In other words, working with a colleague who is mean to you—either by being passive-aggressive, or taking credit for your work, or making unkind comments—inhibits your ability to think clearly.

Our health suffers, too

It may not be particularly surprising that negative relationships cause stress, but stress often has serious consequences for our health. (Unfortunately, that awareness hasn't spurred many of us, including myself, to get a handle on it.) For example, scientists have established a direct connection between working with someone difficult and heart disease. A group of Swedish scientists followed three thousand workers over three years and asked them questions about the competence of their managers. The less competent they perceived their managers to be, the greater the risk of experiencing heart issues. And the risk of serious heart problems increased, the longer participants worked at the company.[16]

In another study, researchers looked at the impact of our relationships on the time it takes to recover from a wound. Working with forty-two married couples, they made small incisions on participants' arms and then measured the rate at which the incisions healed. The wounds inflicted on the couples who reported having animosity in their relationships took twice as long to heal, showing that the stress caused by negative interactions hinders the body's ability to repair itself.[17] Working with a difficult colleague can make you sick and make it harder to bounce back from illness or injury.

Negative relationships are bad for our colleagues and organizations

When you and a colleague don't get along, there are ripple effects. The people in your orbit are subject to what I call the "emotional shrapnel" of your dynamic. This includes the coworkers who directly witness the animosity, of course, but also your friends and family who may offer a sympathetic ear and absorb your stress. When my husband worked for an immature, micromanaging boss, *my* mood and productivity took a hit even though I never met her in person.

University of Michigan professor Jane Dutton talks about this phenomenon in her book, *Energize Your Workplace.* She writes,

"Incivility rarely stays contained. It spirals and spreads within the work organization's boundaries at the same time that it spreads and spirals into people's lives outside work. . . . In one study of the experiences of more than twelve thousand people who encountered incivility in the workplace, virtually every target of incivility described telling someone else about the experience. When news of incivility spreads it increases people's expectations that these behaviors are normal, further increasing their occurrence."[18]

The stakes for organizations are clearly high. One rude person, or one dynamic that is marked by incivility, can hurt the entire team—and perhaps even those who only see or hear about the tense interactions. And if employees are distracted, stressed, struggling to focus, making mistakes, and mentally and physically unhealthy, work outcomes suffer. This is true for organizations of all sizes. Harvard Business School professor Noam Wasserman studied ten thousand founders for his book *The Founder's Dilemma* and observed that 65 percent of startups fail as a result of conflict between the founders.[19] Porath's research at an engineering firm found that those who perceived their coworkers as difficult were twice as likely to quit. And the flight risk was greatest among top talent.[20]

Negative relationships have stronger effects than positive ones

Part of the reason that it's so important to make an effort to improve our negative relationships is that they have a disproportionate impact on our experience at work, because of all the factors I just outlined. Porath found that deenergizing relationships have a four to seven times greater impact on our well-being than energizing, positive relationships.[21]

However, a relationship doesn't have to be toxic or even mostly negative to have deleterious effects. When I think about the difficult people I've worked with, many of the ones that stand out in my mind are those who weren't difficult *all the time*. For instance, I had a colleague who I'll call Tara. We were never friends exactly, but we enjoyed chatting at the beginning of meetings, and at social gatherings, she and I often exchanged stories about our children, who were the same age. I found her funny, personable, and good at her job—most of the time. When I got up the nerve to ask another coworker whether he also found her difficult to read at times, he perfectly articulated what I was experiencing: "You just never know which Tara you're going to get. 'Good Tara' is really nice and seems to have your back. But 'Bad Tara' is grumpy and focused on her career and has no qualms about throwing you under the bus."

Most of our work relationships don't fall into neat categories of "good" or "bad," even if that's how our brains want to sort them. These ambivalent relationships—the ones that feel occasionally positive or mostly neutral, but sometimes veer into alarming territory—are often just as problematic as the unambiguously negative ones. Some research has shown that these relationships are in fact more physiologically harmful.[22]

Of course, having a frenemy is better than having an enemy, and these ambivalent relationships can have upsides too: sometimes they motivate us to work harder on the relationship (whereas we might take a purely positive relationship for granted), and we're more likely to try seeing things from the other person's perspective as we struggle to understand them.[23]

• • •

None of our relationships are fixed. We might assume that the positive ones will always stay that way and the negative ones are doomed to be torturous forever. But that mindset can lead us to neglect our work friendships, and completely dismiss the more complicated ones. If you think about the people you've had connections with over your career, I'm guessing they didn't remain the same over time; they were likely malleable. After all, good relationships can sour, and some of the toughest ones can be transformed, as long as you put in the time and effort.

That said, we could all be smarter about the ways in which we direct our energy. I know I've wasted hours (more than I care to add up) mulling over an exchange with a difficult coworker, rethinking an email I sent or received, even waking up in the middle of the night and rehearsing conversations I wish I could redo (and "stick it to you" things I wish I could say). In the next chapter, I'll talk about what's happening in your brain when you're stuck in a negative dynamic with a coworker, why it takes up so much psychological space, and how to cultivate understanding and self-awareness so you can respond in a productive way.

2

Your Brain on Conflict

How our minds often work against us.

A few months ago, I was introduced over email to a consultant, who I'll call Brad. The person who made the introduction thought Brad would make a good contributor to *Harvard Business Review*, where I work as an editor. I receive a good number of these introductions, and when this one came in, I was particularly overwhelmed with requests. Brad asked if we could get on the phone to talk. I courteously declined and let him know that an editor would be in touch about the draft he submitted. A few weeks later, he asked again. Again, I sent what I thought was a polite response explaining that because of the demands on my time, I wouldn't be able to have a call with him. Then I got this email from Brad: "We're all busy but human connection is the most important thing. I'm going to take my writing elsewhere. I can't handle the ego."

This wasn't the first time I'd dealt with a frustrated would-be author. But this one got to me. I reread his note a few times, each time my heart rate increasing a bit more, and my shoulders and neck tensing. My mind was spinning with rapid-fire thoughts: "What an a**hole." "Who does he think he is?" "He's such a baby." "Get over it, Brad." I started composing pithy retorts in my mind: "Why do you think you're the most important person in my inbox?" "Good luck taking your crappy writing elsewhere!" (I hadn't even read his draft, but I was feeling pretty judgmental.)

My initial reaction that this was all Brad's fault soon morphed into self-doubt. I started to wonder if he was right. "Do I have a big ego?" "Did I just ruin a valuable human connection?" "Why didn't I prevent his frustration by handling the earlier emails better?"

Then, I took a few deep breaths and did what I thought was the right thing: I deleted the email.

Now, I'd love to tell you that the whole situation ended there. And for Brad, it did. He and I have not exchanged messages since, and we probably won't. But my brain had other ideas.

Long after I hit delete, Brad's email kept popping into my mind. While I was writing to another potential author, the phrase "human connection is the most important thing" echoed in my thoughts. When I was making dinner that night, I thought several times about the line "I can't handle the ego." And at 3:00 a.m. the next morning, when I woke up in the pitch black of my bedroom, instead of falling back to sleep, I pictured myself retrieving his message from my deleted folder and composing a long and eloquent response that would make him regret ever sending such a mean-spirited email and rethink every email he sent from now on. I was going to save Brad from being a jerk ever again.

In chapter 1, I made the case for why it's worth addressing the dynamic between you and your difficult coworker. I wish it was as easy as making that decision and then executing the strategies I've outlined in the chapters ahead. But there's an obstacle that you often need to overcome before you can take any sort of action: your brain.

When we're interacting with someone challenging, our brain wants to protect us from harm. In the process, however, it often holds us back. I had made the decision to let Brad's email go, to shrug it off and move on. But my brain was hooked on the interaction.

This chapter is all about what's happening in your head when you're mired in conflict—why a negative relationship is so painful, and why you can't stop thinking about it. Understanding the neurological processes at work will help you develop the self-awareness you need to respond productively rather than impulsively, with the goal of improving your relationship with the other person.

Calm the Inner Critic

In the middle of the night, while I was preoccupied with Brad, my inner critic jumped in: "This is what I'm thinking about at 3:00 a.m.? This ridiculous email? I already deleted it. Why can't I just let it go? Why do I need everyone—even a consultant who I've never met—to like me? What's wrong with me?" This clearly wasn't a helpful line of thinking, so I reminded myself what I've learned from research: my brain was doing what human brains have evolved to do. My rumination about Brad's email didn't signal that something was wrong with me. On the contrary, it was completely normal.

Before you can begin to work on the dynamic between you and a difficult colleague, especially with someone who isn't going to disappear from your inbox forever like Brad did, you have to understand your own reaction to it: why it's bothering you, why it's painful, why you can't let it go even though you want to. And it doesn't hurt to have a little compassion for yourself.

Getting stuck is both normal and frustrating

A desire to worry less about your difficult colleague is often futile. I know I'm not alone in reviewing (and yes, agonizing over) my interactions with my coworkers when I should be sleeping. In her research, Georgetown University professor Christine Porath found that 80 percent of respondents who were on the receiving end of uncivil behavior lost work time worrying about the incident, and 63 percent lost work time in attempts to avoid the offender.[1]

Conflict often drives us to distraction. In an experiment among customer service reps at a large cellular communications provider in Israel, for example, the reps who experienced a rude interaction with a customer had a more difficult time recalling details of the conversation because they were preoccupied with the incivility. Their mental energy was focused on thinking about the poor treatment, not listening to the customer.[2]

This sort of distress is not something we choose. As Porath writes: "When people experience incivility, the process of consciously evaluating it seems to take precedence over primary tasks, even when an individual does not want to think about the rude incident. It tends to occupy them, even if they do not want it to."[3]

In other words, it's normal for your mind to return to a tricky interaction, even if you've resolved to forget about it. Our brains are designed—evolutionarily speaking—to be highly attuned to difficult relationships, so changing the way we react requires proactive steps. Let's take a closer look at what happens inside our heads during a conflict with a colleague.

Our Brains on Conflict

When we experience or perceive a potential rupture in our relationship with another person—we open a snarky email, our colleague turns off their camera in the middle of our video call without explanation, or we catch our boss subtly rolling their eyes at something we said—our brain reacts as if we're in actual danger. It prepares our body to respond to that perceived threat, while also attempting to make sense of what we're experiencing. Why is my manager annoyed at me? What did I do to upset my colleague? Do I deserve this? And since we've evolved to preserve our cognitive resources as much as possible, our brains use shortcuts to direct our responses—shortcuts that can sometimes get us into trouble.

Amygdala hijack

On each side of our brain, behind the optical nerves, there is an amygdala. One of its functions is to detect fear and then prepare the body to respond appropriately. So when you perceive a threat—whether it's a car barreling toward you on the street or your insecure boss claiming credit for your work in an all-staff meeting—the amygdala begins to react by signaling the release of stress hormones like cortisol and adrenaline.

You've no doubt heard the phrase "fight or flight." These instinctual reactions come from the amygdala, and when they kick in, we go into *amygdala hijack*, a term I learned from Daniel Goleman, author of *Emotional Intelligence*. It's known as a "hijack" because the fight-or-flight reaction dominates our executive functions, and it feels as if we're no longer making choices about how to behave, that our bodies and minds are on autopilot. When there's a disagreement brewing between me and a colleague, an elevated heart rate and shallow breathing are my brain's way of preparing me to run if I need to. I now know the warning signs: I feel a tingle at the back of my head, my shoulders start to creep up toward my ears like I'm a turtle retreating into my shell, my jaw clenches, and my palms get sweaty. It isn't fun.

This isn't a glitch though. These mental shortcuts save time and energy and often do keep us safe. If you're standing in the middle of the road and there is, indeed, a car bearing down on you, it would be dangerous if your brain paused to think through the ins and outs of the situation. Instead, you need it to react instinctively, telling your body to get out of the street as quickly as possible.

One of my least favorite parts about this automatic, instinctive response is that, all too often, it happens without us noticing. So we react—perhaps by snapping back at our colleague, raising our voice, shutting down, sending an email we wish we could take back—before we realize that we're in the throes of amygdala hijack. Put simply, we are not in our right minds.

Negativity bias

This fight-or-flight reaction may sound like an extreme response to a rude email, or to your know-it-all colleague talking over you in a meeting, but the brain is highly attuned to incidents, no matter how small, that can be perceived as threatening. This attunement is what's called *negativity bias.*

Essentially, we pay more attention to negative events than positive ones.[4] You might report to your partner or friend that you had a "terrible" day, for instance, when most of the day was fine, but an afternoon meeting with a passive-aggressive colleague spoiled everything. That interaction may have accounted for just a small fraction of your time, but it takes up considerably more mental space.

Negativity bias is probably familiar to you. Think about your last performance review. Do you remember any details about the positive things your manager wrote or does the more critical feedback stand out in your mind? I can recall two sentences of a performance evaluation I received in 2002 (!) about how I lacked understanding of complex business models. Mind you, these were two sentences in an otherwise glowing review. And I can't remember a single positive comment. Similarly, I can recite word for word that nasty email from Brad, but I have no idea who else wrote to me that day or what they said. Only the negative message lingers.

Not only is our attention drawn to more negative events, but our brains react more strongly to them. In extreme cases, negative interactions can even be downright painful.

Conflict hurts

Have you ever thought that an underhanded jab from a know-it-all colleague or an offensive joke from a biased coworker felt like a slap in the face? I've certainly had my breath taken away by some mean-spirited comments that felt like the person just punched me in the stomach. Neuroscience shows that in certain instances, the brain interprets the impact of being devalued, ignored, shamed, yelled at, rejected, or bullied at work in ways that are similar to the experience of physical pain.

Brain imaging research done by a team at UCLA, for instance, shows that feeling excluded activates the same regions of the brain responsible for processing physical pain. We might think that emotional pain, especially when it's caused by our coworkers or people we interact with in a professional context, is "just in our heads," but it's not. Rejection of any kind registers in our brain in a way that is very similar to how we'd experience being punched or cutting our finger.[5]

The Stories We Tell Ourselves

About a year ago, I had an early-morning Zoom meeting with a colleague to prepare for an online panel we were both participating in the following week. This is someone who I mostly get along with, although I find him to be pompous on occasion (he definitely fits many of the know-it-all attributes I talk about in chapter 7). After telling me what he planned to discuss on the panel, he asked for my input. I hadn't said more than two sentences when he put himself on mute and started to look off-screen. I was convinced that he was looking at another monitor, which I knew he had set up in his home office, and was reading, and likely responding to, emails. While I forged ahead with my comments, my inner monologue was going something like this: *Why did he even ask for my input if we're just going to do what he wants anyway? What an arrogant jerk, always focused on himself.* In an attempt to make sense of what was happening, my brain formed a narrative that gave his actions—muting himself and looking away from the screen—negative meaning.

That's often what happens when we are on the receiving end of our coworker's "bad" behavior. We quickly tell ourselves a story about what's occurring, why it's occurring, and what will happen next. And these stories—laden with emotions and critiques—feel truthful to us even when they're based on our brain's sense-making attempts rather than on facts. This is what psychologists call *premature cognitive commitment.*[6] In an effort to conserve resources, our brains make snap judgments about what's going on around us and how we should react.

It turns out I was wrong about my colleague's "rude" behavior. After I finished describing how I thought we should approach the panel, he unmuted himself and asked a follow-up question that made clear that he'd heard everything I'd said. At the end of the call, he apologized for looking distracted and explained that his teenage son (who was doing school online because of the pandemic) had made him pancakes and had come into his home office to deliver them. I felt stupid for assuming the worst, and my brain quickly had to adjust from my original interpretation of rude behavior to a sweet family moment.

As this experience illustrates, we have to be careful about the stories we tell ourselves and how they're influenced by our brain's shortcuts. The good news is that if you can recognize what's happening—and withhold judgment—you can move toward solutions.

The Path Out of Amygdala Hijack: Create Mental Space

There is a famous quote that's often attributed to Viktor Frankl, Austrian psychiatrist and psychotherapist and Holocaust survivor: "Between stimulus and response there is a space. In that space is our power to choose our response. In our response lies our growth and our freedom."[7] Frankl's insight is critical to handling the dynamic between you and a difficult colleague. You must create the necessary space to choose a response that will result in growth instead of conflict.

Observe your reactions

The more you can observe your instinctive reactions when your mind senses a threat, the better you will get at separating the stories your brain cooks up from what's actually happening. With a clearer head, you're more likely to make sound decisions about how to respond.

Personally, I've noticed that I tend to react to an unpleasant interaction with a coworker in three different ways. I blame the other person: "This is all their fault!"; blame myself: "What have I done wrong?"; or try to completely disengage: "This isn't worth my time."

These are not necessarily distinct reactions—sometimes I rapidly cycle through them, like I did in the fifteen minutes after I got Brad's email. But when I found myself awake at 3:00 a.m. on the anxious-thoughts carousel, rather than further suppressing the emotions I was feeling or dismissing the stories I was telling myself, I decided to re-focus my energy on exploring them. I started to ask myself: Why was what Brad said so upsetting? What could my emotions tell me about the situation?

In essence, I tried to see my negative thoughts as useful data rather than distracting noise.[8] What I realized when I took this approach was that Brad's email did two things that I found especially challenging.

First, he broke a norm. I send and receive hundreds of emails each week, and the majority of them are pleasant or neutral. Fortunately, it's rare that any of my exchanges with coworkers, friends, family, or strangers are outright rude. So Brad was violating my expectation that people should treat one another with respect.

Second, the picture he painted of me didn't line up with my self-image. If Brad's email was right, then I had to face the fact that I'm someone with a big ego who doesn't care about human interaction—neither of which are things I believe (or want to believe) about myself. It made me wonder if the way I perceived myself—as caring, thought-ful, humble—was not how others see me.

If you think about your own history with difficult coworkers, ask yourself if one or both of these violations were involved. They often are. We believe our troublesome colleagues are acting in ways they shouldn't (a violation of our sense of community), and their behavior makes us question ourselves (a violation of our self-perception). This creates internal conflict—conflict that we feel as ostracization, exclusion, rejection, and a threat to our sense of belonging, which pulls us into that fight-or-flight mode.

But by observing my reaction to Brad, and interrogating why I was having it, I was able to calm myself down. Instead of giving in to my initial reaction, I was starting to think, *Ah, this makes sense.*

Reappraise the situation

Once you've created a little space from a vexing episode, you can then reappraise it. Psychologists have found that *reappraisal*—reassessing an emotional situation in a more positive or neutral light, or as a challenge instead of a threat—helps people focus and make more considered decisions about how to proceed.[9]

The negative story I constructed around my colleague who was looking off-screen during our meeting caused me to close down. I was less interested in sharing my ideas and resisted the thought of collaborating with him, all of which he likely sensed. Had he not told me that his son had brought him pancakes, which forced me to reappraise the situation, my reaction would've affected our relationship and our ability to work together, not to mention the quality of the panel we were putting together.

Pay attention to the stories you're telling yourself when you're interacting with your difficult colleague. What thoughts are running through your mind? Are they helpful? Is there a way to reframe them so that they're neutral or positive? For example, instead of being laser focused on how your know-it-all coworker's diatribes are excruciating to sit through, can you tell yourself that when you put aside the condescending tone, their rants actually have a nugget or two of useful information? You don't want to sugarcoat a truly negative situation, but is there a different interpretation? Ask yourself what you can learn.

You might also consider what else is going on in your life that may be influencing your negative reaction.

Monitor your stress

It's no surprise that when stress is running high, we are even more susceptible to the pitfalls of amygdala hijack than usual. You've no doubt experienced moments when you're under pressure to meet a big deadline at work or haven't been sleeping well, and you fly off the handle at a colleague's comment or you find yourself feeling completely gutted by a negative piece of feedback on a presentation that you worked really hard on. To find that ever-important space between an upsetting trigger and your response, it helps to assess your overall level of stress.

Having a simple list of questions on hand for fraught situations could be the difference between losing your cool and finding a productive way forward. Here's a mental checklist that I use when I notice that I'm going into amygdala hijack:

- Am I hydrated?

- Am I hungry?

- How did I sleep last night?

- What else am I worried about?

- Do I have any big projects or deadlines weighing on my mind?

- Are any of my important relationships with friends or family strained right now?

- When is the last time I did something that I enjoyed?

Monitoring your mental resources in this way can help you gain perspective. Throughout 2020, I had to remind myself regularly that the cognitive load of living through a pandemic made me much more prone to interpret the behavior of those around me as threatening, mostly because I already felt threatened. And when you're in survival mode, you don't have the reserves to tolerate additional stress. You have less room to feel curious. With this cognitive overload, your brain is focused on making it through the day, not thriving.

Lisa Feldman Barrett explained this beautifully in her book *7½ Lessons About the Brain*: "It's important to understand that the human brain doesn't seem to distinguish between different sources of chronic stress. If your body budget is already depleted by the circumstances of life—like physical illness, financial hardship, hormone surges, or simply not sleeping or exercising enough—your brain becomes more vulnerable to stress of all kinds. This includes the biological effects of words designed to threaten, bully, or torment you or people you care about. When your body budget is continually burdened, momentary stressors pile up, even the kind that you'd normally bounce back from quickly."[10] So take stock of how you're feeling outside of the problems you're having with your coworker. Are there needs you can take care of—going for a quick walk, having a healthy snack, getting a project done—that will reduce stress and put you in a better frame of mind for dealing with conflict?

Give it time

You know the adage "never go to bed mad"? I'm not a fan. Oftentimes, getting a good night's sleep is exactly what you need to change your mindset. Alice Boyes, the author of *The Anxiety Toolkit*, helped me understand that while our initial response to a coworker talking over us in a meeting (*again*) or not following up on a task they promised to get done may be intense, those negative emotions don't usually persist. "We're designed so that emotions extinguish themselves over time—they are warning signals," says Boyes.[11] As we get more information, and reappraise, those feelings often do dissipate.

Let's go back to my incident with Brad. I noticed the next morning when I woke up that I cared a little less about what had happened. I didn't feel the same tightness in my chest when I replayed his email in my mind, and I mostly didn't think about it during the day. And even though I was up again at 3:00 a.m. the following night and my mind immediately turned to Brad, my attention didn't stay there for long (after all, the list of things to feel anxious about in the early hours of the morning is long). And with each day that passed, I spent less time thinking about it. As I'm writing this now, I actually care almost not at all (almost).

Give yourself time away from thinking about issues you're having with a coworker. Consider taking a break—getting outside, listening to your favorite song, thinking about a recent trip you took (or one coming up)—anything that pulls your attention away from your colleague for a bit. Then return to the interaction later and see if you have a different point of view once you've gotten out of amygdala hijack.

That's not to say you should completely ignore conflict, however, or pretend that it doesn't bother you. Boyes says that thinking about tough situations can actually be helpful, as long as your mind is focused on problem-solving and not rumination or perfection. In psychology, this is called *problem-solving pondering*.[12] Boyes helpfully describes this as asking yourself, "Given the reality of the situation, what's the best course of action?"[13] I find it useful to think about the "whys." Why did the person behave the way they did? Why did I react the way I did? Why did we find ourselves in this situation? Just make sure to keep your questions constructive (not "Why is he an idiot?") and be careful that your pondering doesn't veer into negative self-talk that only reinforces a false narrative (not "Why do I always get in my own way?").

I've covered a lot about how our minds often work against us in these moments of conflict with a colleague. But we can use the same brain science in our favor. One way to do this is to remind ourselves that the other person may be going through exactly the same thing. It might not be their intention to hurt you, lash out at you, or make your life miserable; maybe they're in amygdala hijack and aren't thinking clearly. Seeing an adversary as a person with a brain that works in the same, sometimes flawed, way that yours does can be the first step toward creating a better relationship.

PART TWO

THE ARCHETYPES

Cleaning Up Your Side of the Street

A quick note before we dive into the archetypes.

At this point in the book, you may be thinking, "There's an awful lot about how to understand and manage myself in this book. When do we get to the part about the jerk who's making my life miserable?" If this is you, you're not wrong! You've caught on to one of the core principles of my approach: if you're serious about resolving conflict with a coworker, it's essential that you acknowledge your own part in the dynamic. It's far too easy when you're dealing with a trying colleague to focus on them and what the heck is wrong with them (the list may be long). But the tools that I describe in the coming chapters for getting along with a pessimist, a biased colleague, or an insecure boss won't work unless you recognize that while every battle with a difficult person is different, there is one consistent element across them: you.

Some years ago, a dear friend of mine was trying to support her teenage son through a hard time. Her son's therapist told her and her spouse that while their kid worked on himself, they needed to do their own work. He referred to this process as "cleaning up your side of the street" or acknowledging and attending to your part in the struggle. That phrase really resonated with me. (I've since learned that it is commonly used in Alcoholics Anonymous or Narcotics Anonymous when people facing addiction reach out to make amends with those they've harmed.)

I could picture what the therapist meant: imagine that you and the person with whom you're in conflict are standing on opposite sides of a street, firmly entrenched in your perspectives and experiences. If your side of the street is cluttered with trash—volatile emotions stemming from the clash itself, bad blood from previous disagreements, unproven gossip about your opponent, lack of sleep, and so on—it'll be harder to cross the divide. If you approach the other side with all of your garbage, the odds are you'll make the situation worse. But if you get curious about your role in the conflict—how you might be misperceiving the situation, and what you want from the relationship—the path to making amends will emerge from the rubble.

Why should you do all the work when the other person is at least partly (OK, maybe fully) to blame? There are two reasons. First, in any tense exchange, regardless of who's at fault, you can only control *your* thoughts, actions, and reactions. Second, even if you're absolutely certain that you're right and they're wrong, it takes two to tango. Maybe your optimism and tendency to downplay risks spurs your pessimistic colleague to point out more of them. Or perhaps because you've inadvertently signaled to your coworker that you don't like direct confrontation, they've resorted to passive-aggressive tactics to get their point across. The clearer you can be about your role in the dust-up (even if it's minor), the clearer a resolution will become.

In chapter 11, I will share more about how to clean up your side of the street, but for now, keep in mind that your relationship with your coworker isn't something that's happening *to* you. It's a dynamic that you likely participate in and therefore have the ability to do something about. In chapter 2, I discussed at some length the fact that although we can't control how our brain instinctively reacts to a stressful situation, we can reappraise and alter our perception and response. Similarly, you may not be able to change how a colleague behaves, but you can change the way you interpret and respond to their behavior. Remembering that will improve your chances of building stronger, more fulfilling relationships at work, no matter what type of difficult person you're dealing with.

3

The Insecure Boss

"I'm great at my job . . . right?"

When Aiko's new boss, Cora, first joined the company, things were going smoothly. Aiko was happy to have someone she could learn from and who promised to bring new ideas and approaches that would improve her projects. But several months into her new manager's tenure, she started to see some red flags.

Aiko had long been the go-to person on any questions or meeting requests related to the department's initiatives. This seemed to upset Cora, who would ask, "Why aren't they coming to me for answers?" She got angry *with Aiko* whenever this happened, treating Aiko as if she was trying to undermine her. Attempts to redirect their colleagues' inquiries to Cora didn't stick, which only infuriated her further. "It's just what they were used to doing," Aiko told me. "But Cora took it personally." In her previous job, Cora had managed a large team and budget, and now Aiko was her only direct report. "I think that always bothered her," she said.

Cora's overly emotional reactions and snide comments wore on Aiko. "She nitpicked everything I did to the point where I felt I had no power to make decisions, even small ones. I was always afraid she was going to get upset and explode. My confidence in my ability to do my job eroded," she explained.

Aiko had never questioned her competence before. But now, Cora's insecurity was rubbing off on her.

If you've ever doubted yourself because you work for a boss who doesn't have faith in you, shoots down your ideas without explanation, and blames you for their lack of success (like Cora was doing to Aiko), you're not alone. There are, of course, many flavors of bad bosses, but insecure managers wreak a particular kind of havoc. They can be notorious micromanagers who drive you up a wall with their incessant nitpicking, or paranoid meddlers who make you question your every move. They may even go so far as to intentionally hurt your career if they perceive you as a threat.

How do you know if you're dealing with an insecure manager? Here are some of the most common behaviors exhibited by this type of difficult coworker:

- Being overly concerned about what others think of them

- Suffering from a chronic inability to make a decision (or stick with one), even when the choice has little consequence

- Frequently changing the direction of a project or meeting, especially at the suggestion of someone in power

- Taking opportunities to highlight their expertise or credentials, especially when it's not necessary to do so; in its more toxic form, this may include putting others down to make themselves look more important

- Attempting to control everything about a team or project, including when and where and even how people accomplish their work

- Requiring that every decision and detail have their approval

- Not allowing the team to interact with colleagues from other departments or senior leaders in an attempt to control the flow of information and resources

Aiko's boss, Cora, wanted everyone in the organization to go through her because she thought that would prove her value. But she spent so much time trying to manage how others perceived her that she failed to do what she'd been hired to do: provide fresh ideas and mentor Aiko. Instead of innovating, she was micromanaging, and Aiko, as her sole direct report, was the unfortunate target.

Aiko felt stuck. Every time she took even minor steps to advocate for herself, Cora seemed to become only more paranoid and controlling. No one should have to work for a boss like this, ever. But if you can relate to Aiko, and aren't able to leave your job, and want to find a way to work with your self-doubting boss, there are ways to respond that won't further incite their insecurity. The first step is to understand what might be making your insecure manager act the way they are.

The Background on Insecure Behavior

Self-doubt is a universal part of the human condition. We all have times when we wonder if our coworkers think we're smart, if we have what it takes to nail that presentation, if we said something wrong in a meeting, or if strangers are judging the way we dress or look. I'm not proud of this, but when I'm talking with someone who I suspect doesn't respect me or is silently questioning my capabilities, I sometimes mention that I went to an Ivy League school or that I work at *Harvard Business Review*. I have even talked about how busy I am to prove I'm "in demand." I'm cringing as I type, but I do know these are normal reactions to feelings of inadequacy.

Seeking approval and even praise from others stems from the fact that human beings once relied on community to survive and still need it to thrive. As psychologist Ellen Hendriksen explained in an interview with *Vox*, "A little bit of insecurity, a little bit of self-doubt, is helpful because it allows us to monitor ourselves. It causes introspection and self-examination and motivates us to grow and change."[1] There's an instructive label for the 1 percent of people who have no self-doubt: psychopaths. Complete freedom from insecurity is not something to aspire to.

While feeling insecure at times is natural, we start to see problematic behaviors, such as micromanaging, unfairly criticizing direct reports, or constantly seeking reassurance when people attempt to conceal or compensate for their self-doubt.

Leaders may be more susceptible to self-doubt

Research has shown that insecurity increases as you move into leadership roles. A UK-based leadership consultancy surveyed 116 executives, for instance, and asked about their biggest fears.[2] The number one reported anxiety was being considered incompetent. The executives in the study also said they feared underachieving, appearing too vulnerable, and coming off as foolish—all revealing deep insecurities around others' perceptions of their performance as leaders.

Why would managers who tend to have more power and authority than others be more insecure? Shouldn't it be the people without power who worry about their jobs and how others see them? In a series of studies, professors Nathanael Fast and Serena Chen have shown that when powerful people feel incompetent, they tend to act more aggressively toward others, needlessly sabotaging them or being vindictive.[3] Incompetence alone doesn't lead to aggression though. Those in less powerful roles who feel insecure don't typically resort to the same bad behaviors.

The gap may stem from increased pressure to perform when you're promoted to a senior position. "The expectation is that people higher up in the organization will have enhanced leadership ability, knowledge, access to information and data—that they'll be *more* competent than others," says Ethan Burris, the Neissa Endowed Professor at the McCombs School of Business at the University of Texas, Austin.[4] The discrepancy between how confident or capable leaders actually feel and the high expectations that come with their role results in what's called "ego defensiveness," where leaders engage in actions to protect their self-esteem or justify their actions.[5]

Take Ralph, a sales VP at an IT services organization. Ralph had knocked it out of the park as a sales director and earned a big promotion, but he was reluctant to give up his relationships with clients, since he'd worked hard to win their business. He wanted to do two jobs—his old job and his new one—but the company's leadership team insisted that he hire someone to report to him. Roberto was that unlucky hire. When he joined the team, unaware of the full story, Ralph resisted handing over his accounts. He often inserted himself into Roberto's communications with customers and demanded that all decisions related to his previous clients go through him. Roberto was doomed before he walked in the door because Ralph was doing everything he could to protect what had led to success in his previous role.

For people who aren't stereotypically seen as leaders, the problem is even more complex. Women or people of color, for example, may experience self-doubt, not because of any flaw or inability to lead, but because they receive both overt and subtle cues that they aren't equipped to do the job—that they *should* feel like a fraud. Or they're sent conflicting messages, such as "Be assertive but not confrontational" or "Be yourself but don't show any negative emotions." In a wildly popular *Harvard Business Review* article, "Stop Telling Women They Have Imposter Syndrome," consultants Ruchika Tulshyan and Jodi-Ann Burey wrote about this phenomenon. They explain that, in many organizations, women, especially women of color, are blamed for feelings of inadequacy when the real issue is that the workplace culture has signaled that they don't belong or aren't deserving of their success.[6]

In addition to worrying about being outed as incompetent, some insecure bosses may be concerned about job security. If you've ever lost your job, you know how shameful it can be—a feeling that most of us want to avoid at all costs. When you pair the fear of being fired with concern about being perceived as incompetent, it can lead to acute insecurities.[7]

A few months ago, I was talking with a middle manager at a biotech firm about an innovation initiative that had stalled at the company.

One of the obstacles the leader of his division identified was that people were afraid to disagree with anyone senior, not wanting to bring up new ideas that might challenge the status quo. When I asked the middle manager to help me understand this hesitation, he said, "I don't want to get fired. I need this job." When I dug deeper, he conceded that to his knowledge no one had ever lost their job at the company for speaking up. He'd seen people who spoke truth to power go on to be promoted. Still, he was worried. "I don't want to be the first casualty," he told me.

It's possible that your insecure manager feels concerned not only that they're not up to the job they've been given but that they may lose that job at any moment. Fear and shame, as I discussed in chapter 2, can wreak havoc on our minds and provoke us to mistreat others.

The Costs of Having an Insecure Manager

Let's return to Aiko's situation, described at the beginning of the chapter. Aiko's dip in self-esteem wasn't the only consequence of the bad blood between her and her boss, Cora. There were ripple effects. It was difficult for Aiko and Cora to make progress on their team's projects, for instance, with so much confusion around who should be the point person. Colleagues in other departments started to doubt the competence of both people and hesitated to involve them in important meetings about the company's strategy.

There are many other costs associated with having a boss like Cora. First, there are the psychological consequences: an increase in job-related stress, anxiety about your future, and, as Aiko experienced, a creeping self-doubt.

There are also potential consequences for your career prospects, especially if your manager is taking credit for your work or singing their own praises at your expense. In extreme cases, your manager may even intentionally discredit you and your work to make themselves look better. Teresa Amabile, a professor at Harvard Business School, found that self-doubt led managers to give harsher performance reviews. "Those who are intellectually insecure come down hard on others," she wrote, "perhaps as a tactic for proving how smart they are."[8]

Insecure managers are also bad for business in general. Because their egos are fragile, they tend not to listen to other's ideas and resist feedback. In one experiment led by Nathanael Fast and his coauthors, managers at a multinational oil and gas company in the Middle East were asked how competent they felt in their role on a scale of one to seven. The lower they rated their competence, the less likely they were to solicit feedback from their employees, and as a consequence, their employees were less likely to offer up ideas.[9] Insecure managers like those in the study may worry that employees' suggestions reflect negatively on their own competence and ability to do their job. If people believe changes need to be made, the logic goes, then perhaps it will appear as if the manager doesn't know what they're doing. So they send signals that they aren't willing to hear input. And employees who have their ideas ignored or rejected are less satisfied at work, are less creative in coming up with novel solutions to problems, and are more likely to quit.[10]

What can you do to prevent the harm caused to you and your organization by a boss who lacks confidence? Start by asking yourself a few questions.

Questions to Ask Yourself

As with any colleague who fits into one of the archetypes in this book, it's helpful to reflect on the situation before you act. So, ask yourself:

What evidence do I have that my boss is insecure? Could I be wrong in my assessment?

Before you label your manager "insecure," try to be objective. Just because someone doesn't lead in the way that you want doesn't mean that they are unsure of themselves. If the person is acting tentatively, they might have good reason to be risk averse or they might come from a culture where caution is celebrated. Many people, especially women, have been socially conditioned to downplay their successes or positive attributes. It's possible that your manager has been encouraged to avoid bravado and defer to others.

Is the insecurity causing a problem? If so, what is the negative impact?

Your manager constantly seeking reassurance is probably annoying, but is the behavior in and of itself a problem? Perhaps once your boss's ego has been assuaged, other negative consequences are minimal. Consider what, if any, damage your boss's insecurity is doing to you or your team. In what ways is it detrimental? Having a clear sense of the problem will inform if and how you act.

Am I feeding the insecurity?

It's always helpful to explore the role that you may be playing in creating (or perpetuating) a negative dynamic with a colleague. That's not to say that you are the cause of your manager's confidence problem, but could you be triggering it in some way?

Do you generously share the spotlight with your boss? Do you show appreciation for their work? Perhaps, because of your own self-doubts, you try to play up particular skills or expertise you have, which in turn highlights your boss's flaws. Maybe you've challenged their ideas in front of others? Or signaled that you don't trust them to get the job done? Think carefully about whether you are inadvertently feeding your manager's insecurities and possibly making the situation worse.

What does my boss want?

No matter the source of their feelings of inadequacy, what most insecure managers want is to experience less fear and feel surer of themselves. And can't we all relate to that? Everyone wants to feel as if they're good enough. What else might your manager want? What are their goals and aspirations?

As with any situation that requires managing up, it's crucial to understand your boss's objectives. In answering this question, you may instinctively favor negative interpretations: "My boss wants to destroy my career" or "My manager wants everyone else to look bad." But go a step further. Even if they want to "destroy" your career (which is unlikely), what's the motivation behind that impulse? For instance, maybe they're afraid of losing their job in an upcoming round of layoffs or maybe they believe that their critiques (which really come off as harsh criticisms) will motivate you to perform better. Keep asking yourself "why" until you uncover a drive to which you can relate.

With the answers to these questions in mind, it's time to think through the steps you'll take to change the problematic dynamic between you and your self-doubting boss.

Tactics to Try

No one wants to spend their workdays (or sleepless nights) dreaming up new ways to appease their boss's ego or get them to stop weighing in on tiny, meaningless details, like what font to use in a presentation. But having a healthy, positive relationship with your insecure boss will make your work life much easier, and there are some proven ways of making that happen.

After reading through the following tactics, figure out which are most relevant to your situation and try them out. You can make adjustments as you go.

Think about the pressures they face

Far too many bosses are overextended, overwhelmed, underqualified, or undertrained. So step back and look at the big picture. It's possible that legitimate pressures like hitting year-end targets or dealing with constantly changing rules about where and when employees work is raising your manager's anxiety level and prompting them to take out their insecurities on you.

They may have stressors you don't see or fully understand. Exercise empathy. Remember that your manager is human, even if their insecurity is causing problems that need to be addressed.

Sveta's boss tried to control every aspect of how she did her job and would even lie about having important projects coming up to keep Sveta from taking her vacation. Because this was Sveta's first job out of graduate school, she was hesitant at first to push back on her manager. But eventually she felt she had to say something. Confronting her boss only made her double down on the lies though. She tried to shift her mindset instead. "What worked best was thinking of my boss as a child who wasn't aware of the harm she was doing. With that picture in mind, I was able to keep a calm composure as I might with a kid," she told me. Exercising patience took a lot of self-control, especially when her manager got under her skin. But Sveta was careful not to lose her temper, often excusing herself from the room to calm down before going back to a heated conversation with her boss. She never loved working for this manager, but she did learn to live with the relationship, at least temporarily. Controlling her anger kept tensions between her and her boss down and allowed Sveta to do her job—and take her well-deserved vacation time.

Help them achieve their goals

If your insecure boss tends to put you down or take credit for your work, it might spark your own competitive tendencies. But one of the worst things you can do is to retaliate. If your self-doubting manager senses that you can't be trusted or that you have disdain for them, their defensiveness is likely to ramp up. Instead, consider what it might take to appease them and whether you're willing to do that.

This is what Sanjay learned to do with his boss, Vineet. Sanjay was incredibly frustrated by Vineet's lack of trust in him, which was most evident when Vineet questioned Sanjay's data analysis in front of their clients. When Sanjay asked why he was doing this, Vineet said that it was really important to him that they have the numbers right. So Sanjay stepped back to see what he could do to address his manager's concerns. He experimented with a new approach, and a day or two before any appointment with clients, Sanjay made sure to share his data and ask about Vineet's goals. "I wanted to know what he wanted out of the meeting," Sanjay told me. With Vineet's objectives in mind, he would suggest several ways they could achieve them *together*. He used phrases like "We've got this" and "It's good that we're in this together." It felt hokey to say these things, but Sanjay noticed that Vineet started to trust him more as a result. This took extra time and effort, of course, but the payoff was that Vineet stopped undermining him in front of clients.

Framing your work as a joint effort could help to alleviate tension between you and your insecure boss, as it did for Sanjay. Start sentences with "we" as much as possible. And when you succeed, be sure to share the glory.

Be careful that you don't downplay your talents, however. Research shows that employees who are the object of envy will often hide their positive attributes and try to avoid taking credit.[11] But that can backfire. Your insecure manager may feel even more anxious if they think your work isn't up to snuff or that your poor performance might reflect badly on them. And others in the organization may start to think you're not as capable as you are. The goal is for your boss to see you as a trustworthy partner, without damaging your own career and reputation.

Signal that you're not a threat

You want your boss to think of you as an ally, not a rival. It's best if you can do this from the start with your manager, but it's never too late to reset the tone of your relationship. In a meeting, you might say, "I admire what you do and I'm hoping to continue learning from you." At the same time, you don't want to make them think they can walk all over you.

The key is to watch what you say in a way that you don't make them feel even more threatened than they already are. For example,

"I don't understand that" can feel like a challenge to their intelligence, even if it's just a simple statement and you genuinely want to find out what they're thinking.

Lindred Greer, a professor at the University of Michigan who studies conflict, shared this trick with me: when dealing with a superior who sees her as a threat, she imagines herself as a cute little squirrel, and she tries to project the warmth of that persona. She says this picture softens her edges and helps her come off as nonthreatening. This may seem silly—*do I really need to pretend I'm a squirrel?*—but Lindy says she's come to enjoy doing it. It makes her smile and takes her attention away from her frustration with a difficult colleague.[12]

Pay compliments and express gratitude and appreciation

You can also help calm your manager's ego by rolling out the compliments. Research on managers who feel incompetent has shown that genuine flattery helps.[13] Note the word *genuine*. Most people will see right through empty praise. For example, if you're trying to get your boss to ease up on micromanaging, don't tell them how much you admire their attention to detail.

Many people understandably fear coming off as sycophants. Instead of paying compliments, you can also express appreciation for something they've done for you. "Direct reports often don't realize how hungry their leaders are for evidence that they're doing OK," says Nathanael Fast. "People don't like the idea that it's an employee's job to manage their boss's ego. But it does give you a sense of influence." In one of Fast's studies, he saw that when an employee said, "Thank you so much. I'm grateful," it positively influenced an insecure manager's evaluation of their employee's performance.[14] So consider thanking your manager for giving you a chance to work on a high-profile project or for introducing you to colleagues in another division. Doing this in private is great, but it may have more of an impact if you appreciate them in front of people whose opinions they care about. Not only will this put them at ease, but by bringing attention to some of their strengths, you'll help them build confidence.

Buttering up your boss may be the *last* thing you want to do if they're making life hard for you. But hopefully it's a small price to pay for reduced stress and brighter career prospects.

It's a bargain Nia was willing to strike with her boss, Tamara. Tamara was the kind of person who changed her mind easily, depending on who she had spoken to most recently. This gave Nia and her teammates whiplash, as Tamara would repeatedly change course on a decision. Nia's solution was to become Tamara's trusted adviser, the person Tamara turned to when she started to doubt whether they were headed in the right direction. "I had to constantly be on guard about who was whispering in her ear and be available to counter any concerns she developed that might take us off track," Nia told me. "If I took an unflappable approach with her and gave her the dignity she craved, she could find her way. I felt a bit like she needed me to be her Rock of Gibraltar." Although this required artful juggling by Nia, she felt it was worth it. She had her pick of plum projects and helped to run the department more smoothly.

Nia's efforts changed the power dynamic between her and Tamara—a tactic that research has shown to decrease mistreatment from abusive bosses.[15] If you can gain leverage with your manager—perhaps by developing skills that your supervisor will rely on or by becoming a trusted adviser—it might stop some of their problematic behaviors and even motivate your boss to treat you better.

Restore their sense of control

Insecure managers who have trouble trusting others often resort to micromanaging. You can interrupt some of their meddling by helping them feel like they're in charge. You might say things like "What we do is ultimately up to you" or "I trust you to make the right decision" and then make suggestions about how to proceed.

Sharing information is another way to reinforce their sense of control. Many insecure managers are terrified of being out of the loop. Keep them updated as much as possible, and be transparent about what you're working on and who you're talking with, especially in

Phrases to Use

Have some phrases at the ready when trying out these tactics with your insecure boss. You can integrate the following suggestions into your approach. Tweak them so they feel authentic to you.

Demonstrate that you're committed to your boss's success

"I want to make sure we all get credit for the work we put in."

"I know we all want the team to look good here."

"The team has your back on this."

"I know we're all invested in making this a success."

Build their confidence

"I appreciated our conversation about the project last week. It changed my thinking."

"I liked what you had to say in that meeting, and I think others valued your input."

"You have a unique perspective on this. I'd love to hear your thoughts."

Give them a sense of control

"I'll share my two cents so that you can make the final decision."

"What we do here is ultimately up to you."

Reference their ideas before sharing your own: "I'd like to build on your idea . . ." or "As [insert boss's name] just said . . ."

"Do you feel like you're getting enough information from me? It's important to me to keep you in the loop."

other parts of the company. Schedule regular check-ins where you can share progress on projects your boss cares about and make them feel included in the process. While annoying to do in the moment, over-sharing may save you the effort of defending yourself later.

Research shows that asking questions instead of providing answers in a conversation can also boost feelings of control in the other person. Pose questions that start with "What if . . ." or "Could we . ." that invite your manager to share their thoughts.[16]

Keep a compliments folder

When you're working with an insecure boss, you need to find ways to bolster your own confidence so you don't fall into the trap of self-doubt as Aiko did. This could mean keeping a list of your strengths on hand and reviewing them after a particularly tough interaction with your manager or spending time with people in your organization (or outside it) who reflect your best self back to you.

One of the best pieces of advice I've gotten in my career was to keep a compliments folder in my inbox. This is a place where I save any notes that congratulate me on a job well done, praise my work, or point out the impact my efforts have had on coworkers, clients, or readers. I don't look in the folder nearly as often I thought I would when I first created it, but just knowing it's there improves my confidence.

Create a folder in your email now and whenever you receive a compliment from someone—even if it's minor—put it in there. When you need a boost, especially after interacting with your insecure manager, praise is just a click away.

• • •

Unfortunately, no matter how strategic you are, it's unlikely that you will be able to cure your manager of their insecurity. Nor is that your responsibility. While the tactics in this chapter should help smooth out your interactions, don't go overboard. If you become entirely focused on managing your boss, you risk not doing your job well or alienating people in the organization who wonder why you are so intent on making your undeserving boss look good. If progress feels elusive, refer to chapter 12 for a few last-ditch things you can try before throwing in the towel.

Despite Aiko's questioning of herself, she was able to focus her energy on altering the dynamic between her and her manager by emphasizing that they had a shared agenda. She always went to great pains to include Cora in meetings and keep her informed. At the end of each week, before signing off for the weekend, Aiko would send Cora an email listing any developments on their projects or important conversations she'd had that week. These notes did double duty—they helped ease Cora's anxieties, but they also documented the good work Aiko was doing. In the back of her mind, Aiko always knew that Cora's insecurity might result in her trying to take down Aiko in front of others. And she was glad to have a record of the progress she was making to defend herself if this happened. Luckily it didn't come to that. Eventually, Aiko left the company, but she reported to Cora for five years.

Looking back, she thinks she might've handled the situation better, especially if she hadn't taken Cora's behavior personally. Of course, this isn't easy to do. When you have a manager who is always looking over your shoulder, questioning your work, or trying to inflate their own ego at the expense of others', it can feel like a personal attack. But aim for some emotional distance from the situation. Perhaps imagine yourself as a cute, fluffy squirrel.

TACTICS TO REMEMBER
The Insecure Boss

DO:

· Remember that your insecure boss is human. Demonizing them won't help anyone.

- Position yourself as an ally, not a rival.

- Pay your boss genuine compliments, or express gratitude and appreciation—in private, but also in front of others whose opinions they value.

- Start sentences with "we" as much as possible.

- Keep them updated and be transparent about what you're working on and who you're talking with, especially in other parts of the company.

- Schedule regular check-ins where you can share progress on projects your boss cares about and make them feel included in your work.

DON'T:

- Assume you know what pressures your manager is under or what's causing their insecurity.

- Retaliate. If your self-doubting manager senses that you can't be trusted or that you have disdain for them, their anxieties are likely to ramp up.

- Forget to share the spotlight when you succeed.

4

The Pessimist

"This will never work."

Theresa worked two cubicles over from Simran and made a habit of stopping by several times a day. Simran wouldn't have minded these brief visits except that Theresa did nothing but complain. "Every morning when I asked how she was, she would launch into all the bad things in her life," Simran told me. "Her home, her commute, our coworkers, you name it!" At first, Simran thought that listening and asking questions would allow her colleague to vent some of her negativity, but that just made things worse. "I became the go-to for her daily tirades."

Once, after the CEO called an all-staff meeting to announce that she was giving everyone in the company a bonus after a particularly strong year, Theresa went immediately to Simran's desk to point out that the company's benefits package was still inadequate. It tainted the excitement that Simran was feeling, not only about her bonus, but about the organization's successes.

Simran had to work closely with Theresa and wanted to get along with her. But she found it trying, and most days, when she saw Theresa coming, her instinct was to run the other way.

The pessimist, the cynic, the doubter, the complainer, the naysayer, the defeatist.

We've all worked with someone who can't seem to find anything positive to say—ever—and even seems to enjoy pointing out all the ways projects and initiatives will fail. You may be familiar with the *Saturday Night Live* skit featuring the character "Debbie Downer," brilliantly played by the actress Rachel Dratch. Debbie is a drag at any social gathering, regularly bringing up the rates of feline AIDS. Anyone who interacts with her is irritated, and although this is a caricature, a lot of us can relate to the dread of having to deal with someone like Debbie. Pessimists just aren't fun to be around.

Here are some of the behaviors that they frequently exhibit:

- Complaining about meetings, senior leadership, other colleagues, anything and everything

- Proclaiming that a new initiative or project is doomed to fail

- Adapting a "we've already tried that and it failed" mentality, especially in conversations about innovation or new ways of working

- Immediately pointing out the risks of a tactic or strategy

- Finding something negative to say, even when the news or meeting is mostly positive

On days when Theresa was out of the office or on vacation, or was so busy that she didn't have time to stop and chat, Simran felt more focused and productive. She also realized that anytime she heard Theresa coming toward her desk, she would physically brace herself for the onslaught of negativity, or even pretend to be in the middle of something, hoping that Theresa wouldn't interrupt her to complain. But these evasions weren't sustainable, and she found herself wishing that Theresa would change her attitude or at least find somewhere else to direct her negativity.

If you want to get out from under your naysaying colleague's dark cloud, it's helpful to understand what's driving their behavior.

The Background on Pessimistic Behavior

There are a lot of reasons why pessimists see the world the way they do, and gaining a deeper understanding of what makes them tick can help you decide which tactics to use and inspire greater empathy. You may even see ways in which you can benefit from their outlook.

What leads someone like Theresa to be such a downer? There's no single answer to this question. However, there are three elements to consider when it comes to pessimism:

- *Outlook.* A pessimist believes that negative events or results are inevitable. Think of the classic pessimist from children's literature, Chicken Little (or Henny Penny, as she's called in some countries), who told every animal at the farm that the sky was falling. Chicken Little *believed* that disaster was imminent.

- *Agency.* The second aspect is whether or not the person feels they can do something that will affect the outcome of a situation. Michelle Gielan, a researcher who focuses on happiness and success and, therefore, also looks quite a bit at pessimism, defines a pessimist as "someone who doesn't believe good things will happen and has no ability to change outcomes."[1] Negative thinking isn't necessarily bad, she says, and, in fact, may be warranted in some circumstances. But if a person also feels as if their efforts to avert disaster will make no difference, they're unlikely to act.

- *Behavior.* This is where the attitude becomes action. A defeatist's behaviors might include incessant complaining, as with Simran's colleague Theresa, or constantly putting down others' ideas, or talking about how unhappy they are. These actions are the expression of their fatalistic outlook and lack of agency.

All three elements are important to reflect on. Does your colleague have a negative outlook but rarely act on it? Do they feel they have what it takes to change their situation or to influence the results of a project? Those who have a negative outlook but retain agency often fall into a category called "defensive pessimism," which sometimes has benefits.[2]

For example, one study showed that defensive pessimists with chronic illnesses were more likely to take actions that could improve their health, like proactively managing their pain.[3] Researchers suggest that defensive pessimists might fare better during infectious disease outbreaks because their worry leads them to adopt preventive behaviors, such as frequent hand washing or consulting their doctor. People who fall into this subcategory can be easier to work with than someone who feels there's nothing to be done about the impending doom they see everywhere.

There's another category of pessimist—victims—who tend to have a negative outlook, very little agency, and play out their behavior in a way that paints them as the object of scorn or bad luck. I'll talk more about this variation of pessimism in chapter 5.

Prevention versus promotion focus

One of the ways to better understand your pessimistic colleague is to think about what's known as motivational focus. According to this model, prevention-focused people are concerned with safety and often see tasks as a series of obstacles to overcome. Those with a promotion focus tend to think about the future in a positive way and see opportunities where others see insurmountable challenges. Social psychologists Heidi Grant and E. Tory Higgins describe the differences between the two types, as shown in table 4-1.

Neither type is better or worse than the other, but they do function differently on teams and in organizations. Grant and Higgins explain, "[Prevention-focused people] are often more risk-averse, but their work is also more thorough, accurate, and carefully considered. To succeed, they work slowly and meticulously. They aren't usually the most creative thinkers, but they may have excellent analytical and problem-solving skills. While the promotion-minded generate lots of ideas, good and bad, it often takes someone prevention-minded to tell

TABLE 4-1

Differences in dominant motivational focus

Promotion-focused people:

- Work quickly

- Consider lots of alternatives and are great brainstormers

- Are open to new opportunities

- Are optimists

- Plan only for best-case scenarios

- Seek positive feedback and lose steam without it

- Feel dejected or depressed when things go wrong

Prevention-focused people:

- Work slowly and deliberately

- Tend to be accurate

- Are prepared for the worst

- Are stressed by short deadlines

- Stick to tried-and-true ways of doing things

- Are uncomfortable with praise or optimism

- Feel worried or anxious when things go wrong

Source: Adapted from Heidi Grant and E. Tory Higgins, "Do You Play to Win—or to Not Lose?," *Harvard Business Review*, March 2013, https://hbr.org/2013/03/do-you-play-to-win-or-to-not-lose.

the difference between the two."[4] Could it be that your pessimistic colleague has a prevention focus?

If you lean toward a promotion focus (note that it's possible to have characteristics of both types), you might find your prevention-focused colleague especially frustrating. But understanding that there are valuable aspects to their behavior and that pessimism is more than just a pathological insistence that "the sky is falling" could make their vigilance less annoying and may even give you ideas about how to channel it for good.

There are other possible drivers behind your colleague's persistent complaining, including anxiety, a desire for power, and resentment.

Anxiety

For many pessimists, imagining the worst-case scenario can be a knee-jerk response to anxiety. By thinking of everything that could go wrong, they feel like they can guard against those possibilities coming true. Of course, this is only helpful if they then take action to prevent their worst fears.

For example, think about the last time you applied for a job that you really wanted. During the process, you probably told yourself at one point (or maybe several) that you'd "never get an offer." That critical self-talk is certainly pessimistic. However, it can serve a functional purpose if you better prepare for your interview or do more research on the company in response.

It may be that your pessimistic colleague isn't aware that their mind always goes right to the negative, or maybe they think doing so is helpful. Perhaps, for example, they believe that by pooh-poohing ideas up front, they are rescuing the team from the agony of disappointment. Playing out their anxieties in this way can make those around them, especially optimists, uncomfortable. But recognizing that they're doing this because of worry, not because they want to rain on your parade, can make it easier to cope.

Power

Your naysaying colleague may be motivated by a desire for power as well. When I'm in a meeting with someone who is shooting down ideas left and right, I often interpret it as a deflection of responsibility. After all, if they insist, "That's never going to work!" they won't be left holding the bag if the project doesn't pan out as hoped. In some cases, I've also considered it a sign of laziness. If a colleague says, "We shouldn't even try," then they're off the hook for making the project work or contributing to it in any meaningful way.

But research by Eileen Chou at the University of Virginia reveals a different motive. Chou's findings indicate that pessimists find a sense of control in their negativity. Rather than avoiding responsibility, they may be asserting autonomy by disagreeing with the group. Others see them as more authoritative too. As Chou explained to me, "We assume that most people would shy away from naysayers or exclude them because they're a drag. But it's actually quite the opposite. People who have high status are often the people who dole out negative or contrarian remarks."[5] This creates a reinforcing cycle. Pessimists use negativity to feel powerful, and their cynicism makes others likelier to perceive them that way, and even to choose them as leaders, which turns the perception of authority into reality.

Resentment

Perhaps your glass-half-empty colleague is expressing disgruntlement. Take Phillippe. He and his colleague Audrey were both up for a promotion in the marketing department at the pharmaceutical company where they worked. Phillippe had been there for seven years and had had his eye on leading the team for a while. Audrey was a relative newcomer, having joined the organization eight months earlier. But the senior vice president of marketing believed Audrey had more potential, so gave the position to her. Phillippe spent the next six months putting down every idea that Audrey had and claiming that any new initiative she proposed had "already been tried" before her time and was "a complete failure."

In Phillippe's case, his behavior wasn't a matter of an anxious disposition or motivational focus. It was his resentment that led him to undercut Audrey and hinder the team's progress. You often see this cynical and jaded attitude in people who, like Phillippe, have been passed over for promotion, don't feel valued by the organization or their boss, or sense that they aren't earning the respect they deserve. So, unconsciously or not, they try to bring down those around them.

However, in some cases, a pessimist might be right to suspect foul play—especially given what we know about how people from underestimated groups, such as women and people of color, are frequently overlooked for promotions.

Regardless of what's motivating a cynic's behavior, there are costs to you and your organization.

The Costs of Working with a Pessimist

Research shows that pessimists themselves suffer great costs. They are more likely than optimists to experience anxiety and depression. They tend to report more stress and take longer to recover from illnesses and other setbacks. Some studies have shown that a negative outlook makes you less creative. There's even evidence that pessimists experience greater financial trouble: they are less likely than optimists to have put money aside for a major purchase or to have started an emergency fund. They also tend to worry more about money and finances than people who are optimistic.[6]

Since emotions, both positive and negative, are contagious, it's easy to get dragged into a pessimistic colleague's outlook, and you might experience some of the costs discussed earlier as a result.[7] You may become demoralized, worry about negative consequences more than usual, or start to feel like your actions won't make a difference at work. Or you might be irritable and stressed-out as you try to avoid the pessimist. The more time you spend with your negative colleague, the more likely you are to start seeing the world through their eyes.

This is what happened to Jamal when he had a manager, Courtney, who constantly criticized the company's leadership. This was one of Jamal's first jobs, so he didn't think to question Courtney's perspective. Instead, he began to see the company's leaders as Courtney portrayed them. "The constant negativity sapped all my enthusiasm, excitement, and optimism about the future," he explained to me. "I internalized her criticism and believed in the flaws of the leadership and our product." He says that he even doubted some of their teammates because whenever people didn't show up to work, Courtney accused them of faking sick. Even though their team consistently met or even exceeded their targets, "Courtney always made us feel as though we weren't working hard enough. This really created a divide among us. You can't successfully sell as a team when these fissures exist."

Just one pessimist on your team, especially one with authority like Courtney, can change how everyone interacts. Constant complaining can create divisions on a team, reduce everyone's satisfaction at work, erode trust, and foster negativity that pollutes the team—or organizational—culture.

None of us want to bear these costs. So how can you get along with your downer colleague? Start by asking yourself a few questions.

Questions to Ask Yourself

Answering the following questions will help you begin to map out a plan for improving the dynamic between you and your pessimistic colleague.

What are the possible sources of their pessimism?

Knowing what's leading a cynic to shoot down ideas or resist trying new approaches may point you to a solution you hadn't thought of. What's the underlying reason for the complaining? Do any of the motivations I just described—prevention focus, a need for power, or anxiety—seem to fit the bill? Might they be resentful of something?

If your colleague is anxious about a project failing, you might reassure them that they won't be penalized for trying something new. If they're afraid of "wasting time," reiterate why experiments can be valuable, even if they don't work out. If they're just burned-out or too busy and aren't keen to stretch themselves further, then maybe help troubleshoot how they can manage their workload (or reduce it if you're their boss).

Be proactive about figuring out the underlying reasons for their attitude. That's what Lucas did with his colleague Joe who complained nonstop about how their consulting team was sizing the market for a new medical device. The team met several times to go over the project, clearly divide up the work, and set goals and milestones. Joe did not productively contribute to any of these discussions. He would cross his arms and say things like "I don't see how this is useful for the client." Lucas pulled him aside and asked what was going on. After some back-and-forth, it became clear that Joe didn't fully understand what was expected of him. His pessimism was a defense mechanism. Lucas spent half a day with Joe going over what he needed to do and practicing the work with him. Together they sized five of thirty sub-segments of the market so Joe would then be comfortable doing the other twenty-five on his own. This approach worked. Lucas told me that Joe's "skepticism evaporated," and he stopped pushing back during their meetings.

Are their concerns legitimate?

A little cynicism is healthy, even necessary. Pessimists play an important role in society and in most workplaces, because of the balance they bring. They can helpfully point out risks that many of us—especially the optimists—tend to miss. They encourage caution when others are quick to push an initiative forward. We need dissenting voices to check our assumptions, advance our ideas, and prevent us from costly missteps. And negativity is sometimes warranted. When you look at what's happening around the world—soaring economic inequality, racial injustice, a rising wave of populism and nationalism—it's understandable that some people don't feel hopeful about the future. And insisting on positivity when we have lots of good reasons to be concerned about what comes next can make your head spin.[8]

Consider whether your team or organization has fallen into a "cult of positivity" where only agreement and optimism are rewarded. Do you leave room for people to openly disagree or express doubts? Maybe you are mislabeling a colleague a pessimist because they are simply willing to speak up when others are not.

Which of their behaviors are problematic?

Try to avoid painting your coworker and their gloomy attitude in broad strokes and pinpoint the exact behaviors that are creating issues for you. Is it that their negative comments discourage the rest of the team from speaking up? Or that they won't take on work unless they're 100 percent sure it will succeed?

I often hear people describe pessimists as "taking the air out of the room," and I've certainly worked with coworkers who have this effect. But get specific about what they're doing that's causing trouble. As Heidi Grant told me, "You want to be sure there is an actual problem. You might not like their way, but maybe you can just tune that out, roll your eyes, groan a bit, and then move on."[9]

Knowing exactly which behaviors are causing trouble for you and other colleagues will help you decide which strategies to employ.

Tactics to Try

If Winnie the Pooh, with his incessant optimism, wasn't able to change Eeyore's worldview, chances are you won't get your colleague to *always* look on the bright side. But there are steps you can take to make working with a pessimist more pleasant and productive.

Reframe cynicism as a gift

Assuming your colleague doesn't have malicious intentions, try to view them as having a special gift. When they point out yet another reason that the initiative you're working on is doomed to fail, tell yourself, *They are using their unique talent to help us see the risks.* This ability to point out potential flaws is often an undervalued attribute. Take a look at any number of the big corporate disasters that have taken place in the past several decades, from Enron, to Wells Fargo, to the BP oil spill, to the Boeing 747 Max tragedy. Experts who examined what caused these and other catastrophes consistently found that many employees were aware of the mistakes being made (or the crimes being committed) but didn't speak up about them.[10] Oftentimes, people stayed mum because organizational culture discouraged employees from raising concerns, and they feared the repercussions of doing so.[11]

Accepting pessimism for what it is will also build a connection. Finding common ground with your naysaying colleague and seeing logic and even value behind their gloomy disposition can help you get to a place where you can relate and, maybe, eventually get along. But changing your perspective is just the beginning—compassion alone is unlikely to stop your coworker from spreading their gospel of negativity.

Give them a role to play

If your colleague is a natural at pointing out risks, consider making that part of their formal role. You've undoubtedly heard the advice to appoint a devil's advocate who is tasked with raising difficult questions and challenging a group's thinking. Research shows that giving at least one person the right to push back in this way leads to better decision-making for the team as a whole.[12] This is a perfect task to assign to a pessimist. Since "devil's advocate" can have negative implications for some people, I like to call it "disagreer-in-chief."

One advantage of this tactic is that it helps the group avoid vilifying the pessimist and recasts them as a productive team member. Nilofer Merchant, a former tech executive and innovation expert, is a big proponent of the idea that divergent voices are key to both individual and corporate growth. As she writes, "Some leaders demonize people [who raise objections], accusing them of being the problem instead of solving the problem that is being raised. The reason is simple: It's not comfortable to see your shortcomings. It is this discomfort that causes leaders to deflect and defend. And, of course, when leaders do this, they limit whether the organization advances."[13]

Challenge their assumptions

> **Pessimist:** "This is doomed to fail."

> **You:** "Actually, I think this might work."

> **Pessimist:** "You're just being naive."

Trying to force a pessimist to see things your way can further entrench them in their perspective. Instead, engage with their underlying ideas and assumptions. Ask for clarification or more information about what they mean. For example, if your coworker says, "This project is never going to make it past Finance," ask them to explain why. Better yet, ask for alternative solutions: "What can we do to make sure the project does win their approval?" (Watch your tone so you don't come off as dismissive or condescending.) You can even model this behavior by using "but" statements. For instance, you might say, "It's possible that Finance won't go for this, *but* it's worth laying the groundwork now because next year, they're apt to approve more tech projects."

Heidi Grant says that there is a magical combination when it comes to engaging with pessimists: "You want to make clear that you believe it's going to be hard *and* that you believe you can be successful."[14] If you act like it's going to be easy, the pessimist will dismiss you. Conveying that you understand why they feel the way they do will improve your chances of nudging them toward a different perspective.

You can also reframe their complaints, while acknowledging them. For instance, if the pessimist grumbles that another team member is lazy, you might say something like "It's a busy time for everyone. I bet they're doing more than we can see." You don't need to be patronizing or mean, but it's helpful to present an alternative view. Or ask your downer colleague to be constructive. For example, you could say, "I can see why you're frustrated. Do you think there's anything we can do about this now?" Or "What could we try next time?" You don't need to come out and say, "Well, do something about it!" But you can increase a cynic's sense of agency by pointing out actions they can take, or even telling a story of a time when you encountered similar circumstances and responded productively.

Help them understand when their pessimism helps and when it hurts

Because a healthy dose of cynicism can be helpful to a group, your defeatist colleague may not be aware of the negative impact their words and actions are having on others. Help them see the light. For example, you can say, "When you make negative comments, the team gets stuck."

This is what Byron did when his colleague Morgan kept saying that their joint project wasn't going to work. Their team had been tasked with organizing the company's sales inventory and identifying operational efficiencies that might lead to new sales. Morgan worked for another department and was skeptical of the project from the beginning. Byron could see that Morgan's attitude was aggravating the other team members, and he was concerned it would impede their progress. He set up a one-on-one meeting with Morgan and explained, as diplomatically as he could, that whenever Morgan made negative comments, the team looked deflated and the conversation stopped. Morgan doubled down, reiterating his skepticism that the numerous departments involved could pull off the plan. Byron asked him to offer alternatives to the ideas being proposed in addition to raising concerns. "I explained that what he was doing felt like continually putting up roadblocks, without providing a detour sign," he told me. Morgan took Byron's advice, and when team members responded positively, seemingly relieved, it reinforced the new behavior. Byron told me that the team's recommendations were implemented with many of Morgan's alternative solutions. He believes the process was more rigorous because of his contributions.

Lean in to positivity

Positive peer pressure might help, too. Although singling people out is sometimes counterproductive, you can set norms for the whole team to observe that will nudge a killjoy in the right direction. For example, you could agree as a group that everyone will ask themselves before they speak, "Will this comment be helpful?" You might also agree that criticism should be accompanied by a suggestion of what to do instead, as Byron encouraged his colleague Morgan to do in the previous example.

It's especially important to take action if a cynic's negativity is swaying the team. Eileen Chou found in her research that even one pessimist can influence a group's decision-making process. Because of a group's inherent drive to maintain harmony, she explains that "if there's one outlier, the group moves toward the outlier to appease them." You can counter this tendency, she says, by agreeing that decisions shouldn't be driven by just one person's perspective.[15]

Fostering an atmosphere of positivity is another way of using peer pressure to encourage pessimists to look on the bright side. Michelle Gielan suggests, for example, that you might start meetings with a positive prompt, such as "What's one way that a colleague has made your life better or easier lately?" The specific prompt you use is less important than helping the team focus on something good.

Watch for polarizing

When experimenting with these tactics, watch that your actions don't inadvertently make your problem colleague dig their heels in deeper. As Grant says, "Many pessimists think optimists are idiots and they'll be eager to dismiss you as a wide-eyed moron. We think we can come at them with a fire hose and drown them with our optimism!"[16]

But pushing too hard for positivity could make them double down on the gloom and doom. Instead, respect their motivational style and even acknowledge what's right about their point of view. It helps to admit that you also have negative feelings or thoughts, and then validate their perspective—or some aspect of it that you agree with. You don't have to say, "You're absolutely right; this project won't succeed," but you can say, "I hear your concerns, and I share some of them. Help me understand what has led you to these conclusions."

Phrases to Use

Choosing the right words so you don't set off or alienate your pessimistic colleague is tricky. Here are some phrases to try out.

Refocus them on taking positive action

"What can we do to prevent the outcome you're predicting?"

"What would need to be true for us to succeed?"

"If you're unhappy with [person, leader, project], let's discuss what steps you can take to change the situation. I have some ideas, but I'd love to hear your thoughts first."

Don't let them get entrenched in their perspective

"There's a part of me that agrees with you that this might not work. And another part of me thinks it will. Let's tease out both perspectives."

"I hear your concerns, and I share some of them. Tell me more about what led you to that conclusion."

"I can see why you're frustrated. Do you think there's anything we can do about this now? Or what could we do differently next time?"

Reframe their perspective

"I wonder what another way of seeing this might be."

"You're good at identifying the downsides. What might we be missing here?"

Hang with the positive crowd

Spending time with more positive coworkers is a good way to bolster yourself against a storm of negativity. Seek out people who lift you up, as opposed to drag you down, and invest in building relationships with them.

Jamal, whose boss, Courtney, turned him against the company's leadership and his own teammates (see "The Costs of Working with a Pessimist"), used this tactic. Once he realized the negative impact that Courtney was having on him, he tried to avoid contact with her as much as possible. Instead, he focused his time on colleagues who were enthusiastic about the future. As he explained, "It helped me quite a bit to spend time with coworkers who were excited about their work and the company. They wanted to get out into the field and shout about our product from the rooftops!" Although Courtney never really changed her tune, Jamal was able to flourish with support from like-minded friends.

• • •

Let's return to the story of Simran and her colleague Theresa, who had nothing but complaints when she stopped by to chat. Simran told me that she made subtle changes to how she interacted with Theresa, and she tried to emphasize the positive. For instance, after three months of asking Theresa, "How are you?" every morning and getting a "negative earful every single day," she started asking, "What's good today?" The first few times, Theresa was taken aback and didn't have a response. But soon, she started answering the question. Simran says that she never asked, "How are you?" again. Instead, she'd inquire, "What went well in the meeting you had with that client?" or "Tell me about the best parts of your presentation."

She also learned to excuse herself when Theresa started on a tirade: "I'd politely get out of the conversation as quickly as I could." Simran admits that she was surprised that such small actions worked. Theresa didn't ever become a ray of sunshine, but Simran stopped dreading their interactions, and she says that she learned a lot about how to deal with negativity—not just from coworkers but from other people in her life as well. "I feel more able to stay out of the fray and not get dragged down," she says.

TACTICS TO REMEMBER
The Pessimist

DO:

- Encourage them to play disagreer-in-chief as part of their formal role.

- Engage with their underlying ideas and assumptions, asking for clarification or more information about what they mean.

- Convey that you understand why they feel the way they do and nudge them toward a different perspective.

- Help them understand when their pessimism helps and when it hurts.

- Set constructive norms for the whole team—for example, you could agree as a group that everyone will ask themselves before they speak, "Will this comment be helpful?"

- Acknowledge that you also have negative feelings or thoughts and validate their perspective or some aspect of it that you agree with.

- Spend time with more positive coworkers to bolster yourself against a storm of negativity.

DON'T:

- Try to drown them in positivity; that can further entrench them in their pessimism.

- Dismiss their perspective as unhelpful or illogical.

- Ignore their complaints or their concerns; they may have valid reasons for their naysaying.

5

The Victim

"Why does this always happen to me?"

There's a certain type of pessimist that is common enough and vexing enough to warrant its own archetype: the victim. This is the colleague who feels like everyone is out to get them. They don't take accountability for their actions and quickly point the finger at others when things go wrong. And when you try to give them constructive feedback, they respond with a "woe is me" attitude or a laundry list of excuses.

Like the pessimist, the victim believes that bad things are going to happen and that there's little they can do to change that, but they also believe—and complain—that these negative events happen to *them* in particular. While the pessimist will insist that "the sky is falling," the victim says, "The sky is falling *on me*."

Take Gerald. He had been brought in to manage a retail store that was lagging behind the company's other stores in the same area. The regional manager, Carlotta, was keen on hiring Gerald because, according to his résumé and references, he had engineered successful store turnarounds in the past. She imagined he'd be a "breath of fresh air" for the faltering store and its staff. But he turned out to be the opposite. "More like a wet blanket," she told me.

Right from the beginning, Gerald pushed back on the targets Carlotta set, claiming they weren't realistic, even though they were based on results that similar stores had been able to achieve. When she visited the store, she could see that he was bringing down the mood of the employees. "It was like a gray cloud whenever he walked in the room," she says. When Carlotta tried to push him to be more upbeat or to embrace the challenge of turning around the store, Gerald said that he simply couldn't do what was being asked of him. "He never took ownership or responsibility. Someone or something else was always to blame—the staff, the store location, the weather. You name it."

Gerald saw himself as a victim of circumstances, powerless to direct his own fate. Perhaps you've worked with someone who has the same mentality. Here are some of the behaviors that are common to this archetype:

- Feeling sorry for themselves and expecting others to do the same (pity party, anyone?)

- Evading responsibility for things that go wrong and placing blame on other people or external factors

- Pushing back on constructive feedback with excuses about why they can't be at fault

- Dragging others down with complaining and a "woe is me" attitude

- Wallowing in negative feelings

- Forecasting failure, particularly for themselves

Is it possible to help a colleague like Gerald change their mindset? Is there a way to get them to be more accountable? And how do you handle the emotional toll of working with someone who feels like they always have a target on their back?

In this chapter, I'll talk about this particular type of pessimist, what fuels them, and how to handle them. Since many of the tactics for getting along with someone who plays the victim are similar to those for dealing with a pessimist, this chapter is shorter than the others. I recommend reading both chapters to achieve the best results.

Let's start with what makes someone with a victim mentality tick.

The Background on Victim Behaviors

People who think of themselves as victims share several key traits with pessimists. They have the same negative *outlook* ("bad things will happen") and lack of *agency* ("I can do little to change that"), but unlike pessimists, they believe that other people or circumstances are at fault for the disappointing or distressing outcomes. As you can see from the list of typical behaviors, a victim's core beliefs and attitudes manifest in different ways than pessimists' do. Rather than pointing out risks all the time, victims are often consumed by who is to blame, which never happens to be them.

A team of academics in Israel coined a term that sheds light on this trait: *tendency for interpersonal victimhood* or TIV. The researchers define TIV as "an ongoing feeling that the self is a victim" and it's not just in one circumstance or relationship but across different kinds of relationships.[1] Many people, when faced with unpleasant moments, say, being cut in line at the grocery store or interrupted in a meeting, brush them off or confront them head-on. Those with TIV see these incidents as evidence of their own victimhood—that they are uniquely and unduly vulnerable to bad luck and suffering.

Other experts use the term *victim syndrome*. Manfred F. R. Kets de Vries, a psychoanalyst and professor of leadership development and organizational change at INSEAD, has developed a checklist to help people identify whether they're dealing with someone who suffers from this syndrome (see table 5-1).

Reviewing these questions can help you pinpoint which of your colleague's behaviors are particularly problematic. You can then tailor your approach based on the ones you want to address.

Keep in mind that a victim's habits are often rooted in real pain. Some people adopt a victim mentality as a response to trauma, manipulation, betrayal, or neglect. And it can have serious consequences such as loneliness, depression, and isolation.

Still, many people in this archetype maintain the attitude because it garners them certain benefits. Signaling suffering can be an effective

TABLE 5-1

Victim syndrome checklist

Checklist: Are you dealing with someone who suffers from victim syndrome?

- Does every conversation end up centered on their problems?
- Do they tend to play the "poor me" card?
- Do they engage in negative talk about themselves?
- Do they always expect the worst?
- Do they tend to act like a martyr?
- Do they feel that the world is out to get them?
- Do they believe that everyone else has an easier life?
- Do they focus solely on negative events and disappointments?
- Do they never feel responsible for their negative behavior?
- Do they tend to make others take responsibility for them?
- Do they seem to be addicted to misery, chaos, and drama?
- Is their misery contagious, affecting the mood state of others?
- Does blaming others seem to improve their state of mind?

Source: Adapted from Manfred F. R. Kets de Vries, "Are You a Victim of the Victim Syndrome?," *Organizational Dynamics* 43, no. 2 (July 2012), https://www.researchgate.net/publication/256028208_Are_You_a_Victim_of_the_Victim_Syndrome.

way to get attention or sympathy. It can also justify seeking retribution. As de Vries points out, "It's nice to be noticed and validated; it feels good when others pay us attention; and it's pleasant to have our dependency needs gratified."[2]

But when it comes to feeling like a victim or working with one, the costs outweigh the benefits.

The Costs of Working with a Victim

One of the differences between pessimism and victimhood is that there are upsides to the former, but not so much to the latter. While a pessimist's outlook can be helpful in identifying potential risks or pointing out pitfalls that others are missing, a victim's attitude rarely does more than irritate and alienate their coworkers.

The primary cost of working with someone with a victim mentality is emotional contagion. Carlotta's feeling that Gerald's presence was like a "gray cloud" is a common experience. A victim's insistence that things are bad and there's no way to change them can be contagious—you might begin to wonder if people or circumstances are pitted against *you*. Carlotta told me that Gerald's doubts had her focused on all the reasons the store couldn't succeed rather than the actions they could take to mount a comeback.

It's also exasperating working with someone who deflects responsibility. You might experience exhaustion from their constant negativity or burnout from trying to counter their influence on group morale. There's also a good chance of becoming resentful if you're having to do a victim's work for them or taking on the emotional burden of constantly persuading them that they're OK.

To improve your working relationship, start by asking yourself a few questions.

Questions to Ask Yourself

There are several questions about this woe-is-me behavior that you should consider as you develop a thoughtful response.

Are they truly a victim? Are they being targeted by colleagues, senior leaders, clients, or others?

Consider your coworker's complaints. Is it possible that their claims of ill treatment are true? There's a difference between being justifiably upset by ostracization or abuse in the workplace and unjustifiably feeling like the world is against you. There are many people who experience sexism, racism, ageism, and other inappropriate behavior at work whose complaints about unfair treatment are legitimate. Sometimes a statement like "she always plays the victim" can be used to dismiss egregious behavior from others and to even gaslight employees who are on the receiving end of mistreatment. That's why it's important that we carefully consider complaints and do our part to stop or remediate microaggressions, sexual harassment, and any other forms of discrimination and injustice. (There's more about responding effectively to microaggressions in chapter 9.)

Be careful of outright dismissal of your coworker's claims that they've been wronged and look closely at what's going on. To find out, pay closer attention to dynamics in meetings or talk to a trusted colleague who has better insight into what your colleague is experiencing—perhaps a longtime collaborator or friend of the victim. If you do discover that their assertions are legitimate, or even if you suspect they are, consider what you can do to support them, such as referring them to someone internally who can take action.

What triggers your colleague's victim attitude?

Some people, like Gerald, feel like a victim almost all the time. Others fall into the mindset only under certain circumstances. Does your colleague play the victim when they get tough feedback? Or when they are solely responsible for something consequential (perhaps because they buckle under pressure)? Are there particular people who seem to bring out the worst in them?

Observing their behavior will give you clues about which tactics to experiment with.

Tactics to Try

Many of the tactics that work with a pessimist, such as keeping the group positive to counteract their doom and gloom and providing a counternarrative to their "I never get what I want" complaints, will help with victims, too. (Refer to chapter 4 for more on these.) There are other strategies that are specific to this archetype, such as offering a different perspective and reminding a victim that they do have control over some outcomes. Let's take a closer look.

Offer validation

Often a victim wants to be seen or heard, and they see complaining as the only way to get that validation. Offer some positive reinforcement and openly express appreciation for the value your colleague brings to the team. Of course, you don't want them to feel like they only get compliments when they complain, so save your praise for a time when they're not griping.

My daughter learned this lesson with a friend who was acting like a victim and once told her, "I feel like no one likes me." Looking to make him feel better, my daughter started listing all of the things that their classmates appreciated about him—his wry sense of humor, how he was willing to push back on a teacher who was being unfair. The conversation seemingly cheered him. But he kept coming back to my daughter, repeating his belief that people didn't like him. She would again list his positive attributes, adding to the list each time, but this exchange exhausted her, and she eventually started to resent him. So she changed tactics and found ways to compliment him *before* he came to her seeking validation, which disrupted the cycle. He seemed less needy overall, and she wasn't getting sucked into a regular conversation where she was expected to shower him with flattery.

With your coworker, recognize their accomplishments, even if they're small, or tell them what you most appreciate about them. The only rule is that whatever you say must be genuine. False compliments won't work.

Help increase their sense of agency

If they say, "That's out of my control," and you say, "No, it's not!" the conversation is likely to stall out quickly. Instead, say something like "I hear you. I don't react well either when I feel powerless." Then, ask what they would do if they had the authority or capability to take action and help them think of ways they can follow through with their ideas. For instance, you could say, "I understand that you feel like the leadership team hasn't been willing to dedicate the resources you need to make this project a success. That's frustrating. If you got to make the decisions, what would you do differently?" You can even offer to help make a list of steps they can take. If your coworker can't get out of their own way, try a different tack with a question like "How would someone who was known for getting what they want act in this situation?" By taking someone else's perspective, they may be able to brainstorm more effectively.

Anat's colleague Sheila frequently complained about how she was left out of important meetings by their mutual boss, Noni. Initially, Anat told Sheila that he was sure it was just an oversight, and she shouldn't take it personally. But those attempts to reassure her only made Sheila double down on her claim that she was being intentionally singled out. So he tried a different approach, asking her to express all the reasons she should be at those meetings. She had a ready list, to which Anat responded, "That all makes sense. Have you tried explaining that to Noni?" Sheila said she had, and Anat countered, "What if you tried again?" To his surprise, Sheila took his advice and, in her next one-on-one with Noni, mentioned the reasons why she should be on the invite list. Noni hadn't realized that Sheila wanted in on the meetings but was happy to include her going forward.

Encourage them to take responsibility

A victim loves to deflect responsibility. Nothing ever seems to be their fault or in their control. When they resort to pointing fingers, try a direct approach: "I see this as your responsibility—let's talk about why you don't see it that way." When you frame the issue clearly, they may have a tough time diverting blame. Or try a gentler way and see if offering to share responsibility—assuming that's warranted—helps them ease up on the defensiveness a bit. You might say, "The entire team is on the hook for the success of this project, including you and me. While no single person will be blamed if we fail, we all need to take responsibility for pushing things forward." Assuaging their fear about being blamed may help them take ownership.

This is what Carlotta did with Gerald. After his ninety-day employment trial, Carlotta was honest with Gerald about her concern that he may not work out. Not surprisingly, he became extremely defensive. Unwilling to give up on him, she tried to be clearer about the changes she wanted to see. She explained to Gerald that the staff was looking to him for inspiration and motivation and that his complaints had ripple effects. She also asked him to be more constructive. "I didn't want to cut off his complaining completely because some of what he was unhappy about was valid, but I did ask that whenever he brought a problem to me in the future that he also present at least one potential solution," she says. Carlotta laughed the first time Gerald did this because he quickly followed up his recommended solutions with "I'm not sure if this will work." But over time, he got better at leaving out the caveats.

Turn their focus to helping others

This may seem counterintuitive, but when a victim (or anyone else, for that matter) feels stuck and unable to help themselves, you can sometimes nudge them out of a rut by encouraging them to help someone else. There's lots of research that shows that giving to others—whether it's in the form of time, money, or support—improves our own happiness.[3] For a coworker with a victim mentality, suggesting they mentor a colleague, lend their expertise to another team, or even volunteer outside of work can deter wallowing and give them a greater sense of agency.

Protect yourself

It's possible for one person who thinks that the world is against them to convert an entire team to their point of view. I've seen this happen in organizations where a particular department—often led by

Phrases to Use

Here are a few phrases that can help you put the tactics in this chapter into practice.

Offer validation

"It sucks to feel like you're not getting what you need."

"It sounds like the situation is still bothering you. I'm sorry."

Nudge them toward solutions

"Have you considered talking to your boss about this?"

"That's too bad. What do you think you could've done differently? What have you learned?"

"I can see that this is not a great situation for you. Are you interested in talking through what we could do differently going forward?"

"What would you like to see happen now?"

"Sometimes we have more control than we think. What's one step you can take to see if you can make a difference here?"

Reframe their comments

"It sounds like a lot hasn't worked out the way you had hoped. What has gone well so far?"

"When you blame someone else, it's easy to feel like the victim, which isn't helpful to you. What's another way of seeing this situation?"

Redirect

"I hope you don't mind me changing the topic, but have you watched [name of television show or movie] yet?"

"I'm on a deadline so I need to get back to work. But I'll keep my fingers crossed that things work out."

someone with a victim mentality—starts to act as if no one else in the organization understands or appreciates what they do. This becomes a self-fulfilling prophecy because the more defensively people in the unit behave, the less trustworthy they appear, prompting their colleagues to doubt their capabilities or avoid collaborating altogether. All the more reason to set and stick to boundaries with a victim, especially if the person is your manager—you don't want their paranoia, finger-pointing, or failure to be accountable to damage your team's reputation.

One way to protect yourself from emotional contagion is to simply change the subject when they start complaining. If they don't take the hint, you can always excuse yourself to refocus on your work. (There's more on protecting yourself from the negative consequences of any of the archetypes in chapter 12.)

· · ·

Carlotta accepted that she wasn't going to change Gerald's personality. "I don't think he was a particularly happy person," she says. "But the more I offered to co-own things with him, the less he acted like a victim." This meant that Carlotta had to emphasize the fact that Gerald wouldn't be the only one blamed if the store missed its targets. When she did that, he stopped pointing the finger at others, complained less, and proactively began trying to solve his own problems.

These changes were good for everyone: Gerald was able to stay on at the store and he helped the team to turn the underperforming location around. Curbing someone's tendency to see themselves as a victim of fate is difficult, but Carlotta's experience with Gerald shows that time, energy, and a strategic approach can help an ever-suffering colleague become a more productive member of the team.

TACTICS TO REMEMBER
The Victim

DO:

- Provide positive reinforcement and openly express appreciation for the value your colleague brings to the team.

- Ask what they would do if they had the authority or capability to take action and help them think of ways they can follow through with their ideas.

- Offer to help make a list of steps they can take to achieve their goals.

- Take a direct approach and say something like "I see this as your responsibility—let's talk about why you don't see it that way."

- Boost their sense of agency by encouraging them to mentor a colleague, lend their expertise to another team, or even volunteer outside of work.

DON'T:

- Only give them validation when they complain (you'll reward their bellyaching).

- Suffer through their griping sessions—it's OK to excuse yourself or change the subject to something more neutral.

6

The Passive-
Aggressive Peer

"Fine. Whatever."

Malik's new coworker, Susan, was turning out to be a nightmare. Their boss had asked Malik to show Susan how to complete several reports that she'd eventually be responsible for. But when he sat down with her, she acted like she already knew how to do them since she'd done something similar at a previous job. "It was impossible since they were specific to our organization, but when I pointed that out, she told me not to get so worked up," he shared with me. "That was the first sign that something was wrong."

Several weeks later, Malik's boss inquired why he hadn't yet trained Susan on the reports. He didn't want to get defensive, so Malik went back to Susan and offered to walk her through the steps again. She responded that she "had it under control," and then asked him why he was so upset. When he told her that their boss was under the impression that he hadn't done his job, Susan said she had no idea what he was talking about.

Malik, feeling desperate, tried to be straightforward with her, "Is everything OK? Are we good?" Susan smiled and said, "Of course, everything's great!"

Malik was dealing with a passive-aggressive coworker: someone who appears to comply with the wishes and needs of others but then passively resists following through. Sometimes the saboteur will end up doing the task but too late to be helpful or in a way that doesn't meet the stated goals.

When Malik first told me his story, I was reminded of a tactic I employed as a kid. When asked to do dishes, rather than tell my mom I didn't want to do them (which, let's be fair, wasn't really an option), I did a bad job, hoping that I wouldn't be assigned the chore again.

There are many ways that passive-aggression shows up at work. Is your problem colleague displaying any of the telltale signs?

- Deliberately ignoring deadlines after they've agreed to meet them

- Promising to send an email that never arrives

- Acting rudely toward you (say, ignoring you in a meeting or interrupting you) and then denying there's anything wrong when you confront them, claiming "It's all in your head" or "I have *no* idea what you're talking about"

- Displaying body language that projects anger or sullenness but insisting they're fine

- Implying that they aren't happy with your work but refusing to come out and say so or give you direct feedback

- Disguising insults as compliments. For instance, "You have such a relaxed style!" might actually mean "I think you're lazy"

- Twisting your words in a disagreement so it seems like you're the one who's in the wrong

Susan *said* that everything was great, but Malik could tell that something was off. After all, she still didn't know how to do the reports, so Malik had to do them. He was frustrated and didn't want his boss to think that he wasn't able to delegate or, worse, that he was intentionally standing in the way of Susan's success. He was at a loss—what should he do?

The first step is to develop a deeper understanding of why people resort to passive-aggression in the first place.

The Background on Passive-Aggressive Behavior

The term *passive-aggressive* originated in the 1940s in the American military to describe soldiers who didn't comply with superiors' commands.[1] Soon after, it became an official diagnosis called "passive-aggressive personality disorder," but was eventually removed from the American Psychiatric Association's diagnostic manual in the 1990s.[2] The associated behaviors are sometimes seen as a symptom of other mental disorders, such as narcissism, but it's not considered a distinct condition.

Gabrielle Adams, a professor at the University of Virginia who has done several studies on interpersonal conflict at work, defines passive-aggression as not being forthcoming about what you're truly thinking and using indirect methods to express your thoughts and feelings.[3] People often use tactics like the ones listed earlier when they want to avoid saying no to someone or being honest about what they're actually feeling, or they're trying to manipulate the situation in their favor without being obvious about doing so.

Take this text I sent my husband the other day: *It's fine. If that's what you want to do.*

I had wanted him to come home straight after work to help walk the dog, get dinner ready, and supervise our kid's homework, and he wanted to run a few errands first. It didn't really matter what he did. He was coming home eventually, and I didn't really need his help. I'd handled these tasks on my own hundreds of times.

So why did I send the text? It was a last-ditch effort to make him feel guilty and manipulate him into doing what *I* wanted him to do. And it was completely passive-aggressive.

People rarely make the conscious decision to behave in a passive-aggressive way. Rather, it's a reaction, and it's often driven by the fear of failure or rejection, a desire to avoid conflict, or a drive to gain power.

Fear of failure or rejection

Rather than rocking the boat or saying what they're really thinking, your passive-aggressive colleague may be afraid of looking like they don't know what they're doing or of being rejected by you. Malik's colleague Susan clearly seemed invested in appearing like someone who knew how to complete the reports (even though there was no reason she should know).

Rather than admit they might not be able to do what you asked, a passive-aggressive colleague pushes problems back on you. To be on the receiving end of this behavior can be disorienting, and as Malik felt, it can seem like they are intentionally trying to make you look bad or behave deceitfully, when in fact they are often trying to protect themselves from looking bad. Columbia professor E. Tory Higgins told the *New York Times*: "Some of the people being demeaned as passive-aggressive are in fact being extremely careful not to commit mistakes, a strategy that has been successful for them." They become difficult, he said, "when their cautious instincts are overwhelmed by demands that they perceive as unreasonable."[4] Rather than express their feelings, they bottle them up and resent the person making the demands.

I notice myself slipping into this reaction when I feel swamped by requests from other people. Rather than acknowledging that I feel put out and unable to help, I will insinuate that they were wrong to even ask.

Some research has shown that certain types of managers, particularly those with exacting standards, have a knack for triggering passive-aggressive reactions in people.[5] One of my coaching clients worked for an autocratic boss, for instance, who expected everyone to approach work in the same way and was unforgiving of mistakes. As a result, my client and his peers resorted to making excuses and blaming others when projects didn't go as expected. My client had fallen into a pattern of using sarcasm to communicate his frustration with his colleagues, which had garnered him a reputation for being passive-aggressive, when really what he wanted was to not shoulder all the blame when something went wrong.

Conflict avoidance

People who fit this archetype are generally conflict avoidant. Rather than express what they're thinking and feeling straightforwardly, they rely on more subtle methods to communicate their thoughts or dissent. It may be that prior negative experiences in the workplace taught them that it's not safe to openly disagree.

Organizational culture might be a factor, too. In many workplaces, direct, overt disagreement is not the norm, so some people have learned to be passive-aggressive as a way of getting what they need to do their jobs. Research has shown that when a team's goals aren't clear or a manager isn't explicit about what metrics they'll use to evaluate individual performance, employees behave passive-aggressively as they try to sort out what's going on or grapple with uncertainty about their future at the company.[6]

Similarly, big organizational changes such as layoffs, a merger, or restructuring can lead to passive-aggression if people feel vulnerable.[7] This is especially true if an employee feels spurned by the company, if they've been passed over for a promotion or a raise or have otherwise been denied something they felt was owed to them, such as a prized assignment. This violation of the psychological contract between employer and employee is understandably frustrating, and rather than speaking up about what they're upset about, some people retaliate, often in passive-aggressive ways.

I've been there myself: when I was annoyed at a boss who I thought was dragging his feet promoting me, I started leaving work early claiming I had "personal appointments." Eventually he confronted me about bailing early and I admitted my frustration. He explained that my promotion was in process, but it was taking time. I can still hear his voice saying, "Please be patient."

TABLE 6-1

Common root causes of passive-aggressive behavior

Fear of . . .	Desire for/to . . .
Failure	Perfection
Rejection	Be liked
Conflict	Harmony
Being powerless or lacking influence	Exert control

Expression of powerlessness

People who traditionally have less power in an organization may employ passive-aggressive tactics as a way to exercise influence when other, more straightforward approaches could be dangerous to their careers or reputations. In many cultures, for instance, women are socialized to not say what's on their minds. Passive-aggression is, therefore, a more socially acceptable way to get their point across in these contexts. The *double bind*—having to choose between being perceived as competent but not likable, or likable but not leadership material—could also force women into positions where passive-aggression is the only way to make their needs or desires known because being direct or assertive doesn't comply with gender norms.[8] This is not to say that only women behave passive-aggressively. I'm sure you know people of all genders who engage in these tactics. I offer this as insight into why some people who don't always have formal power feel compelled to resort to these behaviors.

Table 6-1 summarizes some of the common root causes of passive-aggressive behavior.

The Costs of Working with a Passive-Aggressive Person

No matter the reason for their behavior, dealing with a passive-aggressive peer is no walk in the park. You often question yourself, wondering, "Am I imagining these attacks? Am I losing my mind?"

You don't know if you can trust your colleague or not. All of the worrying and ruminating about your interactions can hurt your morale and even lead to burnout.

Research shows that the costs are not just to you but to the organization and its bottom line as well.[9] When there's one person (or several people) on a team who behave passive-aggressively, it's more likely that the team will make slower decisions, communicate ineffectively, and engage in unhealthy conflict.

One study showed that organizations with a passive-aggressive culture were about half as profitable compared to their peers. The study authors described companies that fall into that category this way: "In passive-aggressive organizations, people pay . . . directives lip service, putting in only enough effort to appear compliant. Employees feel free to do as they see fit because there are hardly ever unpleasant consequences, and the directives themselves are often misguided and thus seem worthy of defiance."[10]

What can you do to avoid these costs—for yourself and your organization—and put yourself on a path to a better relationship with your passive-aggressive colleague? The first step, as with any difficult colleague, is to do some reflecting.

Questions to Ask Yourself

Ask yourself the following questions about the dynamic between you and your passive-aggressive peer.

Is this behavior about you or might it be triggered by something else?

It's possible that your colleague's conduct has nothing to do with you. Look at the common root causes in table 6-1. Could your coworker be feeling insecure? Afraid to make mistakes? Worried about their own reputation and career? Does the company culture encourage passive-aggressive behavior? Maybe last time they raised a concern or pushed back, another coworker bit their head off. What's the level of psychological safety on your team? Does everyone feel comfortable speaking their minds or are people punished for expressing dissent?

Is your colleague intentionally trying to hurt you?

Be honest with yourself about whether your colleague is truly out to get you. Gabrielle Adams separates run-of-the-mill passive-aggression from "purposeful lying that's meant to obscure a person's intentions."[11] We often assign negative intentions to others where they don't exist. Is it possible that they're struggling and taking out their anxiety on you?

Of course, people's objectives aren't always clear. When your colleague doesn't do their part on a shared project or makes sarcastic remarks about you, they could be trying to cover up their own shortcomings, or they might be trying to make you look bad so that they have a better chance of getting assigned to your boss's pet project. Be generous in your interpretations but also be realistic about what's going on.

Are past experiences with your passive-aggressive peer coloring present interactions?

When someone has acted passive-aggressively in the past, *confirmation bias* primes us to see all of their behavior in the same light. Ask whether you're interpreting your colleague's actions through a tainted lens and assuming they're repeating past mistakes. One way to increase your objectivity is to think of a coworker who you get along with well and ask yourself: "How would I interpret this same behavior from that person?"

When is this person passive-aggressive?

Sometimes people act out under certain conditions whether it's when they're stressed, when they work with particular colleagues, or when they feel like their authority, job security, or their values are threatened. Pay attention to when your coworker is passive-aggressive.

Is it in specific meetings? Or when a certain person is present? Do they communicate better in person than over email (or vice versa)?

Reflecting on these questions will help you understand your colleague better and, most importantly, inform which tactics to choose.

Tactics to Try

While there is no universal script for dealing with a passive-aggressive coworker, the following tactics will improve your odds of getting along. Use whichever ones you think will be most helpful in your unique situation. Try one (or two) things, see what you learn, and adjust accordingly.

Avoid the passive-aggressive label

It's tempting to call out the behavior directly. But saying "stop being so passive-aggressive" will only make things worse. Why? The phrase is loaded, and it's rare that someone would be willing to acknowledge that's what they're doing. I'd be shocked if your colleague said, "Yeah, you're right. I'll stop." More likely it's going to make them angrier and more defensive. You also don't want to assign them feelings they might not recognize—or be willing to admit—they have. Lindred Greer, a professor at the University of Michigan's Ross School of Business, says that labeling people's emotions for them can backfire.[12] As she told me, "The chances of you choosing the right emotion are so small, you're likely to mislabel," further frustrating them.[13] Telling a coworker you're in conflict with their "looking angry" or "seeming frustrated" does little to lessen the tension. What should you do instead?

Focus on the content, not the delivery

Seek to understand what your colleague is really trying to say. What is the underlying idea they're attempting to convey (even if it's wrapped up in a snarky comment)? Do they think that the way you're running a project isn't working? Or do they disagree about the team's goals?

Remember that not everyone feels comfortable discussing their thoughts and opinions openly. If you can focus on your coworker's underlying concern or question, rather than the way they're expressing themselves, you can address the actual problem.

Armed with insight into your coworker's thoughts, *you* can then be direct. Say something like: "You made a good point in that exchange we had the other day. Here's what I heard you saying." Ideally, this will allow your evasive colleague to talk more frankly about their concerns (there's more advice on how to do that in the next section).

This is what Meena did with her colleague Victor, who seemed intent on undermining her whenever they collaborated. Meena, a leadership trainer, valued Victor's expertise and often asked him to be her copresenter, which he was seemingly happy to do. But during their presentations, he would sometimes steal her thunder, interjecting with many of the critical points that they'd agreed Meena would share with the audience. Meena's attempts to deal with Victor directly didn't work—he just denied that he was doing anything wrong. Looking for the motivation behind Victor's sabotage, Meena started to suspect that he didn't like her being positioned as the subject-matter expert.

Based on her hunch, she tried a different tactic, appealing to Victor's expertise during their planning sessions. She'd say things like, "I know you have a lot of experience in this area and want you to have the chance to share what you know." And it helped—their joint presentations went much more smoothly with Meena's efforts to share the spotlight. She acknowledges that what she really wanted from Victor was an apology, but at the end of the day, it was enough that he stopped undermining her.

Don't think of an empathetic approach like Meena's as letting your coworker off the hook for their bad behavior. Instead, see it as a way to nudge them into being more productive in their interactions and for you to get what you need.

Open up a conversation

Of course, you may not fully understand what your coworker really wants. If they express excitement when you ask them to help out with a project, but then never show up to the meetings or respond to your emails, it can be hard to figure out why you're getting the cold shoulder. But spend some time thinking about possible explanations. In negotiation, this is known as assessing the other person's interests. What do they care about? What do they want to achieve?

Then do what Gabrielle Adams calls "hypothesis testing": ask—respectfully and without judgment—about what's going on. For instance, you might say: "I've noticed that you haven't been responding to my emails. Is there something wrong? I don't mean to pry, but I just want to be sure everything's OK."

Social psychologist Heidi Grant says that it's beneficial to "create a safe environment for the person to talk to you about what's bothering them. You want to roll out the red carpet for a direct conversation so they don't feel the need to be passive-aggressive."[14] She suggests making clear that you're interested in their perspective, no matter how hard it may be for you to hear.

The advantage to opening up a conversation like this is that it allows the person to label their own behavior and emotions. If your colleague acknowledges how they're actually feeling (although there's no guarantee that they will), they are one step closer to breaking the habit of responding passive-aggressively.

Don't take the bait in email or text

It's worth noting that email and chat platforms are a horrible medium for any difficult conversation, but especially one with a passive-aggressive colleague. If your coworker makes jabs in writing, keep your response professional and short. For example, if your coworker writes, "Not sure if you saw my last email," you can respond with a simple, "Thanks for the reminder." If they write, "As we discussed earlier," and recap a conversation you both know you had, you can respond with, "Thanks for the recap." Model the respectful candor you wish your colleague would exhibit. Don't take the bait. If it's impossible to stay above the fray, pick up the phone or schedule a video call or a face-to-face meeting. This will force your colleague to talk with you more directly.

Make direct requests

You can be even more direct. As I mentioned earlier, accusing your colleague of being passive-aggressive is unlikely to work, but you can call attention to what's happening. With this tactic, it's best to stick to facts: the things you know for sure, without emotion, judgment, or exaggeration. You might start by saying, "You said that you wanted to help with this project and you haven't joined the three meetings we've had so far. You didn't respond to the email I sent last week about next steps." Then explain the impact these actions have had on you: "I'm disappointed and stressed-out because I'm not able to do all of the work myself and I had hoped to have your help." Finally, and this is the tricky part, make a straightforward request: "If you are still interested in helping out, and I hope you are, I'd like you to attend the meetings. If you aren't able to, I need to know now so I can find an alternative solution."

Keep in mind that a passive-aggressive type will probably deflect responsibility ("I assumed my attendance was optional!" "I said that I might help out, but I never committed!"), so don't be surprised if you get pushback. They may even try to twist your words or take your comments out of context: "I heard you say that you didn't want anyone extra at that meeting." In those cases, calmly respond, without getting defensive, "What I meant was . . ." You can even add, "Sorry if that wasn't clear" or "We must've had a miscommunication." Don't get into a tug of war about who is right and who is wrong. And remember that you can only control your half of the interaction—you can't ensure a productive response. However, by respectfully acknowledging your colleague's behavior, you're letting them know that you've noted their passive-aggression and that you are a straight shooter who doesn't intend to let them get away with it.

Get support from the team

It's easier to get caught up in a never-ending "You're mad," "No, I'm not" war when it's just the two of you. So enlist the help of your teammates. You don't need to gang up on anyone, but you don't have to deal with the situation alone either.

Start by asking whether others are noticing similar behaviors. Frame your inquiries as an attempt to constructively improve the relationship, so it doesn't come across as gossiping or bad-mouthing your colleague. You might ask something like: "I was wondering how Shawn's comment landed with you. How did you interpret that?"

If your teammates confirm that counterproductive behavior is occurring, you can decide together how to proceed. For example, it might help to set guidelines for how everyone on your team will interact. You can decide collectively that when you're discussing next steps, everyone will verbally commit to what they will do, rather than rely on head-nodding or assume silence is compliance. You might also take notes about who's supposed to do what by when, so there are clear action items and deadlines you can circulate afterward.

If your colleague later denies agreeing to something or fails to do their part, the team can help hold them accountable. Even the worst offenders are likely to give in to peer pressure and public accountability.

Take this example from Mitch, who worked in the student guidance office of a public high school. He was struggling with his colleague Alicia. "She would agree to a plan in a meeting but then sabotage it by not following through," he explained. Alicia responded defensively, "That's not how I remember it" or "I didn't think we had finalized the plan." He tried to talk about these "misunderstandings" with her, but she always shrugged him off. "She'd say she was busy or didn't have time to talk," he said.

When Mitch reported to Rita, his and Alicia's boss, that a certain project hadn't gotten done because of this confounding dynamic, Rita said that she had noticed the pattern too. Together, they devised a plan to hold Alicia accountable. "She and I agreed that she would publicly ask for a volunteer to take notes at each meeting, [documenting]

Phrases to Use

Here is some sample language to help jump-start your thinking about how to have productive conversations with your passive-aggressive colleague.

Focus on the content, not the delivery

"What I heard you say was . . ."

"I interpreted what you just said as meaning . . . . Did I get that right?"

"I noticed that you pushed away from the table [or rolled your eyes]. What's your reaction to this discussion?"

"I heard you say [quick summary], but I wasn't sure if you meant something else. Is there something I'm not understanding?"

Get help from the team

"I was wondering how Rachel's comment landed with you. How did you interpret that?"

---

who would be responsible for accomplishing each task and by when," Mitch recalled to me. He was the first volunteer.

The approach worked. After Mitch sent around the task list, Alicia couldn't make excuses. She was accountable to everyone who attended the meetings. And Mitch didn't mind the additional work: "The extra effort I put in was less than the time I was spending fuming about my coworker and picking up the pieces of the things she didn't complete. It actually helped everyone in our department be more productive and was something we should've done a long time ago."

Establishing healthy norms as a team will pay off in the long term. A team-based approach like the one Mitch used has been found in a variety of studies to reduce incivility in general.[15] Together you can

"Let's all make sure we're clear on next steps. Does someone want to take a stab at recapping who is going to do what? I'll take notes to send around afterward."

Be direct

"You made a good point in that exchange we had the other day. Here's what I heard you saying."

"I've noticed that you haven't been responding to my emails. Is there something wrong? I don't mean to pry, but just want to be sure everything's OK."

Managing someone who is passive-aggressive

"I'm concerned that you didn't raise this during the meeting. Are you hoping that the group can readdress this issue?"

"Is there new information that means we should reconsider the decision we already made?"

---

agree to be more up front about your frustrations and collectively model the honest and direct interactions you want to happen.

If you're a manager, you have a responsibility to act

If you lead a team on which one or more members are acting passive-aggressively, don't delay—this behavior corrodes trust and psychological safety. You have a responsibility to make clear that underhanded behavior isn't tolerated. This starts with establishing group norms like the ones mentioned earlier and reinforcing them however you can—in team meetings, at important events, and through recognition. The idea is to empower the group to hold one another accountable for being respectful and to stop rewarding passive-aggression and other detrimental behavior.

You also need to make it OK for people to dissent, debate, and express their true opinions. You don't want people to act like they see eye to eye but undermine one another or disagree behind closed doors. Patrick Lencioni, author of *The Five Dysfunctions of a Team*, refers to this phenomenon as "artificial harmony," and explains that it creates a breeding ground for passive-aggression. "When team members do not openly debate and disagree about important ideas, they often turn to back-channel personal attacks, which are far nastier and more harmful than any heated argument over issues," he writes. "Contrary to the notion that teams waste time and energy arguing, those that avoid conflict actually doom themselves to revisiting issues again and again, without resolution."[16]

Focus on the benefits of addressing conflict directly and set some ground rules. You might say to the group, "I'm concerned that we aren't using our meetings effectively to share all of our opinions." And don't hesitate to confront counterproductive behavior head-on. For example, you could say, "Two or three people come to my office after every meeting to discuss something that should have been raised in the meeting—that's an indication that we're not collaborating effectively, and it's not a good use of everyone's time." By calmly and directly highlighting instances of passive-aggression, without singling anyone out, you help make forthright communication the standard to which everyone will be held.

• • •

Remember Malik at the beginning of this chapter? He tried a lot of tactics with Susan, his passive-aggressive coworker who wouldn't admit that she didn't know how to do the reports he was supposed to train her on. At first, nothing worked. Susan continued to lie. Malik found comfort in his other colleagues. "Luckily for me, I wasn't the only one who she treated poorly. Two other people in our department noticed the same kind of thing, so we were able to commiserate," he says. These weren't unproductive griping sessions. Rather they let him blow off steam. "I had a choice to be angry at work every day or to shrug off her behavior," he says.

He decided to focus on what he could control: himself. When she tried to say she already knew how to do something, Malik would nod and continue to explain how to do it. He found it frustrating to have to pretend she wasn't being difficult, but by focusing on what needed to get done, he no longer looked bad to his boss. And, over time, as Susan got more comfortable in her role, she was less defensive.

Sometimes the tactics in this chapter will really turn things around—and sometimes, as in Malik's case, they won't entirely. But your challenging coworker doesn't have to ruin your day, week, and certainly not your career. Focus on what you do like about your job and the colleagues you enjoy working with. That sort of optimism will help, particularly with someone who is shadowboxing with you.

TACTICS TO REMEMBER
The Passive-Aggressive Peer

DO:

- Try to understand the underlying idea they're attempting to convey.

- Make clear that you're interested in their perspective, even if it's not what they think you want to hear.

- Focus on facts: the things you know for sure, without emotion, judgment, or exaggeration.

- Set guidelines for how everyone on your team—or on a particular project—will interact. For example, when you're discussing next steps, decide that everyone will verbally commit to what they will do, rather than rely on head-nodding or assume silence is compliance.

- Agree to be up front as a team about any frustrations and model the honest and direct interactions you want to happen.

DON'T:

- Take their behavior personally—while you may feel like a target, chances are they treat others similarly.

- Accuse them of behaving passive-aggressively—it'll only make the situation worse.

- Try to guess what they're feeling—mislabeling their emotions can lead to further distrust.

- Take the bait and respond angrily to a passive-aggressive email or text—take the conversation offline.

7

The Know-It-All

"Well, actually . . ."

Lucia dreaded interacting with her colleague Ray. Meetings that were scheduled for an hour would last two. Once Ray started talking, he wouldn't stop. "He loved to be heard, so he would always go on and on and on to anybody who would listen," she told me.

She and her colleagues exchanged knowing glances when Ray launched into one of his monologues. If people tried to interrupt him, he raised his voice to speak over them. The implicit message underlying these diatribes was that he knew what the team and company needed and everyone else should listen. "There's no doubt he was a smart man," Lucia says, "but he did little more than talk about everything he knew. He delegated almost all of his work to others."

Most of us have dealt with a coworker like Ray at some point in our careers. The know-it-all who is convinced that they're the smartest person in the room, hogs airtime in meetings, and has no qualms about interrupting others. They gleefully inform you of what's right, even if they're clearly wrong—or they're lacking information or fail to understand the nuances of a situation.

Here are some of the hallmarks of the office know-it-all:

- Displaying a "my way or the highway" attitude

- Monopolizing conversations, refusing to be interrupted, and talking over others

- Positioning their own ideas as superior

- Refusing to listen to or heed criticism or feedback

- Speaking in a condescending tone

- Explaining things that others already understand

- Rarely asking questions or displaying curiosity

- Stealing or not sharing credit for group successes

- Jumping into conversations uninvited

Lucia felt trapped whenever she was talking with Ray and found herself lying to get out of meetings with him. She didn't like resorting to these tactics, but she wasn't sure how else to handle his condescending manner and the time lost to his pontificating on a daily basis.

Should Lucia point out Ray's domineering style? Or should she find more subtle ways of dealing with him? How do you work with someone who has such a huge ego?

The first step toward a better working relationship with someone like Ray is to understand what makes them tick.

The Background on Know-It-All Behavior

When we talk about our know-it-all colleagues, we often use terms like "egomaniac" or "narcissist." But we need to be careful with these labels. Narcissism is a psychiatric disorder characterized by attention-seeking, a strong sense of self-importance, a lack of empathy, and a tendency to self-promote. Your colleague may exhibit some of these traits (or maybe all of them), but a diagnosis of narcissistic personality disorder is unlikely; pathological narcissism is rare, found in only 0.5 percent of the US population, for example.[1] As with the other archetypes in this book, your efforts are best spent on responding productively to your colleague's arrogance, not on diagnosing them.

The term *know-it-all* was first used in the English language in the late nineteenth century, although arrogance, I'm sure, has existed for much longer. Unfortunately, this archetype has likely persisted, not just in workplaces but in society (hello, American politics), because we often reward the associated behavior. If people who were humble and admitted that they didn't always have the answers regularly rose to power, perhaps fewer of us would have stories about know-it-alls in our lives. But we love confidence—in ourselves and in others.

Overconfidence bias

Scientists who study decision-making consistently find that we tend to rate ourselves as better at things than we actually are.[2] Students overestimate how well they will do on tests.[3] Graduating MBA students overestimate the number of job offers they'll receive and what their starting salaries will be.[4] And the unemployed often overestimate how easy it will be to land a job.[5] Research has also shown that overconfidence is contagious.[6] If someone on your team, whether they're a peer or a leader, has an inflated sense of their abilities, you are more likely to experience excessive self-assurance as well.

One of my favorite measures of just how overconfident we are is the way people rate themselves as drivers. One study found that 74 percent of licensed drivers think they are better than average—clearly, a statistical impossibility.[7]

Confidence is a good thing, as long as it's backed up by competence, but unfortunately, that's not always the case.

Tomas Chamorro-Premuzic, a professor of business psychology, has been on a mission over the past decade to shine a light on the problem of overconfidence in organizations. In 2013, he wrote an article that became one of the most popular that *Harvard Business Review* has ever published called "Why Do So Many Incompetent Men Become Leaders?" In it, and in the book by the same name, he explains that when there are competencies that are difficult to measure objectively, like "leadership," we rely on the way someone presents themselves to assess how well they perform.[8] You can't take a test on leadership and get an unbiased score. So, instead, we let people tell us how good they are, and we end up conflating *confidence* and *competence*, so much so that we tend to believe that confidence, in and of itself, is a trait that makes leaders great—when, in fact, lots of evidence shows that the best leaders, whether in business, sports, or politics, are humble.[9]

As the title of the hit article indicates, there is a gender component to this phenomenon: men are more likely to display confidence (or overconfidence) than women are.[10] This is due to the ways people are socialized and rewarded: women, for instance, are often punished for touting their own capabilities and accomplishments.[11] As Chamorro-Premuzic writes, "The truth of the matter is that pretty much anywhere in the world men tend to think that they are much smarter than women."[12] This leads to a particular type of know-it-all behavior: mansplaining.

Mansplaining

Most of us are now familiar with this phenomenon, which *Merriam-Webster* defines as "what occurs when a man talks condescendingly to someone (especially a woman) about something he has incomplete knowledge of, with the mistaken assumption that he knows more about it than the person he's talking to does." The term has gained popularity over the last decade. The *New York Times* included it in its list of words of the year for 2010, and it was added to the online *Oxford Dictionaries* in 2014. (See the sidebar "A Quick Note about Mansplaining.")

Most people credit writer Rebecca Solnit with naming this phenomenon in her 2008 essay, "Men Explain Things to Me."[13] She didn't use the term *mansplaining* then, but she described the occurrence, which struck a chord with women and people from other underestimated groups.

Research has since revealed that it's more than just an anecdotal nuisance. Studies show that men, especially powerful men, speak more in meetings.[14] When women are outnumbered by men in a group, they speak for between a quarter and a third less time than the men.[15] Men also interrupt others more frequently and are less likely to yield when they are interrupted.[16] A review of fifteen years of the transcripts of US Supreme Court oral arguments revealed that male justices interrupt the female justices approximately three times as often as they interrupt each other.[17]

Whether or not gender is playing a role in your interactions with your know-it-all colleague, there are several other factors that could be contributing to their haughtiness: organizational or regional culture, power, or insecurity.

The possible origins of your coworker's swagger

Many company cultures reward people who act as if they have all the answers. Do employees who state their ideas with conviction tend to get more support for those ideas at your workplace? If people appear uncertain, are they considered weak? In many firms, decision-making is a competitive sport, rather than a collaborative effort, and acting like you know everything is a shrewd survival technique.

National or regional culture can also play a role. Harvard Business School professor Francesca Gino attributes her tendency to interrupt to her native culture. "Italians are often expressive and verbal, and we tend to take interruptions as a sign of interest in the conversation rather than a lack of interest in what someone is saying," she's written.[18] While it's important not to assume everyone from a certain culture behaves in the same way, research has proven Gino out—some cultures, such as Italy, Germany, and Israel, tend to view assertiveness as an expression of engagement.[19] Perhaps your difficult colleague hails from one of these places, or maybe you find grandstanding particularly offensive because you're from a culture that typically values modesty and humility?

Gino uncovered other motivators of brashness in her research as well—in particular, power. In one study, she and her coauthors induced some participants to feel powerful by asking them to write about a time when they had authority over others. These people were more likely than participants who hadn't done the writing exercise to value their ideas over an informed adviser's when making a decision. In another study, the group who had written about a moment of power beforehand dominated discussions and interrupted frequently.[20]

Many of the know-it-alls who I've worked with have been trying to cover up incompetence or insecurities—subconsciously or not. This can be especially pronounced when someone is new to the organization or to a role—think first-time managers.

I worked with a coaching client—a logistics director at a manufacturing firm—who was unknowingly trying to prove himself to his new colleagues. The head of HR had brought me in because of tension that plagued the leadership team in the few months since Boris had joined the company. She explained that Boris was alienating his peers by regularly starting sentences with, "At my last job . . ." This made people think he felt superior to them.

When I sat down with Boris and his colleagues, he repeated this refrain twice in the first fifteen minutes of the conversation. Fortunately, I was able to calmly call it out: "I don't think you're aware of this, but you've mentioned your previous employer two times already." He had no idea. Later, he confessed to me that he was trying to prove his worth. "I thought they hired me because of what I'd done and learned in that previous role," he explained. It was a hard habit to break, and he continued to slip on occasion, but his colleagues, knowing he wasn't bragging intentionally, were much more forgiving.

Talking up your accomplishments is an understandable but misguided tactic often employed by people who, like Boris, are unsure of themselves and want to establish their value in a new role or team. Regardless of the motivation behind know-it-all behavior, however, there are clear costs.

The Costs of Working with a Know-It-All

I'll admit that, of all the archetypes in this book, this is the one I relate to most. Not because I've worked with a lot of these people but because I've often acted like a know-it-all myself. I'm not proud of the times when I confidently proclaimed something that I didn't actually know for sure or acted like I knew more than everyone in the room. I'm aware that when I state something with certainty—even when my projected assurance is out of proportion to how certain I actually feel—people are likely to listen.

But I've also seen the downsides of this approach—how my self-assurance has silenced a colleague's curiosity, or how my condescending attitude has made a friend feel small.

Even worse, working with a know-it-all can hinder your career. Even if your colleague's intention is to help you understand something, it often comes off as condescending and demeaning, which can hurt your confidence and cause you to hold back in important meetings and conversations. When someone talks down to you, especially in front of others, it calls your expertise into question and may give others permission to disregard your insights. All of this can affect how you're treated, not to mention your performance reviews, promotions, and bonuses. It can also hurt team morale by breeding resentment, making it harder to work together.

There are consequences for companies, too. Chamorro-Premuzic told me that "having incompetent people who believe they are better than they actually are puts the companies they lead at a disadvantage. Those organizations don't have the talent they need to rise to whatever challenge they're facing."[21]

So how can you avoid these costs and make your interactions with your know-it-all coworker not just less annoying but less damaging? Let's look at the questions to answer before taking action.

Questions to Ask Yourself

There are several questions you should ask yourself before deciding how to deal with your egotistical coworker.

Are they trying to prove something?

Not every know-it-all is out to prove something, of course, but there's a good chance your colleague's egotism is compensating for some deficiency or fear. Considering their underlying insecurities may give you some clues about how to deal with them. For example, once the head of HR understood that Boris, my coaching client, was trying to demonstrate his value in a new role, she made a point of validating the contributions he was already making, freeing him from the need to tout his past achievements. Is your coworker similarly trying to confirm their worthiness?

Is their confidence warranted?

On the other hand, your know-it-all colleague might have good reason to be confident in their assertions or claims, even if their demeanor leaves something to be desired. Consider the experience or expertise they bring to the table. What are their greatest skills? Is their level of confidence aligned with their level of talent? Do they actually know the things they claim to know? Could it be that their delivery is abrasive, but their underlying points have merit?

Is bias playing a role in how I'm perceiving them?

We all hold biases about who is cut out to hold positions of power. And when someone doesn't fit our preconceptions of leadership—an Asian woman, a young upstart, someone with a disability—we tend to question whether their confidence is justified. For example, research has shown that women of color have to prove their expertise over and over. Is the person you're labeling as a know-it-all from an underestimated group? Do they belong to a culture or demographic that you have unconscious but negative biases about? If you think your coworker is acting "too big for their britches," consider whether their behavior would be perceived in the same way if they were part of a dominant demographic. This technique, called "flip it to test it," was introduced to me by Kristen Pressner, a global HR executive, who confessed, in her TEDx talk, to having certain prejudices about women leaders.[22] To interrupt her own bias, especially when she finds herself judging a woman in power, she substitutes a man in the situation and sees if she holds the same view. Ask yourself, "If my colleague were a white man, would I still think they were acting like a know-it-all?"

Is their confidence pushing your buttons?

Some of us have an allergy to certainty in others. I admit that the stronger someone feels about something, the more I feel resistant to their argument, especially if their view threatens my values in some way. Consider your own sensitivity to confidence. Perhaps you grew up with an arrogant father from whom you've tried to distance yourself. Or you were brought up in a collectivist culture where humility was revered. Ask yourself whether your reaction to your colleague has more to do with you than it does with them. Is it possible that you feel insecure when you compare your accomplishments to theirs? Or maybe you wish that you were as confident or sure-minded as they are?

Is their behavior causing real issues for you or the team? Or is it just annoying?

Distinguish between statements or actions that are irritating and behavior that is preventing you from getting your work done. Not every annoying declaration from a know-it-all needs to be addressed; policing their confidence can be exhausting. Is their manner so disruptive that it needs to be confronted? Is it preventing other people from raising ideas? There are times when it could be best to ignore their arrogance. So consider which battles are worth fighting and which are best let go.

Once you've answered these questions, you're ready to decide which tactics you want to experiment with.

Tactics to Try

The situation with my coaching client Boris was unique in that his colleagues had an impartial third party (me) who was able to call out his perceived pompousness. But you won't always have a mediator. Here are some approaches you can try in the absence of outside help.

Appreciate what they have to offer

It's possible that your colleague is a complete blowhard who has little more than hot air and an arrogant attitude to offer. But I doubt that. Most people have good qualities and contribute *something* to the team or the organization. You may need to dig deep to find it, but there is probably some genuine knowledge or capability behind the know-it-all's overconfidence. Perhaps they grew revenue by 20 percent in their last role. Maybe they have experience with a particular budgeting model that your company needs. Or their sales prowess or their influence might come in handy the next time you need to close an account or secure leadership's buy-in for a project. Sure, they may exaggerate their skills and successes but find the kernel of truth. And if the ultimate goal of their pretentiousness is approval or acceptance, your empathy and appreciation may help them let up on the "Look-how-much-I-know!" routine.

Preempt interruptions

One of a know-it-all's most annoying habits is constantly interrupting people. Earlier in my career, I worked as a management consultant

A Quick Note about Mansplaining

Mansplaining, even when the intention behind it isn't malicious, is rooted in sexism, and sometimes racism and classism. I want to make clear that it's not the responsibility of people who are the targets of such conduct to fix it. Women, people of color, LGBTQ+, people with disabilities, and so on shouldn't have to carry the burden of addressing larger systemic biases by themselves. This is why it's critical that allies step in and disrupt discrimination when they see it. And leaders—whether they manage a team of two or are at the helm of a large corporation—must spend time, energy, and resources on creating an equitable culture that allows everyone to thrive.

If you're a man, it's especially important that you get involved in these efforts. Research shows that at organizations where men take part in addressing gender parity, 96 percent of those organizations report making progress, compared to only 30 percent when women are tackling the issue without male counterparts.[23]

At the same time, if you're a woman who works with a mansplainer, you don't need to wait for allies and senior leaders to confront sexism in your organization. Relying on others isn't always tenable, especially when your career is at stake—you need solutions now. So while the larger cultural issue isn't yours to solve, I hope the advice here will help you address immediate interpersonal challenges. And, of course, much of this advice is applicable to working with a know-it-all, no matter your gender or theirs.

---

on a project in South Korea. One of our clients was accustomed to holding the floor in meetings, as was culturally expected given his title. During a two-hour meeting, he interrupted me multiple times, often talking over me. At first, I was confused. *Didn't he want my advice? Wasn't that what he specifically asked for?* I was young, early in my career, but offering counsel was my job as a consultant. Then I became extremely frustrated. I looked around the room to see if my colleagues would help, but I mostly got subtle shrugs. They didn't know what to do either. I finally snapped, standing up and leaving the conference room. As I took the elevator down to the lobby, I started to cry. It took twelve turns around the block before I could regain my composure and return to the office. I wish I'd been able to keep my cool, but looking back, I fully understand my reaction.

One way to avoid this sort of situation is to preemptively request that people refrain from interjecting. Before you start talking, explain how much time (roughly) you're going to need and say something like, "Please hold any comments or questions until I'm done." If you're not making a formal presentation but are just having a discussion where some back-and-forth is expected, you might say instead, "Interruptions break my concentration, so I'd appreciate it if you'd let me finish my thoughts before jumping in."

A proactive approach isn't always possible. It certainly wouldn't have been culturally appropriate with my Korean client. But in situations with coworkers with whom you have some rapport, it can save you the headache of having to hold your ground against repeated interruptions.

I have two chronic interrupters in my life—my mother *and* my husband—so I've had to use this strategy quite often, and I've also had to learn to let interruptions roll off my back. They do it for different reasons—my mother, because she's worried that she'll forget what she wants to say, and my husband, because it's the style of communication he grew up with. I'm not always as patient as I want to be with them, but they've helped me understand that cutting in isn't necessarily malicious and sometimes people just need a reminder to hold their tongue.

Tactfully address interruptions

If your efforts to preempt interruptions fail, address them directly. But don't just raise your voice. That sets up a power struggle and your colleague is likely to talk louder in an attempt to drown you out. Instead, confidently say, "I'm going to finish my point, and then I'd love to hear what you have to say." Or you can channel Kamala

Harris in her 2020 vice presidential debate with Mike Pence. She seemed to be acting on behalf of all women when she assertively responded to Pence's interjections with the simple, "I'm speaking." This takes courage (which Harris clearly has in spades) and can create tension, especially when done in front of other people. But the hope is that a know-it-all gets the hint and refrains from further interruptions.

If you don't feel comfortable speaking up, enlist allies. It's often easier for someone else to confront rudeness, saying something like, "I'd love to hear what Keith was saying before we move on" or "I don't think Madison was finished with her point." If the know-it-all interrupts multiple people on your team, you could agree to speak up for each other when it happens.

Set norms

It's also important to set norms at the team and organizational levels for an inclusive culture in which everyone feels empowered to take the floor or to stand up for others when a know-it-all tries to take center stage. Appeal to people's sense of fairness. You can start a discussion around the question: "How do we create psychologically safe, collaborative, and inclusive workplaces for everyone?" And encourage the group to reflect on how you communicate and how you can get better.

One norm that I've been using when I'm teaching a workshop or giving a talk to a group where people will be interacting with one another (especially on Zoom) is to "take space, make space." The idea is that if you tend to be someone who stays quiet in meetings, you should challenge yourself to voice your opinions. If you're someone who is prone to holding the floor, try to step back and make room for others to contribute. I've found that sharing this idea at the beginning results in a more equitably distributed meeting. This could be one of several norms you and your team agree on. Having established guidelines will discourage interruptions and make it safe for everyone to speak up.

Ask for facts and data

Another irritating habit of the know-it-all is to proclaim: "Our customers expect us to deliver new features every six months." "Sales are dropping because we aren't quick enough to respond to complaints." "In a year, no one will even be talking about this election." If you're sitting there thinking, *How do they know that? Why are they so sure?* it's OK to ask for sources or data that back up their declarations.

Be respectful, not confrontational, when doing this. You might say something like "I'm not sure we're working with the same assumptions and facts. Let's step back and take a look at the data before we proceed." Of course, you may not interpret the data in the same way or even have data available. If you can suggest gathering some, do so. For instance, if your colleague insists that customers will hate the new feature the R&D team is proposing, is it feasible to run a short customer survey?

Even if your domineering colleague doesn't respond well to these kinds of inquiries the first few times, they may come to expect your requests for evidence and think twice before blurting out unsubstantiated claims. And asking them to explain how they know something may help them see the limits of their knowledge and encourage some humility in the future.

When you're meeting with a know-it-all, show up with verified facts in hand. The more prepared you are to defend your perspective and to counter any misleading statements they make, the better. You'll also be reinforcing the importance of fact-based discussions over posturing.

Model humility and an open mind

Many show-offs act the way they do because it's worked for them in the past, or because implicitly or explicitly they've received messages that projecting confidence is what's expected on your team, in your organization, or in the culture they're from. You can provide a different model by displaying humility and open-mindedness. Try saying, "I don't know" or "I don't have that information right now; let me get back to you." If the know-it-all sees that you suffer no consequences for expressing uncertainty, they may be willing to do the same.

You can even prompt them to be humbler by encouraging everyone to come to meetings having thought through the pros and cons of solutions or ideas they want to propose. Or you can ask questions like:

- What's another viewpoint?

- If we tried to see this from another perspective, what might we think?

- What are the benefits and risks of this approach?

Because some know-it-alls are seeking validation, simply acknowledging their ideas can prevent grandstanding. Thank them for sharing their thoughts or highlight one or two things you appreciate about their perspective before sharing yours or diving in with questions. For instance, you might say, "That's a useful point. I agree with the first part of what you said, and I see the second part slightly differently. Let's talk that through."

This is what Kwame did with his coworker Amara. "During meetings, she'd act like she knew everything and wouldn't ask any questions, but then she'd come to me afterward for clarification," he told me. He was pretty sure that she was afraid of looking stupid. "It seemed like she was worried that people would judge her for not knowing the subject inside and out," he explained. He wanted to tell her outright that asking questions was nothing to be ashamed of, but he suspected she would deny her insecurity, so instead he modeled asking questions in meetings and even occasionally said, "I hope you don't mind me inquiring about these things. This is how I learn." It took several months, but over time, Amara started to feel more comfortable saying she wasn't sure about something or even asking Kwame for an explanation in front of others.

Phrases to Use

It can be hard to choose the right words when talking to someone who thinks they know everything, so here is some sample language to get you started. Adapt it and make it your own.

In direct response to mansplaining

"Thanks, I've got this."

"Your comment makes me wonder if you're familiar with my background in [topic]."

"I'd appreciate it if you would respect that I know what I'm doing. I value your input and I'll definitely ask for it when I need it."

Preempt and address interruptions

"Please hold any comments or questions until I'm done."

"Interruptions break my concentration, so I'd appreciate it if you'd let me finish my thoughts before jumping in."

"I'm going to continue, and I'll address that when I'm done."

"I'm going to finish my point, and then I'd love to hear what you have to say."

"I'm speaking . . ."

Ask them to stop

Your coworker may not be aware of what they're doing and how it's impacting the people around them. In a private, one-on-one conversation, you might say something along the lines of, "Whenever we discuss decisions, you assert yourself with such force that it's hard to continue the conversation. It would help me to know that you're hearing and considering my views, even if you don't agree with them." You could even try using humor and say something like, "Thanks for explaining something to me that I already know!"

Speak up for others

"Before we get there, I'd like to hear the rest of Marcus's point."

"Deidre, were you finished? If not, let's hear you out before we move on."

"I know Daniel has a lot of experience in this area. I'd like to know what he thinks."

"This is your project, Gayle. How do you see it?"

Ask for facts and data

"Tell me a little about where your insights are coming from."

"I'd love to know more about the conclusions you've reached."

Model humility

"Let me tell you what I do know and don't know."

"We're all still learning what we can about this topic."

"I can't tell you that with certainty. I do have an informed opinion, which is . . ."

Bear in mind that when gender plays a role, there may be additional risks to this approach. Women risk being labeled as overly sensitive or accused of "playing the gender card," and these unfair perceptions could hurt your reputation or career. This isn't to say you shouldn't speak up; just keep in mind how things might play out. In cases of biased backlash, consider raising the issue with someone who can (and will) address it—your manager or even HR. Mansplaining has become such a commonly used term that it feels increasingly innocuous, but remember that the condescension and the gender bias behind it can often limit opportunities and corrode team culture. Ideally your organization takes these transgressions seriously. There has been a recent push for companies to formally sanction mansplaining and assess for listening and respect in performance evaluations.[24]

• • •

Let's return to Lucia, who dreaded meetings with her colleague Ray, because he would monopolize conversations with his pontificating. Her initial coping mechanism was to tune him out, and she'd take out her phone or laptop if the meeting ran long and answer emails. But she also recognized that his behavior was more than annoying. With him taking up so much airspace, her opinions weren't getting heard—by him or anyone else. And she saw that others were being similarly silenced.

So instead of ignoring Ray, she engaged with him. At first this meant showing appreciation for what he offered—pointing out moments in his monologues when he made a good point—but these accolades did little to calm his ego. It seemed to spur him to go on longer. So she employed a different tactic: asking clarifying questions about his assumptions. When she did, he soon realized that he didn't always have the answers and would turn to his teammates to respond. This had two benefits: it gave others a chance to show off their expertise and it humbled him. Lucia says one of the most helpful things for her was knowing she wasn't alone. When she and her colleagues exchange glances now, it isn't only to commiserate, but to decide who is going to respectfully cut Ray off, a responsibility they share.

Working with a know-it-all is irritating at best and career-limiting at worst. But you don't need to sit back and suffer. Like Lucia, you can take steps to curb your colleague's bluster—or at least lessen its impact.

TACTICS TO REMEMBER
The Know-It-All

DO:

- Preempt a know-it-all's interruptions by saying something like, "Please hold any comments or questions until I'm done" or "Interruptions break my concentration, so I'd appreciate it if you'd let me finish before jumping in."

- Ask for sources or data that back up their statements.

- Model humility and open-mindedness by asking for other viewpoints.

- Enlist the help of colleagues to stop interruptions and set norms on your team that discourage people from hogging the floor.

- Consider whether your own bias is playing a role in labeling your colleague a "know-it-all."

DON'T:

- Get into a power struggle about who's right and who's wrong.

- Assume they know that they're mansplaining or being condescending.

- Try to address every transgression—it's OK to let some things go.

- Allow your colleague to make you feel small.

8

The Tormentor

"I suffered and you should too."

Julia remembers coming home after her interview with Celeste, the head of hospitality at the hotel chain where Julia was applying to be a marketing manager, and telling her husband that Celeste hadn't smiled once during the interview. She assumed her potential boss wasn't a warm person. Perhaps it was just her style or even a cultural issue? "I've worked with people from different countries, and I've learned not to expect people to behave the same way I do," she explained.

But after getting hired, she noticed that Celeste was "icing her out." Julia didn't meet with Celeste her entire first week. "I was basically doing detective work, trying to find out the information I needed to do my job," she says. And it was clear to her that Celeste didn't trust her. "She was very quick to shoot down my ideas." Julia persevered and after a year felt like she earned Celeste's respect. But Celeste still demanded a lot and expected Julia to be available at all times. "She asked me to cancel vacations, come into the office on my days off, and even work during my honeymoon," she told me. When Julia pushed back on these unreasonable requests, Celeste would tell her: "Personal stuff should never stop you from doing your job."

Celeste seemed to pride herself on her unwavering dedication to work. She bragged about how little maternity leave she had taken after each of her kids was born, explaining that she started working as soon as she got home from the hospital. She made it clear that she hadn't had it easy coming up in their industry, and she wasn't going to smooth the way for Julia either.

Julia was working with a "tormentor"—a senior person (sometimes your boss and sometimes not) who has earned their way to the top, typically making sacrifices along the way, and then mistreats others below them.[1] They appear motivated by the idea that because they suffered, you should too. Their behavior is the workplace equivalent of telling people, "In my day, I had to walk to school and back uphill both ways, in freezing rain."

While *tormentor* might feel extreme, it's an apt term for senior folks who we expect to be *mentors* but who end up making our lives miserable.

Here are the behaviors commonly associated with tormentors:

- Accusing you—directly or indirectly—of not being committed enough to work

- Setting near-impossible standards

- Assigning you needless or inappropriate busywork, or what academics call "illegitimate tasks"[2]

- Proudly sharing the sacrifices they've made in their career and believing you should make similar ones

- Putting down your accomplishments, especially in comparison with theirs

- Denying time off or flexibility for nonwork commitments

- Attributing negative characteristics to a particular generation ("millennials are lazy and entitled" or "Gen Zers are so fragile; they can't handle even an ounce of discomfort")

- Denying the existence of systemic barriers, such as gender bias or institutional racism ("I was able to make it. I'm not sure why you can't.")

- Claiming their mistreatment is some sort of exercise in character-building

If you're working with someone like Celeste, who seems intent on making your life difficult because of what they've gone through, how should you respond? Should you address their abuse head-on? Is it even possible to make them your ally instead of your enemy?

The Background on Tormenting Behavior

If you're dealing with a senior person who questions your commitment to work, treats you harshly, and insists you suffer to earn your stripes, it can be easy to chalk up their behavior to generational differences or even a desire to cause pain, but there are likely other factors that contribute. Next I explore some of the reasons your colleague could be tormenting instead of mentoring you.

A lack of empathy

One of my former coworkers was shocked when he became a new dad and his boss, a mother of three, showed little sympathy for the challenge of balancing work and a young family. His manager's attitude was that "no baby should prevent you from showing up to the office and getting your work done." When my colleague said he couldn't come in because his kid was sick, his boss would ask, "Can't you get a babysitter?" And when he asked to leave early for parent-teacher conferences, she insisted he take a vacation day instead.

There's research that explains this mode of thinking. A team of Kellogg School of Management and Wharton School professors found it's often harder to empathize with someone who's in a tough situation that you've been in before.[3] Their findings suggest that people who have faced significant challenges—say, going through a divorce, working and having young children, or losing a job—were less likely to show compassion for other people enduring the same struggles. Why? The authors offer two explanations. First, while we may remember how challenging a particular experience was in general terms, we tend to underestimate the level of pain and stress we felt at the time. Second, we assume that since we were able to overcome the situation—we found another job, raised children while excelling at work, made it through a divorce—others should be able to do the same.

A tormentor may not accurately recall past hardship, or perhaps they remember it all too vividly and don't believe that you should get off easily. This is how Julia interpreted her boss Celeste's behavior. Celeste's stories about taking an abbreviated maternity leave or working all hours of the night were celebrations of the sacrifices she'd made. While Julia felt like Celeste was unnecessarily hard on her, it seemed she was also trying to show her what it took to succeed in hospitality and specifically at their company, where women often filled entry-level roles (and did the majority of the grunt work) but rarely made it to senior-level positions.

Envy

Your colleague's mistreatment may also be motivated by envy. Many of the people I interviewed for this book suspected that the senior person belittled them simply because they were jealous. Research bears this out.[4] When a junior person has something that someone more senior wants—whether it's strong social skills, close relationships with colleagues, interesting ideas, or specific technical capabilities—it can cause the leader to have what academics call "downward envy" or "generational envy."[5] They fear that up-and-comers might have higher qualifications, reveal their own limitations, or even end up taking their job. Michelle Duffy, a researcher who studies this topic, told me, "The perception that you don't have something, that you're less than someone else, or that they have something you don't have, can trigger low self-esteem and even make you feel threatened."[6]

What to Make of Generational Differences

Be careful when attributing a tormentor's behavior to generational differences. Of course, it's common for people, as they get older and more senior in their careers, to occasionally lament how things have changed. Some experts call this the "kids these days" effect.[7] But, while much has been made of generational stereotypes in the media (*boomers are arrogant; Gen Xers are cynical and disengaged; millennials are entitled*), there's little evidence that people of different generations behave in markedly different ways at work or want markedly different things. People who are twenty-five care about the same things that people who are now fifty cared about when they were twenty-five. And people who are twenty-five now will likely care about similar things when they're fifty.[8] So even if the tormentor is brokering in generalizations about "people your age," resist doing the same to them.

When tormentors feel vulnerable, they act out by consciously or unconsciously putting obstacles in your way.

This is what happened to Orlando when he found himself reporting to Patrick. Orlando had been working for the state government agency led by Patrick for some time and felt ready for a promotion. He applied for several openings at the agency and didn't get them. Each time, Patrick told him he didn't have the "right experience," even though, on paper, Orlando had the necessary qualifications. Orlando took comments like these personally, and he started to wonder if he had what it took to succeed in his field.

Scholar Araya Baker says that repeatedly deciding that a junior colleague is unequipped to move up the ranks is a common tactic among those who experience downward envy. He writes, "Elders might constantly move the goalpost or raise the bar, holding them to ever-changing standards. They're never 'ready' enough because no improvement is ever enough. Meanwhile, mentorship is withheld, and they're labeled impatient for inquiring when things might change."[9] (See the sidebar "What to Make of Generational Differences?")

Social identity threat

It's also possible that your senior colleague is trying to distance themselves from you, especially if you both belong to a group that is traditionally underestimated in the workplace, or if there are few people like the two of you in your industry or field (for instance, women in engineering or Black scholars in academia).

Researchers call this *social identity threat*—the belief that being associated with a devalued group will harm you. Senior women who are underrepresented at the highest ranks of an organization, for example, may see their gender as a liability. As one interviewee told me: "I've been guilty of not supporting other women, and my behavior was fueled by the unconscious idea that another woman's success takes away from mine." Given the continued lack of women in leadership roles, this scarcity mindset makes sense, especially in places where competition for top spots is fierce. A female coworker may distance herself from other women as a way of increasing her chances of getting ahead. (Such behavior has led to the proliferation of the "queen bee" trope; see the sidebar "The 'Queen Bee' Trope" for more.)

It's not just women who disassociate themselves in this way. The same inclination has been observed in studies of gay men, older adults who worry about being seen as out of touch, and ethnic and racial minorities.[10] After all, separating yourself from a group that is underestimated or negatively stereotyped and associating yourself with a dominant group that enjoys more advantages is an understandable survival tactic in contexts where people like you rarely succeed.

Unfortunately, concerns about being identified with an underrepresented group aren't unfounded. One set of studies showed that women and people of color who promoted diversity efforts in their companies received worse ratings from their bosses in terms of both competence and performance. The study authors wrote that their findings "suggest that it's risky for low-status group members to help others like them. And this can lead to women and minorities choosing not to advocate for other women and minorities once they reach positions of power, as they don't want to be perceived as incompetent, poor performers."[11]

Other researchers believe that the reluctance of some people to help others like them stems from what's called *favoritism threat*—a fear that supporting someone similar will be seen as unfair positive bias.[12] Rosalind Chow, a professor at Carnegie Mellon who studies social hierarchies at work, cites another concern that plagues some female leaders: "Women may fear that other women are going to *underperform* and, therefore, reinforce the stereotype that women aren't as competent as men, hurting their own chances of success and making the path to advancement harder for all women in the future."[13] While this doesn't justify cruel behavior, perhaps your colleague is tough on you because they want to keep standards high and show that, despite bias, people like you can succeed at your company.

A fundamental misconception of leadership

There's one other possible explanation for your colleague's behavior that's worth mentioning: a misunderstanding of what effective leadership is. The erroneous belief that leaders must be domineering, demanding, and unsympathetic has haunted workplaces for decades. This "command and control" approach has been shown to have limited efficacy when it comes to producing high performance over the long run, and is not only bad for employees but is also bad for the leader doling out the abuse.[14] Maybe your colleague hasn't gotten the memo and is holding on to outdated notions that in order to succeed as a leader—and gain the respect of others—they must act like a bully, hazing those below them into submission.

The Costs of Working with a Tormentor

Being the object of scorn from someone in a position of power is painful. By now, we know the costs of incivility—to the target, those observing it, and the broader organization.

Having an abusive supervisor has been connected to lack of engagement at work, greater work-life conflict, and psychological distress.[15]

The "Queen Bee" Trope

There is a stereotype that senior women often try to obstruct the careers of younger women coming up behind them. This idea is so prevalent that it's been given a label—the "queen bee" phenomenon—and has been studied by academics.

It's also clearly an experience many share. In my interviews for this book, I heard lots of stories from women like Julia who were being mistreated by other women. And we know from research that women report experiencing more incivility at work than men.[16] A series of three studies, involving large samples of four hundred to six hundred US employers, found that women reported being mistreated—being ignored, interrupted, mocked, or otherwise disrespected—by other women more often than by their male coworkers.[17]

If you find yourself dealing with a colleague who fits the stereotype of queen bee, much of the advice in this chapter will be helpful to you.

However, I want to stress that perceptions of women as queen bees are often influenced by gender biases. There is no doubt that the behaviors associated with the tormentor are damaging and inexcusable—no one of any gender should mistreat their colleagues. Yet women are often held to different standards. We condemn them more harshly for competitiveness, a lack of charity toward others, and other qualities that we either celebrate or simply ignore in men.

Let's take a closer look at competition, for example. Research has shown that competition can spur creativity, innovation, and productivity.[18] And when men engage in it, we might see it as cutthroat or justifiable in a ruthless work environment, or even as a driver of exceptional performance. But when we observe competition—even healthy rivalry—between women, we label it as a "cat fight" or "unprofessional." Research by professors Leah Sheppard and Karl Aquino shows that we often overdramatize work conflict between women in comparison to conflict between a woman and a man, or between men. And this has consequences for the perception of women. If people observing their interactions decide the women don't work well together or are attempt-ing to harm each other's careers, it implies that women are less capable of being productive colleagues.[19]

The notion that women should be generous toward each other, rather than compete with one another, is largely informed by prescriptive ste-reotypes of female communality. And it feeds into the expectation that women should do extra work to take care of other women coming up in the ranks—that they take on mentees, lead the women's employee resource group, and be a tireless advocate for gender diversity.[20] And if a senior woman decides not to take on these roles, she risks being slapped with the queen bee label.

Similarly, because we have expectations that women will be caring and supportive at work, being mistreated by a woman can feel especially hurt-ful. People tend to be less receptive to constructive feedback from women as opposed to men. In a 2019 study, 2,700 people were hired for a tran-scription job and then randomly assigned to a fictitious manager, either a man or a woman. The employees who received negative performance feedback from a female supervisor felt less satisfied with their job and less engaged with the tasks they were assigned, even though the wording of the feedback was identical to that given by the fictitious male manager.[21]

This stereotype doesn't seem to be universally applied. It's important to note that the research on the queen bee phenomenon—and on gender bias in general—has mostly been conducted with white women, so it's unclear how often women of color are accused of the same undermining behavior. According to some research, Black women, for example, may have more leeway to be assertive and direct because we don't associate them as strongly with traditional "feminine" expectations.[22] To be clear, there are plenty of harmful stereotypes about Black women at work, but this may not be one of them.[23]

If you feel like you are working with a queen bee, it's important to ask yourself whether your own biases have informed your interpretation of your colleague's behavior. I'm not suggesting that you're imagining mistreatment, but could you be unfairly attributing it to your colleague's gender? Might you be magnifying your colleague's harshness because she's a woman? Or are you falling into the trap of expecting that women should be nurturing, nice, and selfless team players?

When I think about the bosses I've worked for throughout my career, the majority of them were women, and all but one were fantastic managers—they supported my career goals, promoted my work, gave me advice about how to get ahead, and cared about me as a person. Research supports my experience. When women work with a higher percentage of women, they experience less gender discrimination and harassment.[24] As Stanford University professor Marianne Cooper writes, "When women have female supervisors, they report receiving more family and organizational support than when they have male supervisors."[25] And in workplaces overseen by women, there is a smaller gender pay gap than in those run by men.[26]

If you identify as a man, you could play an especially important role in interrupting the queen bee stereotype and the gender bias that feeds it. Studies show that men have more influence in addressing these issues because they aren't seen as having a vested interest in gender equity.[27] "When it comes to sexism men tend to be more persuasive than other women when confronting bad behavior," says Joan Williams, coauthor of *Bias Interrupted*. "We afford them more credibility because it's not their 'game.'"[28]

Regardless of your gender, proactively counteract the false narrative about queen bees by talking up women who have supported you and your career. One executive I spoke to about reporting to a vindictive female boss told me that the experience inspired her to "be a vocal ally and mentor to younger women in my circle and to find ways of lifting them up and helping them grow." Focus on creating positive experiences—for your own well-being, but also to dispel the myth that women tend to undercut others in the workplace.

There are similar consequences for in-group bullying. For example, research shows that when women suffer mistreatment from other women, it takes a toll on their well-being in the form of lower job satisfaction, lower levels of vitality, and an increased desire to quit.[29] If a senior person, particularly one who is your direct supervisor, distances themselves from you, your career prospects are also likely to suffer. This is especially true if they criticize you in front of others or in performance evaluations. People who share identity markers are likely to be seen as more objective and less biased than others who express similar concerns about your work, so their assessments—even if they're unfair—may be thought of as more credible.[30]

Organizations suffer, too. There are some estimates that abusive supervision costs companies millions of dollars each year in the form of lost productivity, employee turnover, and litigation.[31]

To me, one of the most upsetting consequences of working with a tormentor is the potential damage it can do to your confidence. If you expect that someone will act in your best interest, you may be more likely to attribute their negative feedback or mistreatment to your own shortcomings.[32]

Araya Baker explains that downward envy, however misguided, can have serious consequences. Senior leaders who are jealous of their charges may obstruct promotions, hold younger folks to impossible standards, and insist that they're always right because of rank. These expressions of jealousy reinforce hierarchies and the status quo, validating the structures that put abusive senior people in power in the first place.[33]

What do you do if you're dealing with a colleague who is standing in your way, unnecessarily competing with you, overly demanding or hypercritical, or actively working against your success? As always, start by reflecting on the situation.

Questions to Ask Yourself

I realize it's a tall order to expect someone who is suffering at the hands of a tormentor to have empathy for that person. Rather than thinking of the following questions as a way of being generous to your colleague, see them as a strategic assessment: put yourself in their shoes so you are better prepared to address their behavior.

What else is going on with your colleague?

You won't be surprised to hear that there is *a lot* of research on abusive supervision. People want to make sense of why senior people choose to mistreat those below them. The most appealing explanation might be that your tormentor is a uniquely flawed human. On the contrary, research in this field has shown that, under the right conditions, most people can become abusive bosses.[34] Especially if we keep in mind that many of the hallmarks—accusations that you aren't committed enough or criticizing you in front of others, for example—can be impulsive reactions to stress.

We all know that being compassionate and kind to the people you manage is the right thing to do, but it's easy to slip when your emotional and cognitive resources are depleted. So ask yourself: What is going on with this person? Are they under pressure to hit unreasonable targets? Could they be sleep deprived?[35] Might they be struggling in their home life?[36] None of these excuse toxic behavior, but it may give you a better understanding of what's causing it.

Is your organization encouraging the behavior?

The organizational culture at your workplace may also be giving your colleague tacit permission to mistreat others.

This is what Manuela Priesemuth, a professor at Villanova University, saw in her work on destructive leadership and workplace aggression.[37] She writes,

> Abusive behavior, especially when displayed by leaders, can spread throughout the organization, creating entire climates of abuse. Because employees look to and learn from managers, they come to understand that this type of interpersonal mistreatment is acceptable behavior in the company. In essence,

employees start to think that "this is how it's done around here," and this belief manifests itself in a toxic environment that tolerates abusive acts. More so, studies have even shown that employees who experience abuse from a supervisor are also more inclined to "pass on" this type of treatment in a ripple effect.[38]

Perhaps your tormentor is acting according to the norms that have been set by others at your organization, rather than carrying out a personal vendetta against you. If that's the case, you might also consider whether this is the kind of place you want to work.

Does your colleague think they're helping?
Are they helping?

It may be that your tormentor doesn't have malicious intentions at all, and their hard-driving ways or uncompromising expectations aren't about destroying the competition, or getting you fired, or making your life miserable. Consider what they might be trying to achieve.

Despite how horrible Celeste made Julia feel, Julia believed that her boss was actually trying to help her. "She was hard on everyone in the office, but particularly hard on women, pushing us to prove that we were willing to work as much as she had. By putting so much pressure on us, I think she was trying to help us to achieve things that we didn't know we were capable of," she told me.

Perhaps, like Julia, you'll realize that your colleague's objectives are noble, even if their tactics are misguided and hurtful. Are their actions producing any positive results? For example, have their high expectations made you better at your job?

Some research has shown that working with an intimidating leader who has exacting standards has benefits. Their followers often learn, through observation, how to make quick decisions in high-pressure situations and push themselves to succeed.[39]

Once you've considered the previous questions, it's time to plan your approach to getting along.

Tactics to Try

Your coworker's extreme competitiveness or unattainable expectations may be influenced by the stress they're under or a toxic culture. Even so, if their actions are mean-spirited or harmful, they need to be addressed. Experiment with some of the following strategies.

Encourage their empathy

We are more likely to empathize with people if we identify with them in some way. Rather than trying to distance yourself from your tormentor, find ways to show them that you are more alike than they think. Ask them about what it was like coming up in your industry, or the battles they faced earlier in their career, or obstacles they had to overcome. Then, listen. Expressing interest in what they've been through could disarm them. Also, look for opportunities to talk about any sacrifices you've made or to highlight your passion and drive.

Rosalind Chow suggests asking for your colleague's advice. Approaching them as a mentor or an expert will give their ego a nice boost, and, Chow says, "if they can see themselves in you, they're more likely to treat you better" and to want you to succeed.[40] If your impressive individual or team achievements reflect well on their leadership ability, even better.

This approach may be especially effective with senior women in male-dominated fields. Belle Derks, a psychologist who studies gender and the "queen bee" phenomenon, says that women who fit that stereotype "distance themselves not from women in general, but more specifically from women who have not (yet) made the sacrifices necessary to survive in male-dominated organizations."[41] As Derks told me, "You might have an easier time working with an exacting female superior if you show her you're equally ambitious or willing to go the extra mile."[42]

Focus on a shared goal

In the same vein, consider whether you can align yourself with your colleague so you're focused on the same objective. Joining forces could help you channel your collective talents and energy in positive ways. Is there a project you can tackle together? Or a problem you can help them solve? Of course, teaming up may be unappealing. Who would want to put themselves directly in the line of fire? But having a shared goal could help ease the tension and get you pulling in the same direction.

You can even employ this tactic on a small scale, emphasizing shared goals in your day-to-day interactions:

> "I know we both want to get this project done on time."

> "We both care about our team getting the resources we need."

> "We all want to work in a fair and equitable place."

Using the word "we" in communications can decrease the degree to which your colleague feels you are competitors and can put you, metaphorically, on the same side of the table.

Don't give in to unhealthy competition

If you sense that a colleague feels threatened by you, you may be tempted to up the ante and show them that you're not going to back down. Don't take the bait.

After some reflection, Orlando realized that Patrick's behavior was likely not about Orlando but about Patrick's insecurities over the fact that Orlando had come to the government agency with more credentials. "The underlying theme of our communications was, 'I'm better than you,' and it felt like he was putting me down as a way of making himself feel better," Orlando told me. He noticed that the more he defended himself, the more Patrick mistreated him. So he decided to stop arguing with Patrick.

"Once I stopped vying for a promotion, there was far less tension between us," he says. But he didn't give up on his career goals. He started looking for jobs elsewhere. "I told myself I wouldn't quit until I had something better lined up," he told me. And in the meantime, he focused his efforts on work he cared about. "I decided to care less about the title and focus on the work," he says. He took on special projects that required minimal interaction with Patrick and found satisfaction in helping the agency achieve its mission of making education more accessible.

Instead of engaging in a tug-of-war with your tormentor, save your energy for constructive action, like seeking out interesting projects, working with people who can teach you something, dedicating yourself to the company's mission—or even volunteering outside of work.

Change the balance of power

Another tactic you might try is to shift the balance of power between you and a tormentor. Part of what makes their behavior so painful—and so costly to you—is that they have more authority, but just because they hold a higher rank doesn't mean that you have to accept their insults or hazing. Research shows that you may be able to temper their negative treatment by increasing their dependence on you.[43]

Of course, doing that may seem tough. After all, you probably rely on them, at least in part, for raises, promotions, access to resources, or project assignments. Still, power dynamics aren't fixed, and you can shift things in your favor by demonstrating your value, particularly in relation to what they care about most. Let's say one of your colleague's goals is to ensure your team is using the latest technology to track sales. Knowing that, you might research the technology landscape and assess the challenges of integrating various options with your current system. Perhaps you start following people on social media who specialize in a particular technology or reach out to peers in other companies who make a point of staying on top of the latest developments. You can then share your knowledge and help the tormentor solve their high-priority problem. The key to success with this tactic is to focus on skills and competencies that would be hard for them to find elsewhere. The objective is to send the message: "You need me more than you think, so take better care of me."[44]

Be direct

Addressing a problematic dynamic with a tormentor directly can be a good option. If your colleague is undercutting you, confront them honestly but tactfully. Say something along the lines of, "I could be wrong, but I get the sense that we're not working together as well as we could be. I'd like to have a productive relationship with you so if there's something I did that is negatively affecting our ability to collaborate, I'd like to know so that I can change it." I'm not saying frank encounters won't be awkward—they probably will be—but ideally you'll open up a conversation about how to get back on track. Your colleague may respond with denial ("I don't think anything's wrong with the way we work together") or defensiveness ("Why would you think that?"), but at least you'll have made clear your intention to keep the relationship positive.

Bolster your confidence

Working with someone who's tough on you can test your self-esteem. It's important to stay strong and not give in to imposter syndrome. One woman I spoke to, who was struggling with several colleagues who were icing her out of projects and demeaning her contributions in front of others, said she was ready to quit. But then she was inspired by something a friend told her: "Don't leave until they force you out." Instead of walking away from a job she loved, she doubled down on her resolve to stay. "My job is hard and competitive, and even if others write me off, I have to recognize my worth and deservingness. Even if a few senior people are not going to help me get ahead, and perhaps even try to sabotage me, I can still help myself," she told me.

This wasn't easy, but she focused on what she could do to further her career and rely on her own capabilities, rather than on others. She

Phrases to Use

Whether you decide to disengage from unhealthy competition with your colleague or to address their abuse directly, here are some phrases to help you get started.

Empathize with their sacrifices

"I respect what it took for you to achieve this level of success. I imagine it wasn't easy."

"I recognize that things are probably easier for me now than they were for you when you were in my shoes."

"I know many people who've reached your level in our field have had to make sacrifices. Has that been your experience?"

Address tension directly

"I'm worried that we got off on the wrong foot."

"I'd like to talk about the dynamic between us. At times it feels unproductive and I'm wondering what I can do to change it."

"I'd really love for us to have a stronger relationship. Is there anything I can do to make that happen?'"

Focus on a shared goal

"I know we both care about getting this project done on time. Can we talk about how we can work together to accomplish that?"

"We can both make our team [or department] look good here."

"I think we'd knock it out of the park if we took this on together."

---

said doing this had benefits beyond her self-esteem. "Once I started to trust myself, I began to find mentors who understood what I was trying to do and supported me," she said. Building healthy relationships with other people is always a good way of protecting and fostering your confidence—and your career prospects.

• • •

Let's return to Julia's trials with her boss, Celeste. She found it easier to deal with Celeste's demands when she thought of her as trying to help, but there were a few lines that Julia needed to draw in the sand. For example, she didn't want to work while on vacation or cut her maternity leave short. So she took a direct approach, but not before showing appreciation for Celeste and the sacrifices she'd made. When they wrapped up a meeting early, Julia took the opportunity to tell Celeste how impressed she was with her dedication to her career. "I acknowledged that her generation had far less flexibility and leeway than we have now," she told me. This prompted Celeste to share about why she'd approached her career the way she had, explaining how hard it was for a woman in hospitality management to get ahead. This gave Julia the opening to say that now that things had changed, she was grateful she didn't have to make the sacrifices that Celeste had had no choice but to make—working through vacations, being available all the time, putting herself last. This conversation softened the tension between Julia and her boss, and now when she pushes back on some of Celeste's demands, Celeste is more flexible and understanding.

TACTICS TO REMEMBER
The Tormentor

DO:

- Find a shared goal and focus on that rather than on the negative dynamic between you.

- Ask directly what you could do to improve your relationship.

- Acknowledge the sacrifices they've made or the hardships they've experienced in their career.

- Try to demonstrate that you have value that others don't so that you can shift the balance of power, even slightly.

- Examine how bias and stereotypes may be influencing your interpretation of your colleague's behavior, particularly if she's a woman.

DON'T:

- Forget that most people act aggressively at work because they feel threatened.

- Try to up the ante with a highly competitive colleague; you may be able to disarm them more effectively by refusing to engage in a tug-of-war.

- Allow a tormentor to make you question yourself.

- Assume your colleague's mistreatment is the result of a character flaw; instead consider what else might be going on.

9

The Biased Coworker

"Why are you so sensitive?"

During the seven years that Aliyah worked at a large global media company, she had six or seven different managers. "Honestly, I lost track at some point," she told me. Most of those bosses were "just fine," and a few were supportive of Aliyah and her aspirations to become a director of sales development. But there was one manager, Ted, who she found particularly difficult. She could tell from the start that Ted wasn't entirely comfortable around her. "It was like he was always trying to choose his words carefully, which is ironic because he said a lot of stupid things," she says.

One of Ted's constant refrains was, "You should smile more." When Aliyah pointed out that he probably didn't say this to his male colleagues, Ted told her she was "hard to read." She tried to ignore his remarks, but the more she let them slide, the more Ted dug in. He even said—in a mock confessional tone—that he was intimidated by her. "He tried to make it sound like this was because of my accomplishments, but it was obvious to me that he was also alluding to the fact that I'm a Black woman," she told me.

Ted's comments were biased. They caused Aliyah to question how others might be perceiving her. It was especially damaging when his prejudice emerged in front of others, and when it started to show up in her formal performance reviews.

Perhaps you've been in a situation like Aliyah's. Your colleague says something that immediately makes you uncomfortable. Maybe they think they're just being funny or paying a compliment, but the comment is inappropriate—maybe even sexist, transphobic, ageist, or racist.

We're all guilty of exhibiting bias at times. We may not intend harm. But it doesn't mean that behavior like Ted's—which made Aliyah feel singled out, misunderstood, and stymied—is OK.

Here are some examples of biased statements you might have heard:

"You're so articulate."

"Everyone can make it here if they try hard enough and just do good work."

"Do you know so-and-so?" (when so-and-so is the one other person from an underrepresented group in your workplace)

"I get confused by all of the different pronouns. There were just two genders when I grew up."

"I don't see color."

"When I call something 'gay,' I'm not referring to sexual orientation."

"Your hair looks different today. Is that your casual look?"

"Where are you from?"

"You don't look old enough to be . . . [a professor, a manager, a doctor]."

"I don't like using the singular 'they' because it sounds grammatically incorrect."

Deciding if, when, and how to confront discrimination is complex, especially because you may be fearful that you'll be penalized for how you handle it. This is what makes bias in the workplace particularly corrosive. And the responsibility for addressing bias shouldn't fall to those, like Aliyah, who are on the receiving end. But delivering feedback can sometimes be the right thing, especially if you have to work with a biased coworker regularly.

What should you say or do if you find yourself in a situation like Aliyah's, working with someone who is making insensitive or downright offensive comments? How should your approach differ if you're the target of bias or an observer of it?

One note before we get into the background on biased behavior: my identity as a straight, white woman means that, while I have been subjected to inappropriate comments at work and sexism throughout my career, I don't have firsthand experience with racism, homophobia, and other forms of oppression. Because of that I have relied on the expertise of scholars and practitioners who have direct experience with those injustices to inform my understanding and advice here. You'll see their work reflected and quoted throughout this chapter.

The Background on Biased Behavior

Prejudice can be expressed in explicit and implicit ways. If Ted had said to Aliyah, "I don't like working with you because you're a Black woman," that would've been an obvious example of bias (and likely a violation of company policy and possibly the law, depending on the country or state in which they worked). Instead, Ted indirectly signaled that he was uncomfortable working with Aliyah, and she was left to wonder whether it was because of her race or gender, both, or something unrelated.

In this chapter, I'm going to talk about the subtle forms of bias that often affect our interpersonal interactions at work. These can be particularly painful to experience and vexing to address because they may be ambiguous or disguised as seemingly positive remarks.

Take this example from Stanford University professor Claude Steele. In a podcast interview, he shared two personal experiences with racism, which happened decades apart. First, he recalled a time from his childhood when employees at a golf course told him and his friends, using a racial slur, that they'd never get jobs as caddies there because they were Black. Later, as a graduate student, he never knew where he stood with his white colleagues and professors, whether their mistreatment was racially motivated or not. Steele explained that his response to the earlier incident was "righteous indignation," but the more ambiguous bias he encountered in graduate school made him feel small and caused him to question himself.[1]

"Subtle acts of exclusion"

Instances of covert bias are often referred to as *microaggressions*, a word that has become commonly used over the last several years but was appearing in academic papers as early as 1970. Columbia University professor Derald Wing Sue wrote one of the defining books on this topic. He describes microaggressions as "the everyday verbal, nonverbal, and environmental slights, snubs, or insults, whether intentional or unintentional, which communicate hostile, derogatory, or negative messages to target persons based solely upon their marginalized group membership."[2]

Diversity, equity, and inclusion (DEI) experts Tiffany Jana and Michael Baran offer a different term to describe these actions: *subtle acts of exclusion* (which is also the title of their 2020 book).[3] What I like about their phrase is that it focuses on the impact—exclusion—not the intention. Your biased coworker may not think they're being aggressive or prejudiced when they ask, "Where are you really from?" but implicitly they're communicating, "You don't belong." Also, the "micro" in microaggression implies that the comment isn't really a big deal when, in most cases, it is. I use both terms in this chapter since microaggression is the more familiar term to most people.

Here are some of the most common forms these subtle acts of exclusion take (see table 9-1):

- *Ascription of intelligence.* Comments in this category, like the classic "he's so articulate," convey surprise when a person from a particular group possesses a—typically positive—skill or trait. These statements appear encouraging on the surface, but the implication is that you've exceeded expectations that were low because of your status as a woman, a religious minority, an immigrant, a second-language speaker, a person with disabilities, and so on. Many researchers, including Joan Williams, coauthor of *Bias Interrupted*, have shown that people from underestimated groups have to prove again and again that they are competent, whereas white men and other people with power do not.[4]

- *Mislabeling.* Williams also talks about the "tightrope" that many women and minorities have to walk because there is a narrower range of behaviors that are deemed acceptable for them. Take, for example, the notion that leaders should be assertive and confident, and yet women are often penalized for demonstrating these traits. Similarly, many Black professionals have talked about how their emotions are labeled as "angry" even when they're expressing excitement or disappointment.

- *"Benevolent" bias.* This variety of bias involves someone "looking out for" you when they're actually holding you back. Think about a boss who gives vague feedback to his female direct report because he doesn't think she can stomach constructive criticism—or because he's afraid of looking unsupportive of women of color. This benevolent bias is frequently directed at people with disabilities when a manager assumes they can't handle certain demands of their job.

    When I was new to management consulting, a senior consultant told me, on an elevator to meet with a client, "I've realized that I'm taken more seriously when I wear makeup." I looked at my plain face in the mirrored walls. At that point in my life, I'd worn makeup exactly once (to my senior prom). I don't doubt that my colleague was trying to help me, but instead she eroded my confidence right before an important client meeting and conveyed that, in order to succeed, I'd need to adhere to a gender norm that I wasn't comfortable with.

- *Overfamiliarity.* Sometimes, when addressing or describing a colleague, people use words that are either demeaning or connote a closeness that isn't there. Calling a female colleague "sweetheart" or a Black colleague "bro" falls into this category. This overfamiliarity has been well documented. For example, research done by professors Ella Bell Smith and Stella Nkomo for their book, *Our Separate Ways*, showed that white women often felt closer to their Black colleagues than their Black colleagues felt to them.[5] This assumed familiarity devalues true connection, allowing people to claim a closeness they haven't earned.

- *Assumptions (based on apparent identity).* Comments in this category include misgendering a trans colleague, presuming an Asian colleague didn't grow up speaking English or that a young-looking woman is an assistant—assumptions based on stereotypes that deny people their individual identity. I've committed these kinds of microaggressions, probably more times than I realize. For example, I recently asked a Latina colleague whether she came from a large family. As soon as I saw the subtle furrow in her brow, I realized that I'd made an offensive assumption based on her background. I probably wouldn't have asked a white coworker the same question.

- *Myth of meritocracy.* The final category of microaggressions is the subtle denial that bias exists either in general or specifically in your organization or on your team. Maybe your colleague complains that people focus too much on race or gender or "identity politics." Perhaps they defend the use of stereotypical or derogatory sports team names. They may also admit that discrimination happens elsewhere but not in your company, with remarks like, "I'm glad we work in a meritocracy" or "We're lucky that things like that don't happen here."

What causes someone to fall into these patterns of discrimination?

TABLE 9-1

Subtle forms of exclusion

Type of bias	Definition	Examples
Ascription of intelligence	Commenting on an attribute that you're surprised the person possesses	"You're so articulate." "You speak English so well."
Mislabeling	Labeling a behavior that's deemed acceptable for majority group members as negative or unprofessional	"You might want to tone down your anger." "People are saying you're too bossy."
"Benevolent" bias	Assuming that someone isn't capable of or interested in something because of their identity and that they need protection	"I doubt she'll want to work on that project. It's a lot of travel and she's got a family to think about."*
Overfamiliarity	Using phrases or words that are demeaning or connote a false sense of familiarity or closeness	Calling a woman "sweet-heart" or a Black colleague "bro"
Assumptions (based on apparent identity)	Making assumptions based on stereotypes or denying someone their individual identity	"You don't look old enough to be . . . [a professor, a manager, a doctor]."
Myth of meritocracy	Acting as if bias or discrimination doesn't exist	"I don't see color." "We're lucky to work in a meritocracy."

*Comments like these are often connected to what Williams calls the "maternal wall," where women with children see their commitment and competence questioned or face disapproval for prioritizing their careers. See Joan C. Williams, "The Maternal Wall," *Harvard Business Review*, October 2004, https://hbr.org/2004/10/the-maternal-wall.

Your biased colleague's motivation

In other chapters, I've explored possible motivations behind your difficult colleague's behavior. With this archetype, however, there are no easy explanations. As with other forms of bias, cognitive laziness is partly to blame. If I confuse one of my Indian colleagues for another, even though they don't look anything alike, my brain has taken a mental shortcut to preserve energy. But it's more complex than

Reading about Racism at Work

If you'd like to learn more about racism in the workplace, and what we can do to address it, there are several books that I've personally learned a lot from and that I'd recommend:

- *Race, Work, and Leadership: New Perspectives on the Black Experience*, by Laura Morgan Roberts, Anthony J. Mayo, and David A. Thomas

- *Erasing Institutional Bias: How to Create Systemic Change for Organizational Inclusion*, by Tiffany Jana and Ashley Diaz Mejias

- *How to Be an Antiracist*, by Ibram X. Kendi

- *So You Want to Talk About Race*, by Ijeoma Oluo

- *White Fragility: Why It's So Hard for White People to Talk About Racism*, by Robin J. DiAngelo

- *The Person You Mean to Be: How Good People Fight Bias*, by Dolly Chugh

- *A More Just Future: Psychological Tools for Reckoning with Our Past and Driving Social Change*, by Dolly Chugh

- *Inclusion on Purpose*, by Ruchika Tulshyan

New articles and books on this topic are regularly published, so be sure to ask for recommendations and look for the latest releases.

---

that—and not innocuous. The shortcut is informed by societal, sociological, and historical forces, including white supremacy and systemic racism. (If you'd like to learn more about racism at work, there are plenty of articles, books, and experts to follow, many of whom have influenced my own understanding; see a small sampling in the sidebar, "Reading about Racism at Work.")

As overt bias has become (thankfully) more socially unacceptable in many workplaces, microaggressions and other forms of subtle bias have become the primary outlets for people's prejudice. Psychology professor Lilia Cortina has posited that uncivil behaviors, such as interrupting a colleague or using a condescending tone, can be easily explained away. It's easy for the bully to claim carelessness or attribute a slight to their "brusque" personality, rather than having anything to do with another person's race, gender, or appearance. People often get away with covert discrimination while believing they're unbiased.[6]

We may also see more biased behavior in remote work environments where people are rarely interacting face-to-face. While there are fewer casual interactions happening in hallways or cafeterias, there are plenty of spaces, such as Slack channels or group texts, where people can—and do—make inappropriate comments. Because of a phenomenon called the "online disinhibition effect," people tend to be bolder when they can hide behind a keyboard.[7] We feel less restrained when we're interacting online and feel safer expressing things that we wouldn't say to someone's face.[8]

Sometimes, it's hard to remember how thoroughly racist ideas—and other oppressive systems of thought—permeate our workplaces. Soon after George Floyd's murder by Minneapolis police officer Derek Chauvin, the scholar Ibram X. Kendi offered a helpful metaphor. Living in the United States (though this applies elsewhere as well), we're constantly being "rained on" by racist ideas. As Kendi explains, "You have no umbrella, and you don't even know that you're wet with those racist ideas, because the ideas themselves lead you to believe that you're dry."[9] It's not until someone hands you an umbrella—the awareness of your privilege—that you realize you've been drenched all along.[10]

I share this metaphor not to excuse your biased colleague's behavior but rather to show how deeply entrenched the beliefs that shape those behaviors are likely to be. Everyone holds biases, and they are hard to recognize in ourselves, which makes it difficult to take steps to counteract them and may explain why your colleague struggles to see the harm they're causing.

The Costs of Microaggressions

Research has shown that there are myriad psychological and physiological consequences to being on the receiving end of subtle acts of exclusion. As professors Ella Washington, Alison Hall Birch, and Laura Morgan Roberts write, "Microaggressions seem small; but compounded over time, they can have a deleterious impact on an employee's experience, physical health, and psychological well-being."[11] There are numerous studies on the linkages between microaggressions and negative mental-health outcomes.[12] People who experience discrimination at work are more likely to have symptoms of depression and anxiety, for example.[13] Obesity and high blood pressure caused by stress are just a few of the documented physical ramifications.[14]

There are also potential costs to your livelihood. As Ruchika Tulshyan, author of *Inclusion on Purpose*, told me, comments that exclude people "have impact beyond feelings. When stereotypes are reinforced and perpetuated, there's an impact on your career—how well you're paid, what your advancement opportunities are, who thinks you have leadership potential."[15]

Research shows that subtle bias can cause more harm than blatant discrimination.[16] There are several reasons why. First, processing an ambiguous statement like "You're so articulate" takes up cognitive resources as you try to sort out whether or not it was a compliment or a dig at your identity. Second, microaggressions are much more common than blatant discrimination (in most workplaces), so you're more likely to experience them. The impact of many small slights can build up over time. Third, there is usually little recourse at your disposal. It's hard to report, let alone sue, someone over a microaggression, so you're left to figure out how to handle the situation on your own.[17]

The costs are multiplied if you're made to feel like the microaggression is a figment of your imagination. When dealing with a biased colleague, you may have been told things like:

"He doesn't really mean it."

"She's from a different generation."

"He's just obnoxious."

"Can't you take a joke?"

Characterizing victims of microaggression as overly sensitive or too politically correct furthers the harm, or results in "gaslighting," causing people to question whether what they experienced actually happened or if their reaction is appropriate.

In addition to the potential consequences for you, your health, and your career, a colleague's biased comments also negatively impact your organization by eroding a sense of belonging and psychological safety, and reinforcing exclusion. This, of course, leads to disengagement, decreased productivity, and lower employee retention.[18] All of which means that leadership teams stay very white and very male, since the people who feel like they belong are more likely to rise through the ranks.

Knowing the damage that covert forms of bias can cause, it's important to interrupt these acts when they happen. But confronting a coworker who falls into this archetype isn't always straightforward. Let's look at some of the questions you should ask as you decide if and how to respond.

Questions to Ask Yourself

Typically this section helps you examine the role you're playing in the dynamic between you and your difficult coworker. But when it comes to issues like racism and sexism, you're not doing anything to cause the problem. You're actually doing your colleague a favor if you help them correct their biases. So here, I focus on questions that will inform which of the following tactics are appropriate for your situation.

Were you the target of discrimination?
Or did you observe it?

The burden of noticing and calling out microaggressions typically falls on people from underrepresented groups. And it shouldn't. As

Aneeta Rattan, an expert on mindsets and bias at London Business School, explains, "What we see across a lot of research is that allies are not as quick or ready to recognize bias. They may miss or not notice it at all."[19] It's important that we all be on the lookout for bias and that we believe people when they identify it.

If a microaggression is directed at you, it's up to you whether it's worth the risk of speaking up (more on making that calculation in the next section, "What are the risks?"). However, if you witness the incident, you have a greater responsibility to speak up. Rattan says, "Allies and advocates have to understand that whatever risk there is to you, it is compounded for the member of that group or the recipient of that comment."

The research emphasizes why it's so imperative for bystanders to speak up. If you share an identity marker with the offender, such as race, gender, or role at the company, you are more likely to be seen as persuasive and less likely to be dismissed. In one study, white people were more persuaded when the person speaking up about a racially biased remark was also white. They were also more likely to rate a Black person who addressed the comment as rude.[20]

Keep in mind that experiencing discomfort is not the same as feeling unsafe. As a bystander, you should only choose to ignore a biased comment when your safety—or the safety of the person who has been targeted—is at stake. We all have a moral obligation to speak up, especially if our identities confer privileges that aren't enjoyed by the person or people under attack.

What are the risks?

There's an interesting paradox in many organizations. With the increased recognition of systemic bias, companies are putting more resources than ever before into building diverse, inclusive workforces, and yet for many employees, it often feels dangerous to talk about racism, sexism, or other forms of prejudice. Such conversations can seem like minefields, making discrimination harder to call out than other forms of incivility.

It's useful to think about what could go wrong if you confront your biased coworker as there are material risks involved. But I suggest you also consider the risks of *not* speaking up.

What are the risks of speaking up? Addressing bias openly challenges the status quo and may impact your relationships and standing with your coworkers or boss, your performance reviews, job assignments, or even whether you keep your job. As a result, you might feel social pressure to be polite and not respond.[21]

Think specifically about how your biased coworker might react. Will they be dismissive ("You're overreacting. It was just a joke.") or get defensive ("What are you accusing me of?")? Ask yourself: How does this person normally respond to being challenged? Are they generally self-aware? Open to feedback? Do they have the authority to affect decisions about your raises, promotions, or bonuses? Are they likely to bad-mouth you to influential leaders? Can they block your ideas or hold up your project? How might they hurt your career prospects or reputation? It's important to develop a *realistic* picture of the danger you're facing.

What are the risks of *not* speaking up? At the same time, ask yourself about the consequences of staying silent. Perhaps not addressing a biased statement would violate your personal values. You might inadvertently condone the behavior if you let it pass unremarked. Or miss an opportunity to educate your coworker. Research has shown that direct confrontation of offensive comments can be effective in preventing them in the future.[22]

Are you in a position of influence? If so, the risks of silence are greater. Leaders bear the ultimate responsibility (in some cases, a legal one) for making sure no one feels threatened at work. Tulshyan says those who are "in a position to create a better, more inclusive work environment, where people can bring their whole selves to work, should use their power whenever possible."[23] If people come to you angry or upset about a comment directed at them or someone else, don't dismiss them. Listen. And then figure out the best way to confront the situation.

Ultimately, if you're on the receiving end, the decision to say something or let it go is yours and you should decide what's best for you in every unique circumstance.

Is it important that I respond immediately?

Timing is another important consideration. Is the offense something you need to address right away? A good rule of thumb is to prioritize your safety and well-being. Tulshyan told me about an experience she had with an Uber driver who was making inappropriate comments about her looks. She wanted to tell him to stop, but she considered the fact that she was trapped in a car with him and at the end of the ride, he'd know where she lived, so she decided to ignore the comments to preserve her safety. She only took action by offering feedback on the app after she was safely out of his car.

As Washington et al. put it: "Do not feel pressured to respond to every incident; rather, feel empowered to do so when you decide you should. . . . You control what this incident will mean for your life and your work—what you will take from the interaction and what you will allow it to take from you."[24]

When you witness a microaggression, addressing it sooner rather than later is important. You don't want to tacitly permit the behavior. Confronting the offender after the fact is still worthwhile, but it's not ideal; people who overheard the initial interaction may be unaware of your response and feel unsafe as a result.

Does my company culture encourage speaking up?

Of course, it's far easier to frankly address a colleague's biased behavior if you work in a place where people are encouraged to speak up. Many organizations, especially in 2020 in the wake of George Floyd's murder, made public commitments to anti-racism. A company statement doesn't necessarily make everyone safe, but consider whether company leaders are actively and consistently supporting diversity and inclusion. Have you seen people challenge bias before?

One powerful benefit of speaking up is that you'll be helping to establish healthy, inclusive norms, signaling that calling out prejudice is acceptable and preferable and making it safer and more comfortable for others to point out bias in the future.

Should I report the incident?

Unfortunately, many workplaces don't recognize microaggressions as violations of their harassment or DEI policies. Still, it may be helpful to report the incident to your manager or HR, depending on its severity and whether you feel that escalating the issue will result in productive action.

Before reporting discrimination, Dolly Chugh, NYU professor and author of *The Person You Mean to Be: How Good People Fight Bias*, suggests considering questions like: Is this an isolated incident or a pattern of behavior? Will escalating make things better or worse? Is the behavior preventing you from doing your job—or someone else from doing theirs? "If it's making you more likely to check out job sites and update your résumé, then there's something at stake and it's probably worth bringing it up with your manager," Chugh says.[25] Can you make the argument that your coworker is contributing to a hostile work environment? If so, there may be legal ramifications, particularly in the United States.

Also ask: Do you have a sympathetic ear? Is there someone in a senior position who will want to help and has the power to do so? You could also vet the situation with someone you trust and get their advice on the pros and cons of escalation.

After reflecting on these questions, if you do decide to speak up, the tactics in the next section will help you navigate those conversations.

Tactics to Try

The antibias strategies you use will differ if you are on the receiving end of prejudice or observing it. Throughout this section, I'll point out the scenario to which each tactic applies.

Foster a growth mindset

It would be completely natural, in response to bias, to think, "This woman clearly hates queer people," or "I can't believe I have to work with such a racist." Thinking in absolutes—that people are fundamentally bigoted, rather than that they have biased views that could be altered—is an understandable response when we feel dehumanized. However, Aneeta Rattan's research shows that having a growth mindset, or believing in people's capacity to learn and change, increases our motivation to confront discrimination. In her studies, women and minorities who had a growth mindset and called out bias also had a less negative outlook and thus were better able to retain a sense of workplace satisfaction and belonging than those who had a fixed mindset and didn't speak out. One way to remind yourself that everyone is capable of growth, Rattan suggests, is to stay curious by telling yourself: *I want to understand why they think it's OK to say this,* or *I want to understand how they came to believe this.*[26] Curiosity helps us to reserve judgment until we've gathered more information.

This is the mindset that Daniel, the co-owner of an executive search firm, eventually took with his client Carol, the founder of a youth education organization. He was frequently taken aback by Carol's comments and requests. She once asked Daniel's team to find photos of job candidates so she could see what they looked like. She also requested the age of an applicant, commented that another interviewee "dressed like she was Amish," and expressed concern that the color of a Black woman's skin might prevent people from taking her seriously as a leader. Daniel and his team were upset by these remarks. But rather than assume Carol was a lost cause, he tried to focus on the fact that she needed to learn and could change. "I didn't want to make assumptions about her intentions or moral character. . . . My parents make similar comments sometimes, so I've been exposed to good people who say inappropriate things," he told me. He used that mindset when calling attention to the inappropriateness of her comments (more on that later).

Accept your emotional response

It's normal to feel upset or confused when you are the target of an offensive act or remark. "When someone does something that violates your identity or denies your humanity, getting angry is a natural response," says Tina Opie, a professor at Babson College and coauthor of *Shared Sisterhood*. She advises slowing down and thinking through what happened. Give yourself time to investigate your emotional response before deciding what to do.[27] And don't beat yourself up. As Washington et al. write, "Allow yourself to feel what you feel, whether it's anger, disappointment, frustration, aggravation, confusion, embarrassment, exhaustion, or something else. Any emotion is legitimate and should factor into your decision about whether, how, and when to respond."[28]

Have set responses at the ready

Most of us assume that we will speak up when we encounter bias. But research shows that's not always the case. It's easy, in the moment, to feel unable to respond or to find plenty of reasons not to say something: "I don't want to cause a stir." "It's not a big deal." "They're usually a nice person." To counter those self-protective instincts, it helps to rehearse what you'll say ahead of time and to have a few phrases in your back pocket—such as "I'm not sure you really mean to say that" or "That's an unfair stereotype." Having responses at the ready can make the difference between speaking up and staying silent.

Ask a question

It can be effective to respond with a question, like "What did you mean by that?" or "What information are you basing that on?" You might even ask a biased colleague to simply repeat what they said, which may prompt them to think through what they meant and how their words might sound to others. This should help you discern their true intentions.

Dolly Chugh calls asking such questions "being clueless" and says this approach encourages people to explain themselves, making it harder to hide behind veiled biases.[29] For example, if a new client introduces themselves to your team and one of your colleagues comments on their last name, "Escobar, like the drug lord!" you can ask, "What made you associate her name with a drug dealer?" If he says, "Because it's the same last name," you can point out that many people have that last name. Chugh suggests asking questions with genuine curiosity and starting with "what" instead of "why," which sounds less challenging. "What led you to say that?" is easier to hear than "Why did you say that?" which can sound like an accusation. Keep your inquiry short. "The more words you include, the more it starts to sound like a statement or attack than a question," she says.

Call it what it is

Oftentimes, people have no clue they've misstepped, so you can make it clear that their comment was inappropriate by either explaining why or sharing the effect it had on you. Use statements that start with "I," which tell your colleague how you feel and invite them to consider your perspective, or "it," which can establish a boundary that's not OK to cross. For example, "It's disrespectful to call a grown woman a girl" or "That comment was offensive to Muslims." Avoid "you" statements that accuse the person of being a bigot. When people feel ashamed, attacked, or mislabeled, they're less likely to hear you or change their behavior.

This is how Aliyah approached her boss, Ted, who kept encouraging her to smile more. She said to him, "When you tell me that, it makes me feel like I need to fake a persona to make you comfortable." She was convinced that he was being racist or sexist (or both), but she knew that if she used those terms, he would shut down.

Be explicit about your intentions. For example, you might say, "I'm raising this because I feel comfortable doing so with you and I want us to be able to communicate, even about sensitive issues." It can also help to acknowledge that some microaggressions are committed unintentionally, giving your colleague the benefit of the doubt. This reduces the amount of shame they feel, which, in turn, should reduce their defensiveness.

Planning ahead increases the chances of tactfully getting your message across. The situation-behavior-impact feedback model provides a useful framework:

- Point out when and where a specific behavior occurred (*the situation*): "During our Zoom meeting on Monday, when we were getting ready to sign off . . ."

- Then, explain in detail what you observed, being as specific as possible (*the behavior*): "I heard you say that you were concerned our new client wouldn't take Alan seriously . . ."

- Describe the consequences of the behavior (*the impact*): ". . . and it made me uncomfortable because I assumed you were implying that because Alan is older, he will be perceived as out of touch."

Share information

If a colleague doesn't understand how they've caused offense, offer information that challenges their assumptions. For example, if they suggest that a female colleague is slacking off by leaving work early, you might say something like: "I read an interesting study the other day that found that when working moms leave the office, we assume they're taking care of their kids. But when working dads leave the office, we don't even notice. Do you think that could be the case here?" (That's a real study, by the way.) It's important to avoid coming off as passive-aggressive. The more genuine you are about sharing information—rather than trying to trap someone in an act of bias—the more likely they are to question their rationale.

This is what Daniel did with Carol. "I felt the need to tread carefully since she was a client, but I also couldn't let her insensitivity slide," he said. Instead, he was direct and honest with her and focused on explaining why her behavior was problematic. For instance, when she asked for inappropriate information about candidates, he replied, "We don't request that information because we won't make a decision based on that. We focus on competencies." And, at times, he responded more firmly. When she asked for applicants' photos, he said, "Please don't ask us to do this again. It's not OK."

Anticipate defensiveness

The best-case scenario is that your colleague hears you and thanks you for your feedback. In my experience, it's more likely they get defensive, at least at first. That was the reaction Carol had when Daniel called her out. Sometimes she denied she'd been offensive and said, "You must've heard me wrong."

Your biased coworker might respond similarly, dismissing what you're saying or claiming that you misunderstood them and their intentions. But if pain is caused, it doesn't matter whether the perpetrator had good intentions or not.

If they accuse you of being overly sensitive or defend themselves by saying they didn't mean any harm, make clear how their statement or question landed with you. For example, you might say, "Your comment, however you meant it, made me feel like you don't value me as a colleague."

If the behavior you're calling out isn't directed at you, it's especially important to persist even if a biased colleague responds defensively. Daniel said that his interactions with Carol were uncomfortable, particularly when she denied any wrongdoing. But over time, his input seemed to help. "She says fewer offensive things now," he told me. "It's gotten a lot better."

Form a coalition

Many experts suggest working with others to combat biased behavior. Join forces with people on your team or in your company and make an explicit pact to respond to microaggressions. When something troubling but ambiguous happens, everyone in the group has a sounding board to help determine whether it warrants action.

This is a tactic that several women working in the Obama White House used when they were outnumbered by men in meetings. In an effort to make sure their ideas weren't drowned out or ignored (or co-opted by men), they agreed to use an amplification strategy. When one woman made an important point, another would repeat it and attribute it to the woman who had originally suggested the idea. This forced everyone in the room to recognize the contribution and prevented others from stealing credit.[30]

Research has shown that speaking up about injustice as a group is more effective because those in charge can't dismiss the complaints as coming from "one disgruntled employee."[31] You might also feel safer raising an issue if others have your back. So reach out to people who may be similarly upset by your colleague's actions. If you aren't the target of biased comments, you can still offer to form a coalition with those who are. This allows coworkers from underestimated backgrounds to turn to you when they notice bias that you might've missed.

Call out bias even in private

Some microaggressions and other acts of bias happen behind people's backs. It might be a sexist side comment from another man, or a backhanded compliment during a performance discussion with a fellow manager. Don't let these incidents slide just because they're private. It's equally important to address bias when the person who is being targeted isn't present or didn't hear the offensive remarks. If, in a meeting, someone says, "We're lucky to have an older woman on the team to keep us in line," you could counter by highlighting her accomplishments and skills: "Well, her age and gender don't seem relevant, but I do know that since she's been leading them, her product lines have increased profits by 20 percent."

Phrases to Use

Ask questions, buy yourself time, assess intent

"What was your intention when you said . . . ?"

"What did you mean by that comment?"

"What specifically did you mean by that, because I'm not sure I understood?"

"That could be taken the wrong way—can you explain what you meant?"

"What information are you basing that on?"

"Could you say more about what you mean by that?"

"Can you clarify what you meant when you said XYZ?"

"Hold on, I need to process what you just said."

Address intention

"I imagine it wasn't your intention."

"I know you wouldn't want to inadvertently offend a woman by suggesting she should smile more."

"I know you really care about fairness. Acting in this way undermines those intentions."

It's up to each of us to create a more inclusive, supportive work environment at every opportunity, not just when the people potentially harmed are there to witness injustice.

• • •

Aliyah finally got through to her boss, Ted, but it wasn't until he crossed yet another line. In a meeting where their team was discussing how to respond to complaints from customers, Ted felt like people

Be direct

"It's disrespectful to say . . ."

"That comment is based on a stereotype."

"I'd prefer that you not say that around me again."

"That's not OK with me, and I respect you enough to let you know."

"I'm not comfortable with that."

"That's not funny."

"Do you hear how you sound?"

Educate your colleague

"I know you meant that as a compliment, but unfortunately it connects to a larger history of people being surprised that [Asian people, women, disabled people] can't [or shouldn't] . . ."

"I noticed that you said X [biased comment]. I used to say that too, but then I learned . . ."

"I wonder if you've considered that [women, people of color, queer people] might experience this differently?"

were overreacting and, in a moment of frustration, said, "What are we worried about? A public lynching?" There was an awkward pause and Aliyah quickly exchanged glances with the only other Black person in the room. She told me she was trying to figure out what to say when Ted just carried on as if nothing happened. Fortunately, one of her other colleagues spoke up: "I'm feeling uncomfortable, and I think we need to talk about what just happened."

Initially, Ted tried to explain that he hadn't meant anything by his comment. But after Aliyah's team members explained why it was upsetting, Ted took a deep breath and apologized for what he said. He also apologized for trying to gloss over it. They ended the meeting there, and several of Aliyah's colleagues emailed or stopped by her desk to check on her. Ted steered clear of her for a few days but eventually asked to meet. He told her that he now saw how his comments about her being tough to read and not smiling could be hurtful. He asked her to continue to point out times when he was being biased and said he was committed to learning.

Aliyah was surprised. "I had all but given up on him," she told me. She admits that she's not sure he would've changed had their white colleagues not pointed out his transgression, but she's not sure it matters what caused his shift in perspective. "He got out of my way and that's what I cared most about," she said. Another round of organizational changes meant that Ted was soon moved to another division and Aliyah had yet another new boss. But Ted reached out to her regularly and even recommended her for a promotion, which she got.

TACTICS TO REMEMBER
The Biased Coworker

DO:

- Think carefully about whether you want to speak up, weighing the costs and benefits of doing so.

- Recognize that if you are in a position of power or privilege, you have a responsibility to address offensive comments and create a safe, inclusive work environment.

- Ask questions that encourage a biased coworker to reflect on what they said and clear up any misunderstandings.

- Have a few phrases ready that you can use if you are caught off guard by a microaggression.

DON'T:

- Presume that your colleague is incapable of change.

- Neglect to think through the political costs of calling out a microaggression, especially if you're the target.

- Assume the person knows they're being offensive; it's possible they have no idea.

- Level accusations of racism, sexism, or any other form of prejudice; that will put most people on the defensive and it's unlikely to change their behavior over the long term.

10

The Political Operator

"If you aren't moving up, you're falling behind."

Owen thought his colleague Clarissa was on his side. After the birth of his second child, he took a semester's paternity leave as the chair of the English department at a small university, and Clarissa agreed to fill in temporarily. Then, a few weeks into his leave, he heard from two different colleagues that Clarissa had said in a meeting that she was hoping to take over as chair when Owen was "ready to step down" or if "he decided not to come back." That made Owen a bit nervous (he had every intention of returning to his role), though he was pleased that he'd have a competent successor if and when he was ready to step aside.

Then, two weeks later, Clarissa called to say that the department would need to complete an evaluation for the university review board that they'd originally agreed to put off. "She was completely stressed-out," he recalled. It was a high-stakes review that would determine the department's funding and would put Clarissa in front of several senior leaders at the college. So he spent hours on the phone with her explaining what needed to be done and agreeing to help. "On the call, I signed up to do three-quarters of the work, but I could tell right away that there were going to be problems with who would get credit," he explained. She wanted everything to go through her and "was already calling it 'my report' and bemoaning 'all the legwork I need to get done.'"

Owen suggested that he and others working on the report meet by video to go over it before submitting it to the review board. In the meeting, Clarissa began by "representing the draft as hers." When a few of their colleagues pushed back on aspects of the report, Clarissa responded by saying, "As chair of the department . . ." It rubbed Owen the wrong way that she didn't acknowledge that she was "acting chair" or that he had "done the lion's share of the work," he says.

Owen lost trust in Clarissa and felt like she was playing political games to advance her own career—at his expense.

Of course, everyone has to engage in office politics to some degree. We compete with one another—for promotions, raises, plum assignments, and C-suite attention. We need to advocate for our ideas, and our accomplishments, to secure support and funding. But what if your colleague is fixated on getting ahead and has a take-no-prisoners approach to doing so?

Here are some of the behaviors you might be dealing with from a careerist colleague:

- Bragging about their successes

- Taking undue credit

- Currying favor with people in power or those in a position to help their career

- Acting like they're in charge, even when they aren't

- Gossiping and spreading rumors, particularly about coworkers who they believe are standing in their way

- Pushing their own agenda, often at the expense of team or company goals

- Hoarding information to appear powerful

- Purposely undermining you by not inviting you to a meeting or sharing critical details about your work

Dwight Schrute, the character from the TV show *The Office*, often comes to mind when I think about this archetype. He was in an endless (and fruitless) competition with his fellow salesman Jim. He insisted he was the "assistant regional manager," not the "assistant TO THE regional manager." And he constantly kissed up to his boss, Michael Scott. When Dwight was given any sort of power (like getting to choose the company's health-care policy, in one of my favorite episodes), he relished it and lorded it over his coworkers. While Dwight's character made for good entertainment, it's hard to imagine *anyone* would enjoy working with him day in and day out.

So how do you react to a hypercompetitive colleague who sees work as a winner-takes-all competition? Can you ever trust them? How do you avoid getting dragged into their game? And are there any lessons you can learn from the way they operate?

There is some overlap between this archetype and a few of the others—in particular, the passive-aggressive peer (chapter 6), the insecure manager (chapter 3), and the know-it-all (chapter 7). You may want to review those chapters for additional background and advice on how to deal with a political operator.

Now, let's take a look at what motivates a careerist to be so calculating—and at times disingenuous.

The Background on Politicking

First things first: all offices are political. Work involves dealing with human beings who are driven primarily by emotions rather than logic. We have conflicting wants, needs, and underlying (often unconscious) biases and insecurities. Working with others means negotiating clashing motives and often reaching compromises.[1] In addition, our work increasingly depends on others. Researchers have found that in the two decades since 2000, the time spent by managers and employees in collaborative activities has ballooned by 50 percent or more.[2]

Most of us recognize the need to play some politics. A 2016 Accountemps survey showed that 80 percent of people believe office politics exists in their office, and 55 percent said they take part. More than a quarter of those same respondents said they felt that "politicking" was essential to getting ahead.[3] Research backs them up. Numerous studies show that there's a connection between political skill and career success.[4]

It's important to understand what makes your coworkers tick (I've certainly advocated for doing that throughout this book), and it's politically savvy to use that knowledge to advance your and the organization's objectives.[5] You might leverage your understanding of what your marketing colleagues care about to convince them to get behind your project or present ideas to your boss's boss in a way that makes them most likely to approve. Understanding who has power and influence and tapping your network are necessary, even aspirational skills, as long as you use them for more than just personal gain.

But that's probably not the version of office politics that your colleague is modeling.

Good versus bad office politics

It's not always easy to distinguish between acceptable forms of playing office politics and more toxic varieties. To some people, the idea of sending your boss flowers to congratulate them on a promotion may seem obsequious; to others, it might just be a kind gesture. And still others might consider it a smart political move, knowing that a positive relationship with your manager is likely to help your career.

To discern what's appropriate and what's not, I ask myself: Is someone pursuing success at the expense of others? If the answer is no, then it's likely a shrewd approach to advancing their career. For example, speaking up in a meeting to share what's going well on your team's project is a great way to increase your visibility and enhance your reputation. And as long as you don't interrupt others to do it, or speak badly about another team, there should be no harm done. But if your colleague intentionally takes up the majority of a meeting so that others can't present their ideas, that's a different story.

One person I spoke to while writing this book described their "highly manipulative" coworker this way:

> His agenda always comes first. He's goal-oriented and financially driven. He can be the greatest person to have on your side because he will get what he wants at all costs. But when you're on opposite sides, the war begins. He will say things to make you feel insecure and try to turn you against other colleagues. He always frames his story to make it fit his needs. He might say, "I'm telling you this because I like you and care about you," but that usually means he is looking out for himself and he needs you on his side.

What compels people to behave so ruthlessly?

Scarcity, insecurity, and power

Of course, different people will be motivated by different things, but there are a few common reasons why your colleague is engaging in cutthroat politics, including a sense that resources are limited and must be fought over, insecurity or feeling threatened, and a desire for power or status.

One of the main factors that drives hypercompetitiveness is scarcity, or the idea that there isn't enough to go around. If everyone got exactly what they wanted at work—the salary they dreamed of, the budget for all of their pet projects, endless attention from higher-ups—there would be little need to engage in politicking. But resources are finite, and we're often made to compete for them. Your colleague may be focused on winning those resources to further their own agenda and bolster their position.

People who engage intensely in office politics sometimes do so because they're insecure or feel threatened. A friend of mine once noted that most of the political operators in the media company where she worked were people who weren't particularly good at the technical aspects of their jobs. Driven by a fear of having their incompetence exposed, they adopted underhanded tactics such as agreeing with everything their division head suggested and trying to steal clients away from their peers. (You can read more about how bravado is often a cover for incompetence in chapter 3.)

Finally, many careerists are simply driven by a desire for status or power. Jon Maner, a professor at the Kellogg School of Management, was inspired by a friend's complaints about a bad boss to research why some people sabotage their colleagues. He and a doctoral student found that leaders willingly undermined their own team members by limiting communication or pairing people together who don't collaborate well so that rivals would look incapable of filling a leadership role. These strivers cemented their status by eliminating any competition. Power-hungry leaders were even more likely to sabotage their team if they believed that their position wasn't secure and the hierarchy wasn't stable.[6] In other words, in a politically charged work environment where people are angling for influence, your colleague's natural inclination toward making others look bad may be intensified.

Many people play these games because it works for them. They keep their job as the boss, they get promoted, or they get the funding they want. But office politics doesn't work for everyone in the same way.

Who gets to play?

Women are more likely than men to say that they dislike engaging in office politics and more likely to experience what researchers call "political skill deficiency."[7] This is not to say that women are politically naive. They may be opting out because playing the game doesn't garner them the same benefits. There is some evidence that women and people from other underrepresented groups who engage in identical political behaviors as white men don't experience the career advantages that accrue to the white men.[8] In one survey, 81 percent of women and 66 percent of men said that women are judged more harshly than men when they are seen as "engaging in corporate politics."[9]

This leaves many women and racial minorities in a particular dilemma. On the one hand, they recognize it's not possible to stay out of office politics altogether and still be effective at their jobs. On the other hand, they feel uncomfortable engaging in political operating, often as a result of seeing other people like them suffer punishment when they do engage.

This double bind is something to keep in mind when dealing with your opportunistic colleague. They may have the privilege and leeway to play politics because of their gender or race, or they may be acting out because they feel stuck on the sidelines.

What happens in virtual work environments?

The shift to working virtually, greatly accelerated by the Covid-19 pandemic, may exacerbate your colleague's competitiveness. Not being able to keep tabs on everyone or to observe who is interacting with who or who is getting time with the top brass may deepen your coworker's insecurity about their standing. And there may be unusually limited resources for which everyone must jockey because of a tighter and more uncertain economy.

Working over email and Zoom also makes it harder for you to know what a political operator is doing behind the scenes to get ahead. Leadership consultant Nancy Halpern, who has developed a tool to measure the health of office politics on teams, told me, "There are so many conversations happening off-camera, and you have no way of knowing if and when they're taking place. Sometimes a colleague will just pop up on your screen during a meeting and you don't know who invited them or what role they've been asked to serve."[10] I've definitely had this experience. When I've used the private chat during a meeting to say hello to a coworker I haven't seen in a while or to compliment someone on their sweater, I've wondered who else is having side conversations and what they're saying.

But in some cases, ignorance is bliss. Not having to witness your coworker buttering up the boss or talking about people behind their backs may make it easier to get along with them.

A note on gossip

Gossip is one of a careerist's most common weapons. They will often intentionally spread rumors, mine for information, and strategically decide whether to keep intel to themselves or pass it along, often in exchange for juicy details from others. Being the target of such machinations is frustrating at best and career damaging at worst.

But gossip is one of those behaviors we all engage in occasionally, and while you might find it distasteful in your overly political colleague, it's not always wise to avoid it altogether. If you have a blanket rule of staying out of discussions about other people, for instance, you may be missing out. Listening to office banter is a great way to learn what's going on at your company—what group recently landed a big deal or what initiatives the CEO is likely to approve, for instance.[11]

But there are costs, especially when gossip is personal (talking about someone's divorce, for example) or negative (questioning a colleague's ability to do their job). Studies have shown that negative gossip can lead to lost productivity, erosion of trust, divisiveness, not to mention hurt feelings.[12] I suggest you ask the same question about gossip that you ask about other political behaviors: Is your colleague spreading it at someone's expense?

That will help you decide whether to engage or not. There are several other questions you should ask before settling on an approach to dealing with a ruthless striver at work.

Questions to Ask Yourself

As with any of the archetypes, it's important to begin by recognizing which of your power-hungry colleague's foibles are causing problems.

Which behaviors are problematic? And how problematic are they?

You don't want to unfairly judge or punish ambition. If someone is intensely focused on furthering their career—and you aren't—that's

OK. Don't assume bad intentions. Instead, consider what your colleague is doing that's rubbing you the wrong way. Is their go-get-'em style just irritating? Or does this person pose a real threat—to the organization, the team, or to your career? Are they stealing credit? Lying? Spreading rumors? Throwing others under the bus? What is the negative impact of their actions? How have you or others suffered because of their behavior?

Frequency of politicking also matters. Nancy Halpern has a good rule of thumb to follow: "If they do something once, forget it and let it go. If they do it twice, take note. And when they do it a third time, now there's a pattern."[13] For example, if you catch your colleague in a minor lie, which doesn't have serious consequences, you might ignore it. But if it happens again or it's causing harm, then it's time to take action.

What do the people in power care about?

Organizational culture plays a big part in whether or not employees engage in office politics—and whether they're rewarded for doing so. If you work in a cutthroat environment, your colleague's behavior may not be considered abnormal, especially if the people in charge of deciding who gets ahead have sensitive egos or are political players themselves. Look at who gets promoted and recognized. Is it people like your colleague who try to game the system?

Should you be playing office politics more?

A somewhat counterintuitive consideration is whether you could benefit from doing more politicking yourself. Would it help your team if you improved your persuasiveness or made new connections with influential leaders? Or would a shot of a careerist's confidence help you ask for the promotion you deserve or seek a stretch assignment that could boost your visibility? Of course, we all want our work to speak for itself, but that's not how most offices work. So consider what you might learn from your colleague. Of course, you shouldn't cross ethical lines or adapt tactics you find smarmy, but observe how they win favor with decision-makers and figure out which strategies are worth emulating.

Having answered these questions, you can now decide which tactics have the best chance of improving your relationship.

Tactics to Try

Keep in mind that it can be tough to hold a political operator to account, precisely because they have important connections at work and know how to make themselves look good. They also have little incentive to change their ways because overconfidence (as we learned in chapter 7) is often rewarded. So, instead of trying to take your colleague down a notch, which is probably unrealistic, start by removing yourself from the entanglement.

Don't get dragged in

If you have even a small competitive streak (I know I do), then you'll likely be tempted to try to beat your colleague at their own game. When they spread rumors about you, for example, you may want to turn around and do the same. Don't. Engaging in unhealthy competition or gossiping, even about a gossiper, will reflect badly on you. You don't want to appear petty or do something that's not aligned with your values.

Akila's boss's boss, Rajeev, cared a lot about how he was perceived in their organization and often sought the spotlight. Akila was particularly frustrated when Rajeev would overcommit just to make himself look good and then pressure the team to meet the unrealistic goals he'd set. Akila admits that she occasionally gave in to the temptation to fight back. "Sometimes, out of spite, I would try to 'get back' at him by not responding to him for days," she told me. "But that backfired and made me look irresponsible." And when Rajeev would lose his cool because the team wasn't able to keep up with the promises he'd made to the company's executives, Akila understandably struggled to stay calm. "If I was at the receiving end of one of his shouting bouts, I would try to justify myself immediately, but that would only make him even more worked up." So Akila focused on putting emotional distance between her and Rajeev. "When things went south and he was rude to me, I would just go somewhere quiet to let out my emotions through tears or prayers. That didn't change the immediate situation, but it did help me feel better."

Make your good work known

As Akila discovered, your colleague's politicking can negatively affect your reputation or career, so find productive—and ethical—ways to make sure that the right people know about your accomplishments. This can include keeping your manager up to date on your projects and how you're contributing time, ideas, and effort to other teams, or volunteering to share an overview of the initiative you're leading at an all-staff meeting.

When I found myself helping out as an informal adviser on a project that I wasn't officially assigned, I would occasionally mention it to my manager, saying something like "I've been fortunate to have some input into the decisions so far." And when the team presented at a division meeting, I asked a question that demonstrated to people in the room that I'd been involved. These subtle ways of increasing my visibility have also helped me guard against some of my more political colleagues taking credit for my work.

Of course, it's not always easy to toot your own horn—and research shows that women in particular tend to engage in less self-promotion than men because they're often penalized for doing it.[14] So find a colleague who understands your contributions and can speak on your behalf in a meeting or when your projects come up in conversation. You might approach a coworker and say: "I worked really hard on this report but sometimes find it hard to promote my own work. I'd appreciate it if you asked me questions at the meeting so I can talk about the key takeaways." This kind of peer advocacy benefits both parties. You get credit for your work, and your colleague gets a reputation boost for being curious, engaged, and selfless.

If your careerist colleague tries to take credit for your accomplishments or downplay your involvement in high-profile initiatives, it also helps to document what you're working on—either in emails to your boss or other forms of hard proof. A paper trail can often stop careerists from undermining you.

Offer help

Offering help to a political operator can be surprisingly disarming. They're accustomed to seeing everyone as competition, and they may not receive a lot of generosity or support. You could suggest working together on a project, offer to brainstorm about an initiative they're leading, or provide them with information or insight they'll find valuable. Because most people are inclined to help those who help them in return—the law of reciprocity—you could gain their favor.

One note of caution on this approach: be mindful of how others perceive your colleague. In your efforts to align yourself with this person, you don't want coworkers to see you as a political operator too. But if you have a positive reputation, people may appreciate your efforts to turn a notorious self-promoter into a collaborator.

Ask for advice

Research on negotiations points to another counterintuitive tactic: asking your hypercompetitive colleague for advice. Seeking their counsel on anything from how to phrase a tricky client email to how to persuade a senior leader to support your latest proposal could help you earn their trust. If they know you value their opinion, they may begin to see you as an ally as opposed to a rival. Studies have shown that asking for advice makes you seem cooperative, rather than competitive, and can win someone over, perhaps even encouraging them to become a champion; if you take their advice, they're more likely to feel invested in your success.[15]

The other advantage is that asking something as simple as "What would you do if you were in my shoes?" nudges your colleague to see things from your perspective. This is what Akila did with Rajeev. If she anticipated any snags with the project they were working on, she'd immediately alert Rajeev and ask for his thoughts. "By involving him, I noticed he would become a little more friendly with me. I think it made him feel I was not his 'enemy' after all," Akila told me.

Be wary of an attitude reversal

Proceed carefully if a careerist starts to take you into their confidence. It will probably feel like a relief to be aligned rather than at odds, but keep your antenna up. They might be using you for their own gain, perhaps feeding you information about other people in the hope that you'll pass it on or trying to make themselves look good by "playing nice" with others. Be wary of their intent and consider asking about it outright: "I'm a bit confused. What are you hoping I'll do with this information?" or "What's your intention in telling me this?" Posed in a humble and genuinely curious way, these questions won't sound like accusations.

Bring up what's bothering you

Since power-hungry colleagues are rarely straight shooters, being explicit might catch them off guard. And, as with many of the other archetypes, a political operator may not be aware of the impact they're having on others. Holding up a mirror can give them a sense of how they're perceived and encourage them to change. In conversation, keep your language neutral and devoid of emotion or judgment.

Of course, they may deny that they're engaging in toxic politics. That's fine. At least they will know that you're aware of what's going on and that you're not an easy target.

If you have any concern that your colleague will use such a conversation against you, perhaps as fodder for the rumor mill, then skip this tactic and employ one of the others instead.

Kirk, who worked for HR in a military infantry unit, noticed while reviewing self-assessments for his division that one of his colleagues,

Bernard, had taken credit for an idea that Kirk had come up with. It was a time-saving report for teams to document their work, a report that "helped us avoid duplicating efforts," Kirk explained to me. But Bernard had listed the report as one of his accomplishments for the review period.

Kirk decided to approach Bernard directly and asked him why he'd said he'd implemented the reporting change. Bernard was a bit taken aback, but mostly "he was indifferent and acted like it didn't matter who got the credit," he says. Kirk found the response odd since Bernard was the type of person who was "quick to make sure people knew what he did [and] became quite petulant if he didn't get credit for his efforts."

From that point on, Kirk made sure to copy others when he responded to Bernard's requests for input. "And if it was a project that included units beyond my own, I blind-copied superiors I knew in the chain of command," he explains. "I had to protect my contributions." This nipped the behavior in the bud because Bernard could no longer take credit when others knew better.

Tailor your approach to the political strategy

There are three specific tactics that political operators often employ that I want to address here: lying, gossiping, and stealing credit. Let's take a look at how you might respond to each ploy.

If you're dealing with lying: Confronting a careerist who is a frequent liar can quickly turn into a battle over who is telling the truth. If it's possible to gently point out mistruths and present contrary evidence, go ahead and do that. At first, try doing so in private. For example, you might send an email (which will also serve as documentation of your good-faith efforts later) that says something like "I'm confused about why you said your team wasn't aware of the rollout of the new feature, when, as you can see from the email chain below, we discussed it back in September." This can gently expose deception and make clear that you won't let them get away with it in the future.

If they don't respond positively (or at all) to these one-on-one inter-actions, you might go to your manager or correct your colleague's lies when they occur in front of others.

If you're dealing with gossip: Whenever possible, interrupt negative gossip when you hear it. If an opportunist says something that could harm another person's feelings or reputation, speak up. This takes courage, of course, but doing this even a few times will put the political operator on notice. If they try to bend your ear about someone else on the team, you can respond with, "Have you told them you feel this way?" Or go a step further and neutralize rumors by providing contrary information. For example, if the careerist speaks poorly of a colleague's performance or rolls their eyes when another coworker is brought up in conversation, you can mention a specific time you were impressed with their work.

If you find out your colleague is spreading harmful gossip about *you*, deal with it directly. Be specific and don't make accusations. You might say, "I've heard on several occasions that you're uncomfortable with how I'm running these meetings. Is there something you want to tell me?" Again, they may play dumb, but at least you've shown them that you're not going to let their behavior go unchecked.

If you're dealing with stealing credit: If you find that your careerist coworker is claiming they did all the work on a project that they were barely involved in, start by asking questions, something along the lines of: "I noticed that when you talked about the project, you said 'I' instead of 'we.' Was that intentional? Why did you present it that way?" Asking questions shifts the burden of proof to your colleague: they have to explain why they felt justified taking credit.

Sometimes credit-stealing happens unintentionally. So allow for the possibility that your colleague may realize and acknowledge their mistake, and if they do, refocus the conversation on how you can make things right together. Perhaps they could send an email to the group thanking you for your contributions, or you could both talk to your manager to set the record straight.

Phrases to Use

Your colleague's attempts to get ahead at any cost may understandably leave you tongue-tied. Just because you expect bad behavior from someone doesn't mean that it won't fluster you. Here are some phrases you can try while testing tactics.

Emphasize collaboration or offer to help

"We're on the same team."

"I'd love to discuss how we can help each other and the team [or company]."

"I'm not sure if you realize how you come off in those meetings. Sometimes it seems like all you care about is your project and your team, rather than the collective."

Handle lying

"I remember this situation differently. Can we go back and look at our emails, [meeting notes, or Slack messages] to be sure we're all on the same page?"

"I'm confused about why you said your team led the rollout of our new feature, when, as you can see from the email below, it was my team that was in charge."

If your colleague is notorious for trying to take credit, be proactive to prevent it. Make a point of agreeing up front about how credit will be allocated. Who will present ideas to the senior team? Who will field questions? Who will send the announcement of a new product release to the rest of the company? It can be helpful to write down these agreements and share them with everyone involved in the project in an email so there's no room for misunderstanding.

Handle gossip

"This sounds like gossip. Is that what you intended?"

"Do they know you feel this way?"

"I learned you had some concerns about the approach we're taking. I'd welcome hearing them."

"Next time, please come to me directly."

Handle credit-stealing

"I saw that my name wasn't on that presentation. Please send it to me so I can add myself before sharing it with others."

"I noticed that when you talked about our project, you said 'I' instead of 'we.' Was that intentional? Why did you present it that way?"

"It's unclear to me how our teams are dividing and conquering this plan. Can we discuss who is doing what before the next meeting?"

"How can we make sure that everyone gets the credit they deserve?"

Model generosity

As always, model the behavior you want to see from others. Give credit generously and speak highly of your colleagues in meetings. This not only builds trust and positivity on your team but also encourages others—including your problem colleague—to follow suit. Someone who is prone to backstabbing may actually ease up if you're kind to them. And, if they don't, at least you'll have allies who will come to your defense if your colleague does attempt to undermine you. At the same time, don't go overboard. If you thank everyone who worked on any little part of a project, for instance, you risk coming off as disingenuous. Focus your recognition on the people who truly deserve it.

• • •

Owen did return from his paternity leave and resume his position as chair of the department. Clarissa continued to have her eye on his role, but he decided to not let her get under his skin. The reality was that she was the best successor, so he focused his efforts on making sure she was ready when the time came. He included her in meetings with the college president's office and often sought her advice on decisions. Enlisting her as an ally demonstrated that he was invested in her success and tempered her need to compete with him.

When I think about what approaches work best with a political operator, I think about how Jim handled Dwight on *The Office*. He never stooped to Dwight's level but always approached their relationship with a sense of humor and playfulness. Sure, he teased Dwight, and even pranked him on occasion, but he behaved ethically, found comfort in other people, continued to do his job well, and even saw the humanity behind Dwight's sometimes absurd behavior. Dwight was often just looking out for Dwight, but Jim knew that he also cared genuinely about his colleagues. Dealing with someone who seems like they are out for themselves can be tricky, but it helps if you can remember that they're human too.

TACTICS TO REMEMBER
The Political Operator

DO:

- Choose collaboration over retaliation.

- Find productive—and ethical—ways to make sure that people know about your accomplishments.

- Create a paper trail of who did what on a project so your colleague can't take undue credit.

- Offer to help: suggest working together on a project, offer to brainstorm about an initiative they're leading, or provide them with information or insight they'll find valuable.

DON'T:

- Assume that your good work will speak for itself, especially if your colleague is bad-mouthing you.

- Stoop to their level and try to beat them at their own political game.

- Always trust them when they try to align with you—proceed with caution.

11

Nine Principles for Getting Along with *Anyone*

Change is possible.

I've made my fair share of mistakes when it comes to getting along with coworkers. I've hurled passive-aggressive digs in the heat of the moment. I've sent unkind emails that I wish I could take back. I've rolled my eyes at someone who I thought was being unreasonable. I've smiled to a colleague's face while thinking, "I hate you; I can't believe I have to do this. I wish you'd quit." And, yes, I've talked behind coworkers' backs when my attempts to make things better weren't reciprocated.

None of us is perfect when it comes to navigating the complexity of human relationships. But I've learned that there are certain touchpoints—key concepts to help you clean up your side of the street—that I return to over and over, whether I'm dealing with someone who fits neatly into one of the eight archetypes or who defies categorization.

The following principles should sound familiar—they're interwoven in the previous chapters. I draw them out and expand on them here because, together, they form the basis of how I think about interpersonal resilience. I hope these principles will strengthen your resolve and boost your effectiveness in the face of conflict, no matter who you're at odds with.

I recommend reading this chapter before you begin to plot out the steps you'll take with your difficult coworker. For example, if you're struggling with a passive-aggressive peer, you'll make a plan using the tactics outlined in chapter 6. But before you take action, consider the advice here as well. (Once you're familiar with the nine principles, use table 11-1 at the end of this chapter as a quick reference to test the soundness of your strategy.)

As we learned in chapter 2, our brains often work against us in moments when we're struggling with a colleague. In times of stress—when we feel threatened—even the workplace veterans among us are motivated by short-term goals: *I need to look good in front of my team. Get me out of this conversation! I have to win. I want everyone to like me.* And it's easy to lose sight of how we know we should behave.

Returning to these principles in those moments—and thoughtfully and carefully preparing yourself to navigate rough interpersonal seas—will help you reach the long-term goal of getting along.

The Principles

Principle 1: Focus on what you can control

Paola was struggling to get through to one of her direct reports, Franco, who she found incredibly stubborn. He refused to accept that anyone else on the team had expertise or insight that could be helpful to him in his technical role (a classic know-it-all). Paola had pointed out the behaviors that were bothering Franco's teammates and hurting his performance, including using a condescending tone and interrupting others, and asked him to stop. But he didn't—it seemed her feedback fell on deaf ears.

If there was an easy way to convince an aggravating coworker to change their ways, this would've been a very short book. The reality is that few people alter their behavior because someone else wants them to. They do it if and when *they* want to.

I've been in many situations where I thought, *If I can just explain this to the other person, surely they'll understand.* We've all fantasized about saying or doing the perfect thing that forces a rival to see the light, to realize the error of their ways and vow to completely reform. But, Wharton professor Adam Grant, author of *Think Again*, says that sharing our logic doesn't always work. He writes: "I no longer believe it's my place to change anyone's mind. All I can do is try to understand their thinking and ask if they're open to some rethinking. The rest is up to them."[1] Hear, hear!

Even as Franco's boss, Paola didn't have the power to *make* him change. Instead, she focused on what *she* could do differently. She decided to give Franco more-frequent feedback, dedicating five minutes of their weekly one-on-one meetings to pointing out how his behavior impacted the team and his effectiveness. Then, she simply had to hope that this adjustment in her approach would motivate him to alter his attitude. He eventually toned down his arrogance some, and Paola felt better knowing that she was doing the right thing even if he didn't budge as much as she'd hoped.

To be honest, I don't fully agree with the oft-given advice: "You can't change another person." I've seen many professionals who successfully persuaded a passive-aggressive peer to be more direct or convinced a colleague who played the victim to take responsibility for their failures. But if getting along with your colleague entirely depends on your ability to convince them to become a different person, you're taking a big risk. They may not have the capacity to change, or they might not want to. The only control you really have is over yourself.

Principle 2: Your perspective is just one perspective

Several years ago, I was working with a colleague who I'll call Cara. We were butting heads over how long we thought a project would take. When asked for our estimates, I was shocked that she expected it to take four times as long as I had assumed. But instead of thinking, "Wow, we're seeing this completely differently," I thought, "She's out of her mind!" I went into our conversations convinced there was no way she was even close to correct. And it became clear that she felt the same about me. Our judgment about each other's perspective was obvious, and things got tense.

We were facing one of the realities of difficult conversations: there's rarely an objective truth. We all come to the workplace with different perspectives and sets of values. We disagree on everything from whether it's OK to be five minutes late to a meeting, to whether interrupting someone who's going on and on is justifiable, to the appropriate consequences for making a mistake. It's not realistic to think you'll work with people who see eye to eye with you all the time.

There's a concept from social psychology called *naive realism* that explains just how different our perspectives can be. Naive realism is the tendency to believe that we're seeing the world around us objectively, and if someone doesn't see it the same way, they're uninformed, irrational, or biased.[2] One study in this area looked at what happened when participants were asked to tap out the rhythm of a well-known song, such as "Happy Birthday," and listeners tried to guess the song. Those doing the tapping thought that the listeners would guess the tune around 50 percent of the time, which was a huge overestimation given that they only guessed right 2.5 percent of the time.[3] Once we know something, like the tune of a song or the perfect solution to this quarter's budget shortfall, we find it hard to imagine that others won't recognize it too.

Naive realism is connected to another relevant cognitive bias: *fundamental attribution error.* This is the inclination to observe another person's behavior and assume it has more to do with their personality than it does with the situation in which they find themselves. So if your colleague is late to a meeting, you might presume it's because they're disorganized or disrespectful, not because they were caught in traffic or in another meeting that ran over. But we do the opposite when it comes to ourselves. When you're running behind, you probably focus on all the circumstances that led to your tardiness, not the idea that you're fatally flawed.

It's important to remember these two concepts in your dealings with your coworker. You're likely making assumptions that aren't necessarily true. The divide between your perspective and theirs can feel insurmountable, especially if you insist on a single view of what's happened and who's to blame. You can spend hours debating whose interpretation is correct, but reaching agreement on the "facts" is very unlikely. Instead of rehashing the past—a tactic that usually leads to nothing but hard feelings and deadlock—try to focus on what should happen going forward.

You don't have to agree to get along. You only have to respect each other's perspective enough to decide on a way forward. Rather than convincing Cara that she was completely off base (which I tried), I acknowledged that her perspective—informed by her own experience—was equally valid. In the course of our conversations, she made several points that shifted my thinking. And because I demonstrated a willingness to change my mind, she did the same. We came to a compromise—a schedule that she felt was a bit ambitious and I thought was slightly padded, but we could both live with. What we needed was a path forward, not a shared worldview.

To avoid wasting energy trying to convince my colleagues to see things my way or obsessing over being right or what the "truth" is, I now spend time challenging my own perspective:

- What if I'm wrong? How would I act differently?

- How do I know that what I believe is true? What assumptions have I made?

- How would someone with different values and experiences see things differently?

The answers to the questions matter less than the exercise of asking them. They are an important way of reminding myself that my view is just that: *my view*. Others see things differently—and that's OK.

Principle 3: Be aware of your biases

Interactions with our coworkers are not only influenced by our values and experiences, but also by our biases. Even our definition of "difficult" behavior can be shaped by the prejudices that we carry into the workplace.

I'll share an example I'm not particularly proud of. When I was working as a consultant, I had a client, a Black woman, who I was hesitant to push back on because I worried she would get angry. One of her direct reports—a white woman—stopped me in the hallway of their offices one day and mentioned that I seemed to be holding back with her boss. She was kind and seemed genuinely curious about why I was acting differently than I had in past meetings. I can't recall exactly what I said, but it was something about wanting to keep the client happy. I do remember her response clearly: "She's not going to bite your head off."

When forced to reflect, I realized that I'd seen my client's direct reports challenge her multiple times and she took it well. Sure, she spoke her mind and wasn't afraid to ask tough questions, but I'd never seen her irate. I was allowing stereotypes—specifically the "angry Black woman" trope—to influence my behavior. Not only was I doing her a disservice by typecasting her, I was also failing to do my job as a consultant, which was to present new ideas and challenge the status quo, because of some imagined backlash.

Ultimately, my hesitation to speak up wasn't about the client at all. It was about me and my prejudices.

The tricky thing about biases is that we're often unaware of them. As I discussed in chapter 2, our brains are wired to conserve resources, so they take shortcuts, rapidly putting people and things into categories, and assigning attributes to those categories informed by societal, sociological, and historical constructs of race, gender, sexual orientation, or class. Certain groups are labeled as easygoing, others as smart, still others as threatening.

There are two specific types of bias that are particularly helpful to understand when it comes to navigating difficult relationships: *affinity bias* and *confirmation bias*.

Affinity bias is the unconscious tendency to get along with people who are like us. In other words, we gravitate toward people with similar appearances, beliefs, and backgrounds. When colleagues aren't like us—perhaps in terms of gender, race, ethnicity, education, physical abilities, position at work—we are less likely to want to work with them. That's why it's critical when we're struggling with a coworker to ask ourselves: "What role could bias be playing here? Is it possible I'm not seeing the situation clearly because we're different in certain ways?"

Another form of prejudice that often seeps into workplace relationships is confirmation bias. This is the tendency to interpret events or evidence as confirmation of existing beliefs, and it plays out with vexing coworkers in two ways. First, if your view of a colleague is negative, you are more likely to interpret their actions as further evidence of your belief about them—they're not up to the task, they're unkind, or they only care about themselves. Second, if you've started to believe that your coworker falls into one of the eight archetypes—or a different category altogether—it will be increasingly difficult for that person to prove you wrong. You are preprogrammed to see "jerk-like" behavior from someone who you already think is a jerk.

So how do you interrupt these biases? There are a few things you can do:

- *Get to know your biases.* Taking a quiz online to get a better sense of your susceptibility to hidden biases is a good place to start. There are tons to choose from. I like the one from Project Implicit, a nonprofit started by researchers at Harvard, the University of Washington, and the University of Virginia.

- *Explore different perspectives.* There are lots of exercises you can do to help elucidate implicit assumptions. Listen to podcasts or read articles and books written by people who aren't like you. Learn about different cultures by doing your own research or attending educational events in your area. Practices like this will also help you understand your privilege, or the ways that you experience advantage as a result of your gender, race, sexuality, religion, and so on.

- *Ask for help.* When you face a conflict with a coworker, consult someone you trust—someone who is willing to push back on you—to reflect on the ways that you might be seeing the situation unfairly. You could even be explicit and ask: "What role might my biases be playing here?"

- *Question your interpretation.* Play devil's advocate with yourself, repeatedly asking whether you are seeing a contentious situation impartially. Use the "flip it to test it" approach I talked about in chapters 7 and 8: if your colleague were a different gender, race, sexual orientation, would you make the same assumptions? Or be willing to say the same things or treat them the same way?

I used this last tactic when I examined my reaction to my client. Would I assume she was going to be "angry" if she was a white woman, or a white man, or even a Black man? The answer was clear: no. If the client were a man, I might've interpreted the same behavior as "passionate" or "committed" or maybe "curt" at worst. But anger wouldn't have come to mind. This was an important exercise for me to recognize my own flawed logic and to move beyond it. That's not to say my biases went away. But I was able to monitor them more carefully.

Principle 4: Don't make it "me against them"

In a disagreement, it's easy to think in terms of two separate parties, even enemies at war. Lots of advice about navigating a dispute uses the word *counterpart*, which implies that there is someone opposed to or working against you. I used this wording in my last book about conflict, but I've come to think of this frame of mind as detrimental.

If it's "me against you," the situation becomes polarizing. There's someone who's being difficult and someone who isn't, someone who is right and someone who is wrong. As I explained in chapter 2, this type of storytelling is part of our brain's natural response to negative emotions like anger, fear, pain, or defensiveness. The narrative of "victim versus villain" can be comforting, but it's rare that we are blameless.

To get along with your colleague, you need a different mental model. Instead of seeing two opposing factions, imagine that there are three entities in the situation: you, your colleague, and the dynamic between you. Maybe that third entity is something specific: a decision you have to make together or a project plan you need to complete. Or maybe it's more general: ongoing tension between you or bad blood because of a project gone wrong. Either way, this approach separates the people from the problem, which is advice you might've heard before; it's one of the Harvard Negotiation Project's core principles for handling difficult conversations.[4]

Andre struggled with his pessimistic colleague, Emilia. He felt like whenever he proposed a new idea, Emilia had a list of reasons why it could never work. For a long time, Andre told me, he saw the two of them as opponents and pictured a dark cloud over her head and a bright sun over him. This visualization reinforced his view of things, but it didn't help him get along with Emilia, especially since he went into every conversation bracing himself for a battle. So he tried to change the image, picturing the dynamic between them as a seesaw that each person was choosing to get on and balance out whenever they were at odds. This helped shift his attitude. He stopped seeing Emilia as an adversary and thought of her as a collaborator instead.

Consider choosing your own image to represent the troubling dynamic between you and your coworker. For example, you might visualize yourself and the other person on the same side of a table, working on a problem—your unhealthy relationship—together. No one wants a nemesis at work. So put that idea away and think about how to engage your colleague in problem-solving, which is inherently collaborative instead of combative.

Principle 5: Rely on empathy to see things differently

"Try to see it from their perspective" is advice you've probably heard before. I don't know about you, but the last thing I want to do when

I'm dealing with an insecure boss or an overly political peer is to think about their feelings. When people are passive-aggressive, conniving, or mean, why should I care how they feel?

For starters, we often perceive slights to be worse than they were intended to be. This is what Gabrielle Adams, a professor at the University of Virginia, found in her research. People who feel like they've been wronged by a coworker overestimate how much the wrongdoer intended to harm them.[5] As Adams explained to me, "We imbue others' actions with a lot more intent than is usually there."[6]

This goes both ways. In another study, Adams found that both the "transgressor" and the "victim" are liable to assume the worst about one another. As she summarizes, we all "make erroneous attributions about each other's intent to do harm, how much harm was caused, how severe the issue is, how guilty the other person feels, etc."[7] Telling yourself that your politics-playing colleague meant to take credit for your work (and is therefore undeserving of your empathy) is not only potentially unfair to your colleague, but it nudges you toward wallowing, revenge, or other unproductive responses rather than getting along.

It's far better to give your coworker the benefit of the doubt. Assume there is some rationale behind their prickly behavior (even if you don't agree with it). What might they be thinking? What are they trying to achieve? What pressures are they under? What else do they have going on—at work or at home? Seeking compassionate explanations for hurtful actions (even if they're not 100 percent true) will give you the space—having deescalated feelings of threat—to respond thoughtfully.

This is a lesson I learn over and over from my daughter. When she was nine, we were driving on the highway not far from our house. As we slowed down because of traffic ahead, two motorcyclists came whizzing by in between lanes. They were easily going ninety miles per hour, maybe even a hundred, and neither one was wearing a helmet. Thinking this was a teachable moment for my daughter, I started to lay into the motorcyclists: "I can't believe how fast they're going, and without helmets! That's so dangerous." My daughter joined in, also acting incensed. "They should know better, they're adults!" I smiled, feeling content that she had learned something about safety. After a few moments of silence, she said, "Mommy, maybe they're on the way to buy helmets."

Now, I'm 99 percent certain those motorcyclists were not on their way to buy helmets, but her comment was a perfect reminder to try to see a tense situation from the other person's perspective, with a generous spirit. And, true or not, her observation softened the conversation and our stance toward those humans on their motorcycles.

One word of caution: seeing a hostile situation from your coworker's perspective does require mental resources, so be careful that you don't get so focused on walking a mile in someone else's shoes that you forget to consider your own needs. Start by giving yourself a dose of self-compassion for what you're going through before you turn your attention to your colleague. (For more on the importance of self-care in the midst of conflict, see chapter 14.)

Principle 6: Know your goal

Whenever you're trying to address an unhealthy dynamic between you and a coworker, it's important to be clear with yourself about what you want. Identifying your goal will help you avoid getting pulled into any drama and stay focused on constructive tactics.

Do you want to move a stalled project forward? Complete the initiative you've been working on together and move on? Have a healthy working relationship that will last into the future? Feel less angry or frustrated after interacting with them? Or do you want your colleague to stop undermining your success?

I recommend making a list of the goals you'd like to achieve (big and small) and then circling the one, two, or three that are most important. Your intentions will determine—subconsciously and consciously—how you act. For instance, if your goal is to avoid getting stuck in long discussions with your pessimistic colleague, you'll make different decisions than if your goal is to help them become aware of how their naysaying is bringing down the team.

It's all right to set your sights low. Often it's enough to focus on just having a functional relationship. It would be a big win if you can get to the point where your skin doesn't crawl when their name shows up in your inbox, or you're not losing sleep at night because they're on your mind. A minimal goal like, "Don't think about this person while I'm having dinner with my family," is absolutely fine.

You may have multiple goals. For example, if you're fighting with your insecure boss about which metrics to report to the senior leadership team and he's sent you some heated emails that challenge your experience with web analytics, your goals might be to: (1) come up with a set of stats that you can both live with, and (2) make sure that the senior leadership team knows about your expertise. You might also set a goal of having less heated exchanges right before important meetings.

Don't let your hidden agendas throw you off course. For example, in dealing with your overly political colleague, you may say that your goal is to stop worrying that they're going to undermine you. But what you really want is for them to pay: to be fired, or to feel as miserable as they've made you feel, or to be recognized by everyone in the organization as the dishonest manipulator they are. Ulterior motives often color your interactions, causing you to use language or a tone that is excessively critical or condescending, compromising your ability to achieve your stated goal. It's important to be aware of your secret (or not-so-secret) motivations, so say them out loud or document them, along with your other objectives. Then try to put all ill intentions (no matter how justifiable they seem) aside.

When you've decided on your goals, write them down on a piece of paper. Research has shown that people who vividly describe or picture their goals are anywhere from 1.2 to 1.4 times more likely to accomplish them, and you are more likely to achieve objectives that you record by hand.[8] Refer to your goals before any interaction with your colleague so you can stay focused on your destination.

Principle 7: Avoid gossip, mostly

"Is it me, or is Greta being particularly grumpy this week?"

There are lots of reasons we turn to others when something is off at work. It might be to confirm that you're not misinterpreting a vague email. It could be to determine whose buy-in you need to push forward that stalled cross-department initiative. Or maybe you're seeking reassurance. And when your colleague says, "Yes, Greta does seem grumpy. What's up with that?" you get a little jolt of relief: *It's not just me.*

This type of side conversation, whether it happens digitally or in person, can be particularly complicated when it comes to dealing with difficult colleagues. And let's call it what it is: gossip.

In chapter 10, I talked about how to handle your careerist colleague's gossiping, and I pointed out that there are upsides to being tapped into the rumor mill. Workplace gossip can play an important role in bonding with coworkers and information sharing. When you find out that Marina also finds Michael from finance difficult to work with, it fosters a sense of connection. If you learn that it's not just the two of you who wish Michael would be more of a team player (or find another job), that bond becomes even deeper. You have essentially formed an in-group which has information that others, especially Michael, don't have. Your perspective has also been validated, so you get the rush of adrenaline and dopamine that comes from feeling like you're "right."

Here's a secret about gossip: studies have shown that it can actually deter people from behaving selfishly. If a team member knows that others might talk badly about them if they're uncooperative or rude, it can prevent them from misbehaving in the first place.[9] I would argue that talking to someone directly about what they're doing and who it's hurting is a better approach, but research has indeed shown that gossiping about people indirectly punishes them and warns others about the pitfalls of working with them.[10]

Does that mean you should talk behind your coworkers' backs? Well, not so fast. There are dangers as well. First, it could make you more susceptible to confirmation bias. Sure, Michael may be exasperating sometimes, but once you and your work friends start talking about it, you're more likely to interpret his future actions as negative. Occasional missteps start to get painted as an inherent trait and the "Michael is difficult" storyline becomes a self-fulfilling prophecy.

When others are invested in a particular story about a colleague, it's exponentially harder to change the narrative. Additionally, gossiping often reflects poorly on the gossiper. You may get the immediate validation you're seeking, but you may also garner a reputation for being unprofessional—or end up labeled as the difficult one.

Before you start spreading rumors about how incompetent your boss is or how unbearable it is to work with the tormentor who heads up your department, think about your goal. Whether it's to improve your relationship, feel better, or get your job done despite resistance, ask yourself whether gossip will help or hurt the situation.

It is perfectly legitimate to seek help sorting out your feelings or to check that you are seeing things clearly with someone else. But choose who you talk to (and what you share) carefully—seek out people who are constructive, have your best interests at heart, will challenge your perspective when they disagree, and exercise discretion.

Principle 8: Experiment to find what works

There isn't one right answer or proven path that you can follow to get your know-it-all colleague to stop being condescending or your passive-aggressive peer to deal with you in a more straightforward way. In this book, I've shared strategies that have been shown to work, but which ones you try and how you apply them will depend on the context: who you are, who the other person is, the nature of your relationship, the norms and culture of your workplace, and so on.

Improving a relationship can be overwhelming; it's no easy feat. But it will feel far more manageable if you start by coming up with two or three ideas you want to test out. Often, small actions can have a big impact. Design an experiment: determine what you'll do differently, set a time period during which you'll try your approach, and see how it works. For example, if you want to improve communication with a passive-aggressive colleague, you might decide that for two weeks, you're going to ignore their tone and focus on the underlying message. Rather than assuming that's going to fix everything between you, see it as a test and acknowledge that you'll likely learn something, even if you learn that the tactic doesn't work. Then, set up another experiment, tweaking your approach over time.

Keep refreshing the approaches you try and be willing to abandon ones that aren't producing results. If you've attempted to handle a colleague's lack of follow-through by sending an email after meetings confirming what everyone has agreed to do, and this hasn't prevented your colleague from saying one thing in meetings and doing something else later on, then don't repeat the experiment expecting different results. A situation like that calls for what conflict expert Jennifer Goldman-Wetzler calls a "constructive, pattern-breaking action," which is a simple act "designed to interrupt the conflict pattern of the past."[11] In other words, try something you haven't tried before, even something the other person might not expect.

Principle 9: Be—and stay—curious

When it comes to confronting a negative dynamic with a coworker, it's easy to tell yourself, "This is the way it's always going to be" or "Why should I expect them to change?" or "We just don't get along." I won't tell you that it's going to be fun or even pleasant to do what you need to do to salvage a troubled relationship, but complacency and pessimism will get you nowhere. Instead, adopt a curious mindset.

Research shows there are a lot of benefits to being curious at work—benefits that will make navigating conflict easier. For example, curiosity has been shown to help us avoid falling into confirmation bias and prevent us from stereotyping people. It also helps us stay out of amygdala hijack, as we're more likely to approach tough situations creatively and be less defensive and aggressive.[12]

Adopting a curious mindset also helps to disrupt the stories we tell ourselves, especially if we can switch from drawing unflattering conclusions to posing genuine questions. When your colleague Isabel starts to pick apart another coworker's proposal, for example, rather than telling yourself, *Here we go again with Isabel's naysaying. Doesn't she know how to do anything else?* you might ask, *What's going on with her? This feels familiar, but what have I missed in the past? Why is she acting like this?*

Assume you have something to learn and believe that the negative dynamic can turn around, both of which are aspects of adopting a growth mindset. Of course, it's not always easy to get—or stay—in that frame of mind when you're feeling frustrated. Try to catch yourself in an unproductive thought pattern, step back, and change the framing. Instead of thinking, *Isabel is . . .* , try *One view of Isabel is that she can be quite negative. What are some other options?* Think about the other people she works with. Is there someone who genuinely enjoys working with her? Try to put yourself in *that* colleague's shoes. Look for disconfirming evidence or instances when Isabel does the opposite of what you expect—taking a positive or neutral stance, for example.

Another way to foster a growth mindset is to remind yourself of times when you or others have changed. Think of previous instances, at work or elsewhere, where you and another person didn't get along at first or hit a rough patch but were able to get past it. Rely on these previous experiences to challenge any preconceived notions about people's immutability. How were you able to persevere? What helped you achieve resolution?

Focus, too, on what you stand to gain from meeting your goals for your relationship. Project into the future. If you achieve your objectives, what will be different? How will your work life improve? Consider posting the intentions that you wrote down earlier in this chapter somewhere you can see them as a reminder of what success will feel and look like. Not only will you have solved your current predicament, but you'll have improved your ability to navigate other tricky relationships you encounter at work.

• • •

Resolving conflict can be a bumpy ride, and some of your experiments will fail miserably. You might even feel like things are getting worse. But don't lose hope—change *is* possible, and the dynamic is *not* set in stone. As the famed Argentinian therapist Salvador Minuchin said: "Certainty is the enemy of change."[13] You can't be certain of what the future holds for you and your colleague, so be curious instead. It'll snap you out of the fixed mindset that might be keeping you from discovering an unexpected solution to your problem.

No matter what type of difficult colleague you're dealing with or what you decide to do next, keeping these nine principles top of mind will improve your odds of building stronger, more fulfilling relationships at work.

Summary of the Nine Principles

Once you're ready to take steps to better get along with your difficult colleague, you can use table 11-1 on the following page to double-check that you're going in with the right mindset and that you've selected tactics that will set you up for success.

TABLE 11-1

Nine principles for getting along with anyone

Principle 1: Focus on what you can control	• Don't waste time trying to convince your colleague to change; people change if *they* want to change. • Focus instead on what you can do differently.
Principle 2: Your perspective is just one perspective	• Acknowledge that you and your colleague won't always see eye to eye. • Forget the blame game; rally around finding a path forward. • Ask yourself: What if I'm wrong? What assumptions am I making?
Principle 3: Be aware of your biases	• Get to know your biases so you can detect when they're affecting your interactions—or causing you to unfairly interpret your colleague's actions. • Note when you might be falling into *affinity bias*, gravitating toward people with similar appearances, beliefs, and backgrounds. • Avoid *confirmation bias*, the tendency to interpret events or evidence as confirmation of your existing beliefs.
Principle 4: Don't make it "me against them"	• Imagine that there are three entities in the conflict: you, your colleague, and the dynamic between you. • Use positive, collaborative visualizations (such as you and your coworker sitting on the same side of a table) instead of combative ones to improve the odds of turning your unhealthy relationship around.
Principle 5: Rely on empathy to see things differently	• Give your coworker the benefit of the doubt, asking yourself, "What is the most generous interpretation of their behavior?" • Assume that there is some rationale behind their prickly behavior (even if you don't agree with it).
Principle 6: Know your goal	• Be clear about what your goals are for the relationship. • Write them down and refer to them frequently. • Watch out for any ulterior motives that might damage your chances of getting along.
Principle 7: Avoid gossip, mostly	• Resist the urge to talk behind your coworker's back. • Choose who you talk to about the situation carefully; seek out someone who is constructive, has your best interests at heart, will challenge your perspective, and exercise discretion.
Principle 8: Experiment to find what works	• Come up with two or three things you want to test; small actions can have a big impact. • Keep refreshing your approaches, based on what you learn along the way, and be willing to abandon ones that aren't producing results. • Try something you haven't tried before, even something the other person might not expect.
Principle 9: Be—and stay—curious	• Adopt a growth mindset; believe that you have something to learn and that the dynamic can change. • Focus on what you stand to gain from meeting your goals for getting along.

PART THREE

PROTECTING YOURSELF

12

When All Else Fails

Don't give up—yet.

I'm going to level with you. Sometimes the tactics I've laid out in this book won't work. You can't convince a know-it-all to recognize and change their arrogant ways because your boss *values* their overconfidence. Your biased colleague refuses to see how their comments are offensive, despite your attempts to educate them. The pessimist on your team is so stuck in their negative ways, it becomes clear that change just isn't possible for them.

If you've persistently taken steps to get along with your coworker, but you aren't seeing progress, there are a few things you can do before you throw in the towel. These strategies won't magically turn things around, but they will help you protect your career, your reputation, and your ability to do your job without losing your mind. In the next chapter, we'll talk about how to avoid common mistakes so you don't make things worse. And in chapter 14, I'll share advice on preserving your overall well-being and finding ways to thrive in spite of conflict.

In the absence of progress, it might be time to try one or more of the following maneuvers: setting boundaries and limiting your exposure; documenting your colleague's transgressions and your successes; escalating the issue to someone with power; and, if *nothing* else works, moving on. First, let's talk about how you can disengage.

Establish Boundaries

There's a corny joke you may have heard before: a man goes to see his doctor complaining of a hurt elbow. The doctor asks him when it hurts, and the man replies, "When I bend it like this." The doctor says, "Then don't bend it like that."

Similarly, if interacting with your problem colleague is stressful, interact with them less. Setting clear boundaries with someone you have to work with every day isn't always easy, especially if there's a good deal of interdependence between your jobs. But it's not impossible.

Author and therapist Nedra Glover Tawwab says, in her book *Set Boundaries, Find Peace*, that "people treat you according to your boundaries," which she defines as "expectations and needs that help you feel safe and comfortable in your relationships."[1] What do healthy limits look like when you're dealing with a difficult colleague?

For starters, find ways to minimize how much you rely on them. If you have an ongoing conflict with a client, you could explain the situation to your supervisor and propose that one of your equally qualified colleagues replace you on the account. If you're having trouble with someone in the finance department, you could build a relationship with a new contact on that team. If your boss is the problem, you might apply for jobs in other departments; start by cultivating a broader network in the organization and connecting with people on teams you may want to join.

Happiness researcher Michelle Gielan describes a tactic for limiting interaction called the "two-minute drill." She suggests asking yourself: What exactly do you need from your uncooperative colleague? A piece of information? Their agreement on a project plan? And what's the least amount of time it will take to get what you need from them? If you know they are likely to do something that will annoy you, say, bad-mouth your shared boss, can you have a response ready? How can you keep your interactions as brief and positive as possible?[2]

For instance, if your pessimistic colleague is prone to stopping by your desk or trapping you on video calls to complain, have a few phrases in your back pocket that you can use to exit the conversation: "I need to get ready for my next meeting" or "I promised that I'd respond to this email ASAP."

This is what Sebastian, who worked as an engineer at a tech company, did when his coworker Gabriel continually got under his skin. Whenever they were alone in the lunchroom, Gabriel would gripe about other engineers. Sebastian told me that according to Gabriel, "either someone was completely incompetent (95 percent of the time) or fantastic (5 percent of time)." He even said things like, "This will never work because they're all morons." Sebastian regularly saw Gabriel bring down an entire team's mood with his naysaying during meetings.

Sebastian tried to help Gabriel be more constructive by saying things like, "Maybe this time it will work," or "I'm sure in the right context, Laurie can contribute." But Gabriel's response was always the same: "You're just an idealist. You'll see how it is with these people, and don't tell me I didn't warn you." Eventually Sebastian decided to just decrease the amount of time they spent together. He avoided working on projects with Gabriel whenever he could. "I asked for his advice occasionally because he had valuable insights and I needed him to feel included so he wouldn't turn on me. But when I did request his help, I went out of my way to make sure it would not require collaborating with others."

The strategy Sebastian employed here is known as "job crafting." It's a process in which you proactively redesign your role to make it more meaningful and less draining, and which research has shown to lead to greater job satisfaction and improved well-being.[3] There are several forms this strategy can take: task crafting, where you alter the type, scope, or number of tasks you take on as part of your job; cognitive crafting, where you change the way you interpret or think of the work you're doing; and relational crafting, where you modify who you interact with in your work.[4] Although relational crafting is the most relevant to dealing with a tiresome colleague, all three approaches can help you shift your work and attention away from a troublesome coworker. To start, consider all the ways you could minimize the amount of time you spend with them and increase collaboration with people who energize, inspire, and support you.

Also, think about the most effective ways to communicate with someone who makes you cringe. Do they tend to be easier to deal with over email? Or are things less complicated when you have a quick phone call? Figure out what will be least stressful for you and stick to clear boundaries. Sometimes a simple "I prefer that we figure this out over the phone" will do the trick.

If there's no way to reduce your exposure to a difficult colleague, try to lighten the tone of your interactions. Find ways to turn them into a game. For example, see how many times you can get a relentless pessimist like Gabriel to say something positive or to smile. When you succeed, consider it a tiny victory. This will give you a small way of regaining a sense of control while maintaining emotional distance.

Document Their Transgressions and Your Successes

It's helpful to have a record of bad behavior, especially if you need to make the case to those in power that your colleague is doing real harm. For every offense possible, note the time, place, what was said or done, by whom, and who was present at the time. And don't just record your colleague's actions; also note what you said and did in response. Leaders will be more willing to intervene if they see a pattern of behavior and know that you—and perhaps others—have already taken steps to address it. This may be painstaking, but keeping a record like this over time helps show that the mistreatment is consistent, destructive, and ongoing.

Document your successes, too, so they don't get diminished by your colleague or the tension between you. Keep a running list of what you're working on and any ideas or pitches you bring forward. Regularly share your wins with your boss, even via a short weekly email. Don't think of this as bragging; it's about building a case for your value at the company. This is an especially important strategy if your colleague is a know-it-all who is trying to steal your thunder.

Find ways to make your good work known to others in the organization as well. Introduce yourself to people in other departments or at higher levels in the company, perhaps by volunteering for a cross-functional initiative or joining a powerful executive's pet project. Cultivating new connections will give you a chance to broadly demonstrate your talents and ideally disprove any false information your colleague may be spreading about you.

One friend of mine smartly keeps a journal where she lists the work she is doing and any notable achievements. She started doing this for herself to counter the negativity of a pessimistic colleague, but she says she finds it useful at review time when completing self-appraisals and whenever she is meeting with senior executives and wants to be able to speak to her accomplishments.

Escalate to Someone Who Has the Power to Do Something

There is always the option of going to someone higher up in the organization, your boss or another manager who can provide you with advice, give direct feedback to the difficult coworker, or even reprimand them if their behavior is out of bounds.

This is a tricky move in any scenario, especially if the difficult colleague is your boss, so weigh the trade-offs carefully. Will escalating the issue make *you* look bad? Do you risk further damaging your relationship with your colleague if they discover you went behind their back or brought in reinforcements? Will the person you appeal to believe you or take your side?

If you do speak to someone about your colleague's behavior, try to avoid coming off as a complainer. Make clear that you're not acting out of jealousy or being vindictive. Approach the discussion as an effort to create a good working relationship with your colleague, not an excuse to throw them under the bus. This is especially important if you're dealing with a political operator who is good at managing up and may have powerful allies. Also, be ready to explain what you've done so far to solve the issue yourself.

It will help if you can tie problems with your coworker to concrete business results. Articulate how they're damaging the team's performance in a way that leaders will care about and provide plenty of evidence to back up your claims. (This is where meticulous documentation comes in handy.) It's more convincing if your account of events can be corroborated, so confirm that others have witnessed the negative behavior and are willing to stand with you if need be.

You should also consider who you are escalating to and what they have the power or motivation to do. Who is the right person or department to go to? Will they be open to helping you? Will they be discreet? Do they have the skills or authority to give your difficult colleague feedback? Are they sufficiently motivated to take action? Turning to other people doesn't always work, especially if they are ill-equipped (or unwilling) to address your colleague's behavior. Plus, if they solve the problem for you—perhaps behind closed doors—you won't develop the skills you need to deal with similar issues in the future.

What about going to HR? Bob Sutton, author of *The No Asshole Rule*, cautions that hoping HR or even your legal department is going to take swift action is misguided. And let's be real: it's rare to hear an account of someone who appealed to HR when navigating a tricky relationship with a coworker and received meaningful help (though it does happen). As Sutton told me, "In most companies, HR is not there to be your friend. They are there to protect the institution."[5] Do your research ahead of time to see how your HR department has handled similar situations in the past. If they haven't helped, then you'll probably have better luck appealing to someone who knows you and the other party.

Before approaching a potential ally, whether they're your boss, your boss's boss, an HR representative, or someone else, think about how they've responded to comparable situations in the past. Did they give good advice? Did they follow through if they offered assistance?

Did they make things better or perhaps worse? The answers to these questions will help you decide whether it's a good idea to escalate or not.

Should You Quit?

Leaving your job because of a conflict with someone is obviously an extreme response, and it's a tactic that I don't recommend lightly. But sometimes, it's justified.

About one in eight people who report being treated poorly leave their job because of the incivility.[6] I'm of two minds about quitting. On the one hand, I realize it's not a possibility for everyone. For financial or logistical reasons, it may not be feasible no matter how dysfunctional your interactions with a coworker have become. You may have a mortgage to pay or family members who rely on your benefits and salary, or perhaps you work in an industry where there are few openings.

If you're miserable but you feel like you can't quit just yet, set up some parameters for how long you'll stay. Seeing a light at the end of the tunnel will make the time until you can leave more bearable. You might tell yourself, "I'll stick it out for four months, and if these three things don't change in the meantime, I'll start sending out my résumé." The key is to avoid feeling like you're stuck, which will only worsen your misery.

On the other hand, if you've exhausted other options, including enlisting the help of senior leaders or exploring possible moves within your company, ask yourself whether it's worth sticking it out. As one interviewee told me, "I had to quit because of the mental torture and its impact on my health." No one should have to suffer like that at work.

I asked Bob Sutton for his take on leaving a job when you're being stifled under the weight of a challenging relationship, and he said it was an "underrated" option. "I'm a big believer in quitting," he said. "Grit is overrated when it comes to working with toxic people, and on average, people decide to quit too late, after they've already suffered the consequences."

He points out that one advantage to quitting is that you get to try different things. "The grass does always seem greener elsewhere," he said, especially when you're miserable. Several years ago, Sutton left Stanford and took a job at Haas School of Business at the University of California Berkeley, hoping it would give him more opportunities and that he could extricate himself from some unhealthy dynamics. But, after only a year, he returned to Stanford, accepting a role at the Engineering School and a 30 percent pay cut. He says, "I consider myself part of the 'grass is browner' club now. I'm one of many people who left their employer and came back because the new experience showed me that what I had wasn't so bad after all." Sometimes it's a good thing to test the waters and see if you will indeed be happier in a different environment. (Follow Sutton's lead and keep the door open at your current employer if possible—it's always nice to have options.)

If quitting your job is a realistic possibility for you, consider what you'd like to do instead before jumping ship. When feasible, it's better to leave for something else—like a more positive culture—rather than running from a bad situation. As research by Boris Groysberg and Robin Abrahams from Harvard Business School shows, rushing to leave is one of the most common missteps people make when changing jobs. They write: "Often, job seekers have become so unhappy with their present positions that they are desperate to get out. Instead of planning their career moves, they lurch from one place to the next, applying artificial urgency to the job hunt rather than waiting for the right offer."[7]

Before taking the leap, think through several questions: How exactly will you be better off if you leave? (Be specific.) What are you going to do with your time and energy after you walk away? (This one's especially important if you don't have another job lined up.) What do you want from your relationships in a new environment?

Bear in mind that quitting usually isn't an immediate solution, and certainly shouldn't be done impulsively. Give yourself time to spruce up your résumé, expand your network, and talk with people who may be able to support you in making the move. However, there are situations in which conflict is so bad that severing the relationship promptly is best. It's not worth endangering your mental or physical health, for instance, or losing your good reputation. Only you can decide when enough is enough.

Keep in mind that all of the tactics in this chapter are meant to be last-resort options, employed only if well-intentioned attempts at improving your working relationship with your colleague haven't turned things around. There are also several strategies that I recommend you avoid at all costs—because they will only make things worse—which I'll cover in the next chapter.

13

Approaches That Rarely Work

They'll only make things worse.

One of my favorite questions to ask people who are dealing with a difficult colleague is: "What would you do about this situation if you could do *anything* you wanted?"

I suggest they put aside financial considerations, societal norms, and any repercussions. The answers range from practical to entertaining to a bit scary (there are lots of people who want to punch an annoying colleague in the face!). Many fantasize about quitting dramatically. Others just want to tell their coworker exactly how they feel without mincing words. God knows I've come up with some nasty comebacks in my head while walking my dog.

There are two reasons I ask this question. First, I want people to think expansively about how they might respond, and often, without constraints, they land on a strategy that might actually work (*not* punching someone in the face).

Second, this can be a useful exercise for venting frustration. I remember driving in the car with my mother several years ago when I noticed she was looking at and moving her hand in a strange way, as if she was in pain. I asked her what was happening. At the time, she was a lobbyist in the Connecticut State General Assembly, representing over thirty nonprofit organizations. Her days were filled with challenging conversations, and she had endless stories about fellow lobbyists, clients, and legislators who fit many of the archetypes in this book. In response to my question, she held up her hand, laughed, and told me: "This is a legislator." She explained that she and her hand-legislator were engaged in a screaming match that she knew they could never have in person. It was her way of letting off steam.

I'll talk a bit more about positive coping mechanisms like this one in chapter 14, but first, I want to look at the less productive approaches that we sometimes gravitate toward, even when we know they won't work or may backfire. Avoiding this short list of tactics will prevent you from making things worse. They may alleviate your pain in the short term but are ultimately bad for you, the other person, and your organization.

Suppressing Your Emotions

When you're at your wits' end with a challenging colleague, and it feels like you've tried everything, well-meaning friends and coworkers may tell you to "just ignore it" or to "suck it up" and move on with your life. This *can* be good advice if you're truly able to let it go. But often we decide we're going to do nothing but actually end up doing a whole lot of things, whether it's stewing about the situation, talking our partner's ear off about it, or becoming passive-aggressive. Suppressing our emotions rarely helps.

Susan David, author of *Emotional Agility*, writes that "suppressing your emotions—deciding not to say something when you're upset—can lead to bad results."[1] She explains that if you don't express your feelings, they're likely to show up in unexpected places.

Psychologists call this *emotional leakage*. "Have you ever yelled at your spouse or child after a frustrating day at work—a frustration that had nothing to do with him or her? When you bottle up your feelings, you're likely to express your emotions in unintended ways instead, either sarcastically or in a completely different context. Suppressing your emotions is associated with poor memory, difficulties in relationships, and physiological costs (such as cardiovascular health problems)," David explains.[2] In other words, sucking it up doesn't usually decrease your stress level. It raises it.

The risk that you'll take out your negative feelings on innocent bystanders isn't the only reason to avoid this tactic. Caroline Webb, author of *How to Have a Good Day*, points out that, while the intention behind pretending you're not upset with a difficult colleague may be good—perhaps you want to preserve the relationship—they are likely to sense your irritation anyway. "Because of emotional contagion, they might not be conscious that you harbor negativity toward them, but it will still have an effect on them. Your passive-aggressiveness is going to come through, even in remote work environments," she told me.[3] Research has shown that it's not just you who suffers the physical impact of suppression either. If you hide anger or frustration, the blood pressure of those around you is likely to rise as well.[4] They may not know exactly what you're feeling and thinking, but they register underlying tension just the same.

Retaliating

Another tempting response to mistreatment is to fight fire with fire. If your passive-aggressive teammate says one thing in a meeting and does something completely different afterward, why not do the same to them? Or if your pessimistic colleague is going to poke a zillion holes in your ideas, why shouldn't you take them down when they suggest something new? Unfortunately, stooping to their level doesn't generally work. You intensify the feeling of being on opposing sides rather than giving the dynamic a chance to change. And retaliation often makes you look bad. Or worse, it violates your values.

To avoid giving in to the (understandable) desire for revenge, commit to behaving in line with your values. Sometimes it's helpful to write them down. What is it that you care about? What matters most to you? If you're not sure, consider looking at a set of universal values, such as those created by social psychologist Shalom Schwartz and his colleagues, and see which resonate with you, listing them in order of importance (see table 13-1). Then, when you're coming up with a plan for how you want to respond to your insecure boss or biased coworker, refer to the list and make sure that the tactics you land on align with your values.

Shaming

When I'm dealing with someone who fits one of the eight archetypes, I often fantasize about sending an email to everyone who knows them, outing them as a jerk. My (flawed) logic is that if the person who has wronged me is humiliated enough, they will be forced to change their ways.

TABLE 13-1

Universal values

Value	Description
Self-direction	Independent thought and action—choosing, creating, exploring
Stimulation	Excitement, novelty, and challenge in life
Hedonism	Pleasure or sensuous gratification for oneself
Achievement	Personal success through demonstrating competence according to social standards
Power	Social status and prestige, control or dominance over people and resources
Security	Safety, harmony, and stability of society, of relationships, and of self
Tradition	Respect, commitment, and acceptance of the customs and ideas that traditional culture or religion provide
Benevolence	Preservation and enhancement of the welfare of people with whom one is in frequent personal contact
Universalism	Understanding, appreciation, tolerance, and protection for the welfare of all people and for nature

Source: Adapted from Shalom H. Schwartz, "An Overview of the Schwartz Theory of Basic Values," *Online Readings in Psychology and Culture* 2, no. 1 (December 2012), https://doi.org/10.9707/2307-0919.1116.

Bob Sutton, author of *The No Asshole Rule*, sums up why this doesn't work: "Calling people an asshole is one of the most reliable ways to turn someone into an asshole—or make them hate you."[5] That's because feelings of shame rarely inspire us to behave better; more often, they make us lash out further.

I like the way that Brené Brown distinguishes between shame and guilt and explains their relative usefulness:

> I believe that guilt is adaptive and helpful—it's holding something we've done or failed to do up against our values and feeling psychological discomfort.
>
> I define shame as the intensely painful feeling or experience of believing that we are flawed and therefore unworthy of love and belonging—something we've experienced, done, or failed to do makes us unworthy of connection.
>
> I don't believe shame is helpful or productive. In fact, I think shame is much more likely to be the source of destructive, hurtful behavior than the solution or cure. I think the fear of disconnection can make us dangerous.[6]

Making your colleague feel as if they're a bad person, labeling them as a racist, a jerk, or someone who plays the victim, is unlikely to improve your relationship.

Similarly, dehumanizing a difficult coworker doesn't help. It's easy to demonize the person who causes us harm, but hating them only pits you against one another. Instead, make sure that every step of the way, you remind yourself that you're dealing with a fellow human, not a robot or an arch villain. As Webb told me, "Seeing them as a human being with frailties—just like you—can be a powerful first step in defusing tension."[7]

Hoping Your Colleague Will Leave

Many of us bank on outlasting our difficult colleagues and focus on making the situation workable until they get fired or move on to another job. But be careful of putting all of your eggs in the "eventually they'll be gone" basket. Sutton warns that sometimes "removing the bad apples" does little to change the underlying issue, especially if your colleague's obnoxious behavior is validated by the organizational culture. Often other things need to change to prevent incivility, he says, things like the "incentive system, who's promoted and rewarded, how meetings are run, and the pressure people are under to perform."

A few years ago, the head of HR for a health insurance company asked me to train its staff on how to have difficult conversations. She explained that the company had a very hierarchical culture and was having trouble getting people to speak up, especially with ideas that challenged the status quo. Nine years earlier, it had done a survey that showed employees felt it was a very "command and control" environment. Determined to evolve, executives led several culture change initiatives and hired new leaders who were known for having a more collaborative and less autocratic style. Those leaders also replaced people on their teams so that within that nine-year period, almost 80 percent of the employee population had turned over, including most of the leadership team. But when they conducted the culture survey again, they got almost exactly the same results. The exasperated HR executive told me, "It's like it's in the water here."

Sometimes it's not individual people who are the problem but the systems that allow, and in some cases encourage, hostility over cooperation. And systems are hard to change. Your dream that your difficult coworker will walk out the door may come true, but there's no guarantee that the culture will shift or that you'll get along with their replacement. Ultimately you're better off trying to create a workable situation with your colleague now than hoping things will improve if they leave.

• • •

Will you always be able to avoid these flawed responses? No. Nobody's perfect. But if you catch yourself trying to put on a brave face, take down your challenging coworker, or wait for someone else to get rid of them for you, take a deep breath and go back to the strategies outlined for the specific archetype you're dealing with or return to the nine principles outlined in chapter 11 and try to set things straight.

Unproductive approaches are seductive. But if you get a flat tire, you don't fix the problem by slashing the other three tires. When you strike out with the first tactic (or several tactics) you choose, try something else—or reach out for help. Maybe your boss, a friend, or a mutual colleague can offer a novel solution. The point is to keep at it; remember, even small improvements can make a big difference.

14

Taking Care

Your well-being is priority number one.

I'm a fan of mantras. I have them written on sticky notes on my desk. I say them out loud to myself when I'm about to tackle a difficult project or write a tricky email. And it's not uncommon for me to text a friend asking, "Can I borrow a mantra for today?" when I'm struggling to find the right one.

Technically, a mantra is a word, a phrase, or a sentence that is repeated during meditation to aid concentration and awareness. I use them a little differently. Repeating to myself that *this will pass* or *everything that has a beginning, has an end* or *you can only control what you can control* reminds me to stay calm and maintain perspective when I'm in the midst of a tense interaction. We could all use more nudges like these to remind us of what matters and keep us out of amygdala hijack, especially when dealing with a passive-aggressive coworker or a boss who seems determined to undermine you.

The road is rarely easy when dealing with conflict at work. There will be times when colleagues won't reciprocate your good-faith efforts at reconciliation. Or you'll wonder why you always have to be the "adult in the room." Or you'll see glimmers of progress and you and a coworker will be getting along, only to have some organizational change or intense project prompt them to revert to their old ways.

That's why it's critical to take care of yourself along the way. Whether you're just starting to address the negativity or you've been trying to change things for years, your health and well-being should *always* be a priority.

In this chapter, I'll share tactics—including a few mantras—for preserving your mental health. My hope is that the advice here will buffer you from the damage that can result from unhealthy relationships.

Control the "Controllables"

No one likes to feel trapped in a bad situation. So take steps to increase feelings of control, even when you can't change everything. Focus on the things that you do have the power to affect, no matter how insignificant they seem.

What's controllable might be fairly basic. Maybe you can't dictate how your coworker treats you, but you can build up your defenses by getting a good night's sleep, eating well, exercising, and spending time outside. I know that achieving this list of fundamentals can feel overwhelming at times; there are never enough hours in the day. Start small, focusing on progress in one area, whether it's increasing quality sleep or committing to a more consistent exercise routine.

The more freedom you have over how you spend your time and energy, the less stuck you will feel. A friend of mine was working at a health-care nonprofit for an insecure boss who micromanaged everything she did. She was able to tolerate her manager's behavior because they worked remotely and she could more or less control when and how they interacted. Her boss would never walk by her desk unannounced.

Plus she felt like her manager's foibles were worth enduring because she enjoyed the work and the job afforded her the flexibility she craved when her two boys were young. But as the kids got older, it got harder to put up with her manager. As the breadwinner in her family, she couldn't quit, and her attempts to find a position that would give her all of the benefits and flexibility she wanted yielded no alternatives at first.

Rather than throwing up her hands, she started small, with what she dubbed the "coffee date offensive." She began inviting friends and acquaintances out for coffee—virtually or in person. She didn't know exactly where these conversations would lead and she didn't have a specific new job or company in mind, but taking this step gave her a sense of control. She'd end every conversation with the same question: "Is there anyone else you think I should meet with?" She tracked these exchanges in a spreadsheet along with notes about each meeting and to whom she'd been referred. A year into this experiment, and after thirty-seven coffee dates(!), one of the people she met with early on reached out about an opening at his company. She landed the job. She was incredibly relieved to get away from her insecure manager, but she told me she was happy she didn't rush into a new gig right away.

When it comes to restoring my own sense of control, I have a sticky note I keep by my desk with a mantra borrowed from my friend Katherine's daughter's school. At the beginning of each day, they all recite this together:

> *My body is calm.*
> *My heart is kind.*
> *I am the boss of my brain and my mind.*

On days when I'm struggling with a nasty email or gearing up for a difficult conversation, I'll read it out loud to myself. It's a good reminder that even when it feels like I'm lost in a tornado of chaos, I still have agency over some things.

Vent Productively

In chapter 11, I talked about why spreading gossip about a difficult coworker is usually best avoided. However, I'm not suggesting you refrain from discussing conflict altogether. Venting can be a healthy way of relieving stress. Sharing your feelings in confidence (with someone you trust) will help prevent negative emotions from leaking into interactions with your colleague or into other parts of your life.

Or consider venting in writing. Over the years, my friend and leadership expert Amy Jen Su has shared how journaling has helped her sort through her thoughts. It's a habit I've now picked up. Open a notebook or a blank document on your computer or phone and spend a preset amount of time, say four or five minutes, describing your feelings about a tough situation. Don't overthink what you're putting down; just document whatever comes to mind—the good, the bad, and the ugly. It might be helpful to refer to what you've written later. Noting how your emotions have evolved about the relationship can provide a sense of progress. Conversely, it might feel good to delete or get rid of your notes in a symbolic gesture of putting the situation behind you and moving on.

Build a Microculture

Even one negative relationship can cast a shadow over your work life. But if you look, you can often find like-minded people who are interested in positive interactions. Emotional intelligence expert Annie McKee calls this creating a "microculture." Rather than allowing toxic relationships to dominate your work experience, determine what you need to be effective and happy in your job and then build a coalition of people who are committed to similar goals and values. As McKee writes, "You're probably not going to be able to single-handedly change the culture of your entire organization. What you can do, however, is to take matters into your own hands and create a resonant microculture where you have the greatest chance of succeeding: on your team. And while it may be easier to do this when you are the team leader, it's not critical that you be in a position of power."[1] Having a posse of people who support—and won't undermine—you can counteract the influence of a trying coworker.

When one person I interviewed realized that her dynamic with an insecure boss was unlikely to change, she made a commitment to herself to foster a more functional and supportive work environment for those who she interacted with. "I vowed that I was going to protect the people who reported to me and asked myself: How can I create a safe space for them to do productive work?" she explained. This made all the difference for her: "I wanted to create a place where other people would be happy to come to work, and it had the same effect on me. Rather than dreading my interactions with my boss, I looked forward to going to work and seeing my team."

Have a Life outside of Work

When work is dragging you down, for whatever reason, it's always good to have somewhere else to focus your attention and find fulfillment. Georgetown professor Christine Porath's research shows that thriving *outside of* work is strongly correlated to thriving *at* work. "Take control over your personal life. Find hobbies, build communities, invest in relationships with friends and family, and you bring a stronger, more resilient self to work. The negative people and interactions won't pull you off track as much," she explains. In a study she did of people who experienced incivility in the workplace, those who reported thriving in nonwork activities also reported 80 percent better health, 89 percent greater thriving at work, and 38 percent more satisfaction with their handling of mistreatment from their colleagues.[2]

Amy Jen Su concurs: "Surround yourself with good people. Healthy and supportive relationships are a critical part of self-care. . . . Don't let work cause you to neglect the most important people in your life. Use breaks during the day, or perhaps your commute time, to call friends and loved ones, and carve out plenty of time outside of work to nurture relationships."[3] These connections will bolster you when you're feeling dragged down by a difficult coworker.

Cultivate Interpersonal Resilience

Because the road to getting along is often bumpy, you'll need the strength to bounce back when you encounter obstacles. Tapping into your emotional reserves when a pessimistic colleague turns your meeting into a gripe session or a know-it-all makes you feel small in front of your boss will help you persevere.

One way to do this is to think about your past. There have almost certainly been times in your life when you failed, faced setbacks, or worried that you didn't have what it takes to succeed. What did you do to get through? What steps did you follow? Who supported you? Remind yourself that you have overcome challenges, even when it felt like the odds were against you.

If your coworker makes you feel like you're not good at your job, recall a moment when you felt valued. Dig up positive performance reviews or revisit your compliments folder (see chapter 3). With some effort, you may even be able to find silver linings to the unhealthy dynamic itself. Perhaps you've learned something useful from it, or it's honed your skills to navigate future tricky relationships. This process is called "benefit finding," and research has shown that uncovering positive meaning in negative events builds resilience, improving well-being and health, and the ability to deal with setbacks.[4]

For me, keeping the big picture in mind—with the help of a few mantras (of course)—replenishes my reserves. These are a few of my favorites:

- I don't see the world in exactly the same way as the people around me and that's OK.

- Everyone is going through something, and we all have different ways of coping with uncertainty, grief, and stress.

- People are under pressures that I don't always see and can't fully understand (and probably aren't entirely my business).

- It's not helpful to me or to anyone to compare our challenges and suffering.

- We are all doing the best we can at this moment. And we can all do better.

I learned several of these through therapy over the years. Kelly Greenwood, an expert on mental health in the workplace, says that when people are dealing with tricky relationships at work, they often see talking with a therapist as a last resort, but she believes it's "something that should happen further upstream." It's especially important to notice if you're feeling distracted, sluggish, angry, or irritable; not sleeping well or sleeping excessively; relying on alcohol or food to comfort yourself; or withdrawing from friends and activities you enjoy as a result of your interactions with a difficult coworker. These could be signs of a mental health condition such as depression or anxiety, which can be triggered by workplace factors. But, says Greenwood, "you don't need to have a diagnosable disorder to benefit from therapy—the bar should simply be whether you're satisfied with your mental health."[5] A trained psychologist can help you develop strategies for resolving conflict and coping mechanisms for maintaining your well-being.

Have Self-Compassion

I've talked a lot in this book about having empathy for a difficult colleague. But focusing on another person can sometimes distract from tending to your own needs. Make sure you're directing empathy inward, too. You might say to yourself: *It's OK to feel hurt* or *Who I am is not shaped by this person's beliefs.* Self-compassion in these moments will help you stay centered.

Instead of ruminating on your failure to improve a relationship or chastising yourself for not having thicker skin, be kind to yourself. Research has established a myriad of benefits from self-compassion, including a stronger desire to grow and improve, higher emotional intelligence, and deeper resilience. It also makes you more compassionate toward others.[6]

Kristen Neff, a professor at the University of Texas and one of the leading researchers on self-compassion, defines it as having three elements.[7] First is *awareness of your negative emotions.* To acknowledge them, you might tell yourself, *This is hard right now* or *I'm feeling tense.* Second is *a sense of common humanity,* or that others face similar obstacles. Remind yourself, *I'm not the only one who has to deal with challenging relationships. I'm not alone.* Third is *being kind to yourself,* and there are many ways to accomplish this. Ask, *What do I need right now?* or *What's the kind thing to do here—for me?*

If this is new to you, it may take practice. Use a short meditation, even just five minutes, at the start of your day or during a break, when you take three deep breaths and reflect on each of the three elements of self-compassion in turn. Or write a letter to yourself. We tend to be kinder to others than to ourselves, so imagine that you're writing to comfort a friend or family member who is facing a similar challenge. Reread the letter when you're done and come back to it a few days later or whenever you need another dose of self-compassion.

Emotionally Disengage

In chapter 13, I talked about how suppressing your emotions isn't a smart coping mechanism, because your feelings are likely to leak out anyway. However, there is a form of emotional disengagement that is productive: *caring less.* If the pattern of dysfunction is deeply ingrained, doing this will take some effort. But mantras can help. Find a phrase that reminds you not to ruminate about your challenging relationship at work. Maybe you tell yourself, *This isn't about me; This will pass;* or *Stay focused on what matters, and* this *doesn't matter.*

You might also try to put the situation in perspective. In the heat of the moment, a challenging dynamic with a colleague can feel all-consuming, but ask yourself how you will feel about the situation in a week, in a year, or in five years. Will it still feel as critical as it does now? Or will it feel like a distant memory?

If you find it difficult to emotionally distance yourself from conflict and you tend to replay troubling encounters over and over in your head, give yourself a time limit. Set a timer for ten or fifteen minutes and allow yourself to go over the situation in your mind until the alarm goes off; then shift your focus to something else. Don't give your coworker permission to take up space in your mind. That's valuable real estate!

When you have to interact, be mindful of what you do before and after. For example, if you know you're going to be spending a lot of time with a tormentor, you might start your morning doing something that reliably lifts your spirits. Michelle Gielan, author of *Broadcasting Happiness*, keeps a compliments folder similar to the one I described in chapter 3 and she'll look through nice notes or even pictures of her kids to get herself in the "right headspace" before dealing with a chronic complainer, for example.

Similarly, do something to help you decompress after tough interactions. Text a friend, go for a quick walk, or listen to music. Choose something that you know will improve your mood and can help counteract the negative impact of dealing with your coworker. This practice will help you recover and make you "battle ready," as Gielan calls it, when you have to engage next time.

There's one other tactic I use to emotionally disengage, and I'll admit, it's not the nicest approach, but I find it helpful in the most distressing cases. I remind myself that every morning my challenging coworker has to wake up as themselves—the unpleasant, likely unhappy, person who has made our interactions so fraught. And I get to wake up as me.

Accept the Situation

Part of interpersonal resilience is accepting that we can't always have the relationships we want. And we can't get along with everyone. Even when you try to say what's on your mind with empathy and kindness, people won't necessarily be happy about it. And while you assume the best of someone, they may not reciprocate. I have one final mantra I'll share that helps me when I'm still at odds with a colleague, despite my best efforts.

This mantra came to me from an old friend named Geeno. A few summers ago, my family hosted a talent show, an annual tradition where kids (and some adults) show off their skills, whether that's playing ukulele, juggling, reading a poem, or doing a darn good impression of a cheetah. Geeno and his partner performed a song. They explained that they had learned it from an old friend of theirs, a member of the Radical Faeries, a loosely affiliated group of queer activists committed to challenging the status quo and celebrating the eccentric.

The song, it turned out, was more like a mantra. It was simple, just a few lines. Geeno and his partner sang it once and then led us all in singing it with them. We sang the final line over and over.

> *Sometimes people are going to be mad at you . . . and that's OK.*
> *Sometimes people are going to be mad at you . . . and that's OK.*
> *Sometimes people are going to be mad at you . . . and that's OK.*

Whether you are asking a know-it-all colleague to stop interrupting you or explaining to someone why their comment was offensive and not just an innocent remark, you may upset, and even anger, people. And *that's OK*. Disagreements are an inevitable, normal, and healthy part of relating to other people. The goal isn't to feel comfortable every step of the way; it's to strengthen your relationship and take care of yourself in the process.

I repeat the words from that song Geeno taught me pretty much every day. Because that's the point of a mantra—even when we know something deeply, we can all use a little reminder.

Remember: It's All about Our Relationships

I've been lucky. The list of people I've enjoyed working with—and have had meaningful relationships with—is long. And the list of people with whom I've had difficult relationships is, thankfully, short. Of course, those in the latter category loom large in my mind, especially when I am in the thick of it. But I feel better, have more confidence, do better work, and thrive on and off the job when I remind myself that a given interpersonal disaster represents only a fraction of my workplace interactions.

Ideally, with the advice in this book, you'll be able to turn a colleague who has felt like a thorn in your side into a collaborator or perhaps even a friend. But the more realistic goal is simply to shift the dynamic—improve it—so that it causes you less strife and you have the energy to do your best work. You can achieve this by first acknowledging the importance of relationships at work, understanding why tricky ones weigh so heavily on your mind, and then taking a close look at yourself, cleaning up your side of the street. By exploring your colleague's motivations and experimenting with tactics to move the needle, you can come up with an approach that feels authentic to you. Of course, you'll also need determination, creativity, and acceptance, especially if things don't work out the way you hope.

Through it all, don't lose sight of the need to prioritize yourself, your health, and your career. It's easy to get swept up in conflict with a coworker and spend your time focused on them. But your well-being is always critically important.

The ability to confidently and calmly navigate friction with other people isn't just a work skill; it's a life skill. We often disagree, and that's OK. As long as we do it with respect, compassion, and kindness, it can lead to new ideas, stronger bonds, and a refreshing level of candor. Isn't that what we all want?

It's not always easy, but we can have better relationships at work and beyond—and we deserve them.

Who Am I Dealing With?

Figuring out which archetype(s)
your coworker fits into.

Sometimes it's obvious which of the eight archetypes your colleague falls into. You know right away that you're dealing with a pessimist who can't get out from under their own dark cloud. Or your boss makes it apparent that they are claiming credit for your work because they're insecure and aren't sure they have what it takes to succeed in their role.

But other times, people's behavior is ambiguous. Maybe your co-worker makes passive-aggressive jabs at you one day and then plays the victim the next. It's possible—and quite common—for people to fall into several of these categories. Your coworker may be a mix (or dare I say, a hot mess) of multiple archetypes.

Find the advice that best suits your situation, review the common behaviors in the table, and highlight the ones that describe your colleague. Then refer to the corresponding chapter(s) for tactics to help with your specific circumstances.

Archetype	Chapter	Common behaviors
The insecure manager	3	• Being overly concerned about what others think of them • Suffering from a chronic inability to make a decision (or stick with one), even when the choice has little consequence • Frequently changing the direction of a project or meeting, especially at the suggestion of someone in power • Taking opportunities to highlight their expertise or credentials, especially when it's not necessary to do so; in its more toxic form, this may include putting others down to make themselves look more important • Attempting to control everything about a team or project, including when and where and even how people accomplish their work • Requiring that every decision and detail have their approval • Not allowing the team to interact with colleagues from other departments or senior leaders in an attempt to control the flow of information and resources
The pessimist	4	• Complaining about meetings, senior leadership, other colleagues, anything and everything! • Proclaiming that a new initiative or project is doomed to fail • Adapting a "we've already tried that and it failed" mentality, especially in conversations about innovation or new ways of working • Immediately pointing out the risks of a tactic or strategy • Finding something negative to say, even when the news or meeting is mostly positive
The victim	5	• Feeling sorry for themselves and expecting others to do the same (pity party, anyone?) • Evading responsibility for things that go wrong and placing blame on other people or external factors • Pushing back on constructive feedback with excuses about why they can't be at fault • Dragging others down with complaining and a "poor me" attitude • Wallowing in negative feelings • Forecasting failure, particularly for themselves
The passive-aggressive peer	6	• Deliberately ignoring deadlines after they've agreed to meet them • Promising to send an email that never arrives • Acting rudely toward you (say, ignoring you in a meeting or interrupting you) and then denying there's anything wrong when you confront them, claiming "It's all in your head" or "I have *no* idea what you're talking about" • Displaying body language that projects anger or sullenness but insisting they're fine • Implying that they aren't happy with your work but refusing to come out and say so or give you direct feedback

Archetype	Chapter	Common behaviors
		• Disguising insults as compliments. For instance, "You have such a relaxed style!" might actually mean "I think you're lazy" • Twisting your words in a disagreement so it seems like you're the one who's in the wrong
The know-it-all	7	• Displays a "my way or the highway" attitude • Monopolizes conversations, refusing to be interrupted and talking over others • Positions their own ideas as superior • Doesn't listen to criticism or feedback • Speaks in a condescending tone • Explains things that others already understand • Rarely asks questions or displays curiosity • Steals or doesn't share credit for group successes • Jumps into conversations uninvited
The tormentor	8	• Accusing you—directly or indirectly—of not being committed enough to work • Setting near-impossible standards • Assigning you needless or inappropriate busywork, or what academics call "illegitimate tasks" • Proudly sharing the sacrifices they've made in their career and believing you should make similar ones • Putting down your accomplishments, especially in comparison with theirs • Denying time off or flexibility for nonwork commitments • Attributing negative characteristics to a particular generation ("Millennials are lazy and entitled" or "Gen Zers are so fragile; they can't handle even an ounce of discomfort") • Denying the existence of systemic barriers, such as gender bias or institutional racism ("I was able to make it. I'm not sure why you can't.") • Claiming their mistreatment is some sort of exercise in character-building
The biased coworker	9	• Commenting on a positive attribute as if they're surprised you have it ("You're so articulate!") • Labeling a behavior that's deemed acceptable for majority group members as negative or unprofessional ("You might want to tone down your anger") • Assuming that you're not capable of or interested in something because of your identity ("I doubt she'll want to work on that project. She's got a family to take care of.") • Using phrases or words that are demeaning or connote a false sense of familiarity or closeness ("sweetheart," "bro," "sister") • Making assumptions based on stereotypes or denying someone their individual identity ("You don't look old enough to be a manager") • Acting as if bias or discrimination doesn't exist ("I don't see color")

(continued)

Archetype	Chapter	Common behaviors
The political operator	10	• Bragging about their successes • Taking undue credit • Currying favor with people in power or those in a position to help their career • Acting like they're in charge, even when they aren't • Gossiping and spreading rumors, particularly about coworkers who they believe are standing in their way • Pushing their own agenda, often at the expense of team or company goals • Hoarding information to appear powerful • Purposely undermining you by not inviting you to a meeting or sharing critical details about your work

NOTES

Introduction

1. Mitchell Kusy and Elizabeth Holloway, *Toxic Workplace! Managing Toxic Personalities and Their Systems of Power* (San Francisco: Jossey-Bass, 2009).

2. "The Truth About Annoying Coworkers," Olivet Nazarene University, accessed December 5, 2021, https://online.olivet.edu/news/truth-about-annoying-coworkers.

3. Esther Perel, host, "Prologue," *How's Work?*, podcast, February 3, 2020, https://howswork.estherperel.com/episodes/prologue.

4. Shasta Nelson, *The Business of Friendship: Making the Most of Our Relationships Where We Spend Most of Our Time* (Nashville: HarperCollins Leadership, 2020).

5. Christine Porath and Christine Pearson, "The Price of Incivility," *Harvard Business Review*, January–February 2013, https://hbr.org/2013/01/the-price -of-incivility.

6. Christine Porath, "No Time to Be Nice at Work," *New York Times*, June 19, 2015, https://www.nytimes.com/2015/06/21/opinion/sunday/is-your-boss-mean.html.

7. Abby Curnow-Chavez, "4 Ways to Deal with a Toxic Coworker," *Harvard Business Review*, April 10, 2018, https://hbr.org/2018/04/4-ways-to-deal-with-a -toxic-coworker.

8. Author interview with Kelly Greenwood, March 2, 2021.

Chapter 1

1. "The State of American Jobs," Pew Research Center, October 6, 2016, https:// www.pewresearch.org/social-trends/2016/10/06/the-state-of-american-jobs/#fn -22004-8.

2. Laura M. Giurge and Kaitlin Woolley, "Don't Work on Vacation. Seriously," *Harvard Business Review*, July 20, 2020, https://hbr.org/2020/07/dont-work-on -vacation-seriously.

3. Martha C. White, "Think You Have Off Monday? No, You Don't," *Time*, February 13, 2015, https://time.com/3708273/presidents-day-work/.

4. Author interview with Emily Heaphy, October 20, 2020.

5. Vivek H. Murthy, *Together: The Healing Power of Human Connection in a Sometimes Lonely World* (New York: Harper Wave, 2020).

6. Marissa King, *Social Chemistry: Decoding the Patterns of Human Connection* (New York: Dutton, 2020); Rob Cross, "To Be Happier at Work, Invest More in Your Relationships," *Harvard Business Review*, July 30, 2019, https://hbr.org/2019/07/to-be -happier-at-work-invest-more-in-your-relationships.

7. Adriana Dahik et al., "What 12,000 Employees Have to Say About the Future of Remote Work," Boston Consulting Group, August 11, 2020, https://www.bcg.com /en-us/publications/2020/valuable-productivity-gains-covid-19.

8. Tom Rath and Jim Harter, "Your Friends and Your Social Well-Being," *Gallup Business Journal*, August 19, 2010, https://news.gallup.com/businessjournal/127043 /friends-social-wellbeing.aspx.

9. Jessica R. Methot et al., "Are Workplace Friendships a Mixed Blessing? Exploring Tradeoffs of Multiplex Relationships and Their Associations with Job Performance," *Personnel Psychology* 69, no. 2 (Summer 2016): 311–55, https://onlinelibrary.wiley.com /doi/full/10.1111/peps.12109.

10. Simone Schnall et al., "Social Support and the Perception of Geographical Slant," *Journal of Experimental Social Psychology* 44, no. 5 (September 2008): 1246–55, https://doi.org/10.1016/j.jesp.2008.04.011.

11. "Jack Needs Jill to Get Up the Hill," *Virginia Magazine*, Fall 2009, https:// uvamagazine.org/articles/jack_needs_jill_to_get_up_the_hill.

12. Christine Porath and Christine Pearson, "The Price of Incivility," *Harvard Business Review*, January–February 2013, https://hbr.org/2013/01/the-price-of-incivility.

13. Porath and Pearson, "The Price of Incivility."

14. Arieh Riskin et al., "The Impact of Rudeness on Medical Team Performance: A Randomized Trial," *Pediatrics* 136, no. 3 (September 2015): 487–95, https://pubmed .ncbi.nlm.nih.gov/26260718/.

15. Christine L. Porath, Trevor Foulk, and Amir Erez, "How Incivility Hijacks Performance: It Robs Cognitive Resources, Increases Dysfunctional Behavior, and Infects Team Dynamics and Functioning," *Organizational Dynamics* 44, no. 4 (October–December 2015): 258–65, https://doi.org/10.1016/j.orgdyn.2015.09.002.

16. Bill Hendrick, "Having a Bad Boss Is Bad for the Heart," WebMD, November 24, 2008, https://www.webmd.com/heart-disease/news/20081124/having-a-bad-boss -is-bad-for-the-heart#1.

17. Gaia Vince, "Arguments Dramatically Slow Wound Healing," *New Scientist*, December 5, 2005, https://www.newscientist.com/article/dn8418-arguments -dramatically-slow-wound-healing/.

18. Jane E. Dutton, *Energize Your Workplace: How to Create and Sustain High-Quality Connections at Work* (San Francisco: Jossey-Bass, 2003).

19. Noam Wasserman, *The Founder's Dilemmas: Anticipating and Avoiding the Pitfalls That Can Sink a Startup* (Princeton, NJ: Princeton University Press, 2013).

20. Christine Porath, "Isolate Toxic Employees to Reduce Their Negative Effects," *Harvard Business Review*, November 14, 2016, https://hbr.org/2016/11/isolate-toxic -employees-to-reduce-their-negative-effects.

21. Andrew Parker, Alexandra Gerbasi, and Christine L. Porath, "The Effects of De-energizing Ties in Organizations and How to Manage Them," *Organizational Dynamics* 42, no. 2 (April–June 2013): 110–18, https://doi.org/10.1016/j.orgdyn.2013.03.004.

22. Jessica R. Methot, Shimul Melwani, and Naomi B. Rothman, "The Space Between Us: A Social-Functional Emotions View of Ambivalent and Indifferent Workplace Relationships," *Journal of Management* 43, no. 6 (January 2017): 1789–1819, https://doi.org/10.1177/0149206316685853.

23. Shimul Melwani and Naomi Rothman, "Research: Love-Hate Relationships at Work Might Be Good for You," *Harvard Business Review*, January 20, 2015, https:// hbr.org/2015/01/research-love-hate-relationships-at-work-might-be-good-for-you.

Chapter 2

1. Christine Porath and Christine Pearson, "The Price of Incivility," *Harvard Business Review*, January–February 2013, https://hbr.org/2013/01/the-price-of-incivility.

2. Christine L. Porath, Trevor Foulk, and Amir Erez, "How Incivility Hijacks Performance: It Robs Cognitive Resources, Increases Dysfunctional Behavior, and Infects Team Dynamics and Functioning," *Organizational Dynamics* 44, no. 4 (October–December 2015): 258–65, https://doi.org/10.1016/j.orgdyn.2015.09.002.

3. Porath, Foulk, and Erez, ""How Incivility Hijacks Performance."

4. John T. Cacioppo, Stephanie Cacioppo, and Jackie K. Gollan, "The Negativity Bias: Conceptualization, Quantification, and Individual Differences," *Behavioral and Brain Sciences* 37, no. 3 (June 2014): 309–10, https://doi.org/10.1017/S0140525X13002537.

5. "Rejection Really Hurts, UCLA Psychologists Find," *ScienceDaily*, October 10, 2003, https://www.sciencedaily.com/releases/2003/10/031010074045.htm (thank you to Paul Zak for directing me to this research); Naomi I. Eisenberger, "The Neural Bases of Social Pain: Evidence for Shared Representations with Physical Pain," *Psychosomatic Medicine* 74, no. 2 (February 2012): 126–35, https://www.ncbi.nlm.nih.gov/pmc/articles/PMC3273616/.

6. Benzion Chanowitz and Ellen J. Langer, "Premature Cognitive Commitment," *Journal of Personality and Social Psychology* 41, no. 6 (1981): 1051–63.

7. While this quote is often attributed to Frankl, it hasn't been found word-for-word in any of his writings, nor has it been definitively linked to anyone else's writing. However, the idea is very much in line with Frankl's work, as well as that of others. For example, American psychologist Rollo May wrote, "Human freedom involves our capacity to pause between stimulus and response and, in that pause, to choose the one response toward which we wish to throw our weight."

8. This "emotions are data not noise" idea is something I've learned from professor Sigal Barsade and psychologist Susan David.

9. Anat Drach-Zahavy and Miriam Erez, "Challenge versus Threat Effects on the Goal–Performance Relationship," *Organizational Behavior and Human Decision Processes* 88, no. 2 (July 2002): 667–82, https://www.sciencedirect.com/science/article/abs/pii/S0749597802000043; Emma Seppälä and Christina Bradley, "Handling Negative Emotions in a Way That's Good for Your Team," *Harvard Business Review*, June 11, 2019, https://hbr.org/2019/06/handling-negative-emotions-in-a-way-thats-good-for-your-team.

10. Lisa Feldman Barrett, *Seven and a Half Lessons About the Brain* (Boston: Houghton Mifflin Harcourt, 2020).

11. Author interview with Alice Boyes, November 20, 2020.

12. Dawn Querstret and Mark Cropley, "Exploring the Relationship between Work-Related Rumination, Sleep Quality, and Work-Related Fatigue," *Journal of Occupational Health Psychology* 17, no. 3 (July 2012): 341–53, https://doi.org/10.1037/a0028552.

13. Author interview with Alice Boyes, November 20, 2020.

Chapter 3

1. Sean Illing, "A Psychologist Explains How to Overcome Social Anxiety," *Vox*, June 26, 2018, https://www.vox.com/science-and-health/2018/6/26/17467744/social-anxiety-psychology-mental-health.

2. Roger Jones, "What CEOs Are Afraid Of," *Harvard Business Review*, February 24, 2015, https://hbr.org/2015/02/what-ceos-are-afraid-of.

3. Nathanael J. Fast and Serena Chen, "When the Boss Feels Inadequate: Power, Incompetence, and Aggression," *Psychological Science* 20, no. 11 (November 2009): 1406–13, https://doi.org/10.1111/j.1467-9280.2009.02452.x.

4. Author interview with Ethan Burris, January 11, 2021.

5. Nathanael J. Fast, Ethan R. Burris, and Caroline A. Bartel, "Managing to Stay in the Dark: Managerial Self-Efficacy, Ego Defensiveness, and the Aversion to Employee Voice," *Academy of Management Journal* 57, no. 4 (September 2013): 1013–34, https://journals.aom.org/doi/10.5465/amj.2012.0393.

6. Ruchika Tulshyan and Jodi-Ann Burey, "Stop Telling Women They Have Imposter Syndrome," *Harvard Business Review*, February 11, 2021, https://hbr.org/2021/02/stop-telling-women-they-have-imposter-syndrome.

7. David L. Collinson, "Identities and Insecurities: Selves at Work," *Organization* 10, no. 3 (August 2003): 527–47, https://www.researchgate.net/publication/238334590_Identities_and_Insecurities_Selves_at_Work.

8. Teresa Amabile, "Your Mean Boss Could Be Insecure," *Washington Post*, July 12, 2012, https://www.washingtonpost.com/national/on-leadership/your-mean-boss-could-be-insecure/2012/07/12/gJQAiIZufW_story.html.

9. Nathanael J. Fast, Ethan Burris, and Caroline A. Bartel, "Research: Insecure Managers Don't Want Your Suggestions," *Harvard Business Review*, November 24, 2014, https://hbr.org/2014/11/research-insecure-managers-dont-want-your-suggestions.

10. Fast, Burris, and Bartel, "Insecure Managers."

11. W. Gerrod Parrott, "The Benefits and Threats from Being Envied in Organizations," in *Envy at Work and in Organizations* (New York: Oxford University Press, 2017), 455–74.

12. Author interview with Lindred Greer, January 12, 2021.

13. Fast, Burris, and Bartel, "Insecure Managers."

14. Author interview with Nathanael Fast, January 19, 2021.

15. Hui Liao, Elijah Wee, and Dong Liu, "Research: Shifting the Power Balance with an Abusive Boss," *Harvard Business Review*, October 9, 2017, https://hbr.org/2017/10/research-shifting-the-power-balance-with-an-abusive-boss.

16. David E. Sprott et al., "The Question–Behavior Effect: What We Know and Where We Go from Here," *Social Influence* 1 (August 2006): 128–37, https://doi.org/10.1080/15534510600685409.

Chapter 4

1. Author interview with Michelle Gielan, January 11, 2021.

2. Fuschia Sirois, "The Surprising Benefits of Being a Pessimist," *The Conversation*, February 23, 2018, https://theconversation.com/the-surprising-benefits-of-being-a-pessimist-91851.

3. Fuschia M. Sirois, "Who Looks Forward to Better Health? Personality Factors and Future Self-Rated Health in the Context of Chronic Illness," *International Journal of Behavioral Medicine* 22 (January 2015): 569–79, https://doi.org/10.1007/s12529-015-9460-8.

4. Grant and Higgins, "Do You Play to Win—or to Not Lose?," *Harvard Business Review*, March 2013, https://hbr.org/2013/03/do-you-play-to-win-or-to-not-lose.

5. Author interview with Eileen Chou, January 14, 2021.

6. Michelle Gielan, "The Financial Upside of Being an Optimist," *Harvard Business Review*, March 12, 2019, https://hbr.org/2019/03/the-financial-upside-of-being-an-optimist.

7. Sigal G.Barsade, Constantinos G. V. Coutifaris, and Julianna Pillemer, "Emotional Contagion in Organizational Life," *Research in Organizational Behavior* 38 (December 2018): 137–51, https://doi.org/10.1016/j.riob.2018.11.005.

8. Susan David, "The Gift and Power of Emotional Courage," filmed November 2017 at TEDWomen in New Orleans, LA, https://www.ted.com/talks/susan_david_the_gift_and_power_of_emotional_courage.

9. Author interview with Heidi Grant, February 1, 2021.

10. Amy C. Edmondson, "Boeing and the Importance of Encouraging Employees to Speak Up," *Harvard Business Review*, May 1, 2019, https://hbr.org/2019/05/boeing-and-the-importance-of-encouraging-employees-to-speak-up.

11. Hemant Kakkar and Subra Tangirala, "If Your Employees Aren't Speaking Up, Blame Company Culture," *Harvard Business Review*, November 6, 2018, https://hbr.org/2018/11/if-your-employees-arent-speaking-up-blame-company-culture.

12. David M. Schweiger, William R. Sandberg, and James W. Ragan, "Group Approaches for Improving Strategic Decision Making: A Comparative Analysis of Dialectical Inquiry, Devil's Advocacy, and Consensus," *Academy of Management Journal* 29, no. 1 (1986): 51–71, https://psycnet.apa.org/doi/10.2307/255859.

13. Nilofer Merchant, "Don't Demonize Employees Who Raise Problems," *Harvard Business Review*, January 30, 2020, https://hbr.org/2020/01/dont-demonize-employees-who-raise-problems.

14. Author interview with Heidi Grant, February 1, 2021.

15. Author interview with Eileen Chou, January 14, 2021.

16. Author interview with Heidi Grant, February 1, 2021.

Chapter 5

1. Rahav Gabay et al., "The Tendency for Interpersonal Victimhood: The Personality Construct and Its Consequences," *Personality and Individual Differences* 165 (October 2020), https://doi.org/10.1016/j.paid.2020.110134.

2. Manfred F. R. Kets de Vries, "Are You a Victim of the Victim Syndrome?," *Organizational Dynamics* 43, no. 2 (July 2012), https://www.researchgate.net/publication/256028208_Are_You_a_Victim_of_the_Victim_Syndrome.

3. Bryant P. H. Hui et al., "Rewards of Kindness? A Meta-Analysis of the Link between Prosociality and Well-Being," *Psychological Bulletin* 142, no. 12 (December 2020): 1084–1116, https://pubmed.ncbi.nlm.nih.gov/32881540/.

Chapter 6

1. Scott Wetzler and Leslie C. Morey, "Passive-Aggressive Personality Disorder: The Demise of a Syndrome," *Psychiatry* 62, no. 1 (Spring 1999): 49–59, https://pubmed.ncbi.nlm.nih.gov/10224623/; Christopher Lane, "The Surprising History of Passive-Aggressive Personality Disorder," *Theory & Psychology* 19, no. 1 (February 2009): 55–70, https://journals.sagepub.com/doi/abs/10.1177/0959354308101419.

2. Christopher J. Hopwood et al., "The Construct Validity of Passive-Aggressive Personality Disorder," *Psychiatry* 72, no. 3 (Fall 2009): 255–67, https://www.ncbi.nlm.nih.gov/pmc/articles/PMC2862968/.

3. Author interview with Gabrielle Adams, January 12, 2021.

4. Benedict Carey, "Oh, Fine, You're Right. I'm Passive-Aggressive," *New York Times*, November 16, 2004, https://www.nytimes.com/2004/11/16/health/psychology /oh-fine-youre-right-im-passiveaggressive.html.

5. Nora J. Johnson and Thomas Klee, "Passive-Aggressive Behavior and Leadership Styles in Organizations," *Journal of Leadership & Organizational Studies* 14, no. 2 (November 2007): 130–42, https://journals.sagepub.com/doi/10.1177 /1071791907308044.

6. Johnson and Klee, "Passive-Aggressive Behavior."

7. D'Lisa N. McKee, "Antecedents of Passive-Aggressive Behavior as Employee Deviance," *Journal of Organizational Psychology* 19, no. 4 (September 2019).

8. There are numerous studies and articles on the double bind that women face at work. I find this article to be one of the most descriptive: Alice Eagly and Linda L. Carli, "Women and the Labyrinth of Leadership," *Harvard Business Review*, September 2007, https://hbr.org/2007/09/women-and-the-labyrinth-of-leadership.

9. Michelle K. Duffy, Daniel C. Ganster, and Milan Pagon, "Social Undermining in the Workplace," *Academy of Management Journal* 45, no. 2 (November 2017): 331–51, https://journals.aom.org/doi/10.5465/3069350.

10. Gary L. Neilson, Bruce A. Pasternack, and Karen E. Van Nuys, "The Passive-Aggressive Organization," *Harvard Business Review*, October 2005, https://hbr.org /2005/10/the-passive-aggressive-organization.

11. Author interview with Gabrielle Adams, January 12, 2021.

12. Jeffrey Sanchez-Burks, Christina Bradley, and Lindred Greer, "How Leaders Can Optimize Teams' Emotional Landscapes," *MIT Sloan Management Review*, January 4, 2021, https://sloanreview.mit.edu/article/how-leaders-can-optimize-teams -emotional-landscapes/.

13. Author interview with Lindred Greer, January 12, 2021.

14. Author interview with Heidi Grant, February 1, 2021.

15. Pauline Schilpzand, Irene De Pater, and Amir Erez, "Workplace Incivility: A Review of the Literature and Agenda for Future Research," *Journal of Organizational Behavior* 37, no. S1 (February 2016): S57–S88, https://doi.org/10.1002/job.1976.

16. Patrick Lencioni, *The Five Dysfunctions of a Team: A Leadership Fable* (San Francisco: Jossey-Bass, 2002).

Chapter 7

1. Rebecca Webber, "Meet the Real Narcissists (They're Not What You Think)," *Psychology Today*, September 15, 2016, https://www.psychologytoday.com/us/articles /201609/meet-the-real-narcissists-theyre-not-what-you-think; Sheenie Ambardar, "Narcissistic Personality Disorder," *Medscape*, last updated May 16, 2018, https:// emedicine.medscape.com/article/1519417-overview#a5.

2. Mark D. Alicke et al., "Personal Contact, Individuation, and the Better-Than-Average Effect," *Journal of Personality and Social Psychology* 68, no. 5 (1995): 804–25, https://doi.org/10.1037/0022-3514.68.5.804; David Dunning, *Self-Insight: Roadblocks and Detours on the Path to Knowing Thyself* (New York: Psychology Press, 2005).

3. James A. Shepperd, Judith A. Ouellette, and Julie K. Fernandez, "Abandoning Unrealistic Optimism: Performance Estimates and the Temporal Proximity of Self-Relevant Feedback," *Journal of Personality and Social Psychology* 70, no. 4 (1996): 844–55, https://doi.org/10.1037/0022-3514.70.4.844.

4. Stephen J. Hoch, "Counterfactual Reasoning and Accuracy in Predicting Personal Events," *Journal of Experimental Psychology: Learning, Memory, and Cognition* 11, no. 4 (1985): 719–31, https://doi.org/10.1037/0278-7393.11.1-4.719.

5. Johannes Spinnewijn, "Unemployed but Optimistic: Optimal Insurance Design with Biased Beliefs," *Journal of the European Economic Association* 13, no. 1 (February 2015): 130–67, https://doi.org/10.1111/jeea.12099.

6. Joey T. Chang et al., "Overconfidence Is Contagious," *Harvard Business Review*, November 17, 2020, https://hbr.org/2020/11/overconfidence-is-contagious.

7. Allan Williams, "Views of U.S. Drivers about Driving Safety," *Journal of Safety Research* 34, no. 5 (2003): 491–94, https://doi.org/10.1016/j.jsr.2003.05.002.

8. Tomas Chamorro-Premuzic, "How to Spot an Incompetent Leader," *Harvard Business Review*, March 11, 2020, https://hbr.org/2020/03/how-to-spot-an-incompetent-leader.

9. Jeanine Prime and Elizabeth Salib, "The Best Leaders Are Humble Leaders," *Harvard Business Review*, May 12, 2014, https://hbr.org/2014/05/the-best-leaders-are-humble-leaders.

10. Katty Kay and Claire Shipman, "The Confidence Gap," *The Atlantic*, May 2014, https://www.theatlantic.com/magazine/archive/2014/05/the-confidence-gap/359815/.

11. Stéphanie Thomson, "A Lack of Confidence Isn't What's Holding Back Working Women," *The Atlantic*, September 20, 2018, https://www.theatlantic.com/family/archive/2018/09/women-workplace-confidence-gap/570772/.

12. Tomas Chamorro-Premuzic, "Why Do So Many Incompetent Men Become Leaders?," *Harvard Business Review*, August 22, 2013, https://hbr.org/2013/08/why-do-so-many-incompetent-men.

13. Rebecca Solnit, "Men Who Explain Things," *Los Angeles Times*, April 13, 2008, https://www.latimes.com/archives/la-xpm-2008-apr-13-op-solnit13-story.html.

14. Victoria L. Brescoll, "Who Takes the Floor and Why: Gender, Power, and Volubility in Organizations," *Gender and Inequality* 56, no. 4 (February 2012): 622–41, https://doi.org/10.1177/0001839212439994.

15. Christopher F. Karpowitz, Tali Mendelberg, and Lee Shaker, "Gender Inequality in Deliberative Participation," *American Political Science Review* 106, no. 3 (2012): 533–47, https://www.cambridge.org/core/journals/american-political-science-review/article/abs/gender-inequality-in-deliberative-participation/CE7441632EB3B0BD21CC5045C7E1AF76.

16. Kim Goodwin, "Mansplaining, Explained in One Simple Chart," BBC, July 29, 2018, https://www.bbc.com/worklife/article/20180727-mansplaining-explained-in-one-chart.

17. Tonja Jacobi and Dylan Schweers, "Female Supreme Court Justices Are Interrupted More by Male Justices and Advocates," *Harvard Business Review*, April 11, 2017, https://hbr.org/2017/04/female-supreme-court-justices-are-interrupted-more-by-male-justices-and-advocates.

18. Francesca Gino, "How to Handle Interrupting Colleagues," *Harvard Business Review*, February 22, 2017, https://hbr.org/2017/02/how-to-handle-interrupting-colleagues.

19. Erin Meyer, *The Culture Map: Breaking Through the Invisible Boundaries of Global Business* (New York: PublicAffairs, 2014).

20. Gino, "How to Handle Interrupting Colleagues."

21. Author interview with Tomas Chamorro-Premuzic, January 21, 2021.

22. Kristen Pressner, "Are You Biased? I Am," filmed May 2016 at TEDxBasel, Basel, Basel-Stadt, Switzerland, video, https://www.youtube.com/watch?v=Bq_xYSOZrgU&vl=en.

23. Matt Krentz et al., "Five Ways Men Can Improve Gender Diversity at Work," Boston Consulting Group, October 10, 2017, https://www.bcg.com/en-us/publications/2017/people-organization-behavior-culture-five-ways-men-improve-gender-diversity-work.

24. Sarah Kaplan, "What Companies Should Do with the Office Mansplainer," *Fast Company*, July 19, 2019, https://www.fastcompany.com/90378694/what-men-and-companies-should-do-about-mansplaining.

Chapter 8

1. This term was first suggested to me by Michael Gutman on LinkedIn, https://www.linkedin.com/in/gutmanmichael/. Mike is a remote work consultant and educator, and clearly a word genius and generous colleague.

2. Norbert K. Semmer et al., "Illegitimate Tasks as a Source of Work Stress," *Work and Stress* 29, no. 1 (March 2015): 32–56, https://www.ncbi.nlm.nih.gov/pmc/articles/PMC4396521/.

3. Rachel Ruttan, Mary-Hunter McDonnell, and Loran Nordgren, "It's Harder to Empathize with People If You've Been in Their Shoes," *Harvard Business Review*, October 20, 2015, https://hbr.org/2015/10/its-harder-to-empathize-with-people-if-youve-been-in-their-shoes.

4. Pilar González-Navarro et al., "Envy and Counterproductive Work Behavior: The Moderation Role of Leadership in Public and Private Organizations," *International Journal of Environmental Research and Public Health* 15, no. 5 (July 2018): 1455, https://www.ncbi.nlm.nih.gov/pmc/articles/PMC6068656/.

5. Lingtao Yu, Michelle K. Duffy, and Bennett J. Tepper, "Why Supervisors Envy Their Employees," *Harvard Business Review*, September 13, 2018, https://hbr.org/2018/09/why-supervisors-envy-their-employees; Manfred F. R. Kets de Vries, *The Leadership Mystique: Leading Behavior in the Human Enterprise* (Hoboken, NJ: Prentice Hall, 2009).

6. Author interview with Michelle Duffy, January 14, 2021.

7. John Protzko and Jonathan Schooler, "Kids These Days: Why the Youth of Today Seem Lacking," *Science Advances* 5, no. 10 (October 2019), https://www.researchgate.net/publication/336596902_Kids_these_days_Why_the_youth_of_today_seem_lacking.

8. Rebecca Knight, "When Your Boss Is Younger Than You," *Harvard Business Review*, October 9, 2015, https://hbr.org/2015/10/when-your-boss-is-younger-than-you.

9. Araya Baker, "10 Signs of Generational Envy," *Psychology Today*, July 22, 2021, https://www.psychologytoday.com/us/blog/beyond-cultural-competence/202107/10-signs-generational-envy.

10. Belle Derks, Colette Van Laar, and Naomi Ellemers, "The Queen Bee Phenomenon: Why Women Leaders Distance Themselves from Junior Women," *Leadership Quarterly* 27, no. 3 (June 2016): 456–69, https://doi.org/10.1016/j.leaqua.2015.12.007.

11. Stefanie K. Johnson and David R. Hekman, "Women and Minorities Are Penalized for Promoting Diversity," *Harvard Business Review*, March 23, 2016, https://hbr.org/2016/03/women-and-minorities-are-penalized-for-promoting-diversity.

12. Michelle Duguid, "Female Tokens in High-Prestige Work Groups: Catalysts or Inhibitors of Group Diversification?," *Organizational Behavior and Human Decision Processes* 116, no. 1 (September 2011): 104–15, https://www.sciencedirect.com/science/article/abs/pii/S0749597811000720.

13. Author interview with Rosalind Chow, February 18, 2021.

14. Zhenyu Liao, "Intimidating Bosses Can Change—They Just Need a Nudge," *Harvard Business Review*, August 31, 2020, https://hbr.org/2020/08/intimidating-bosses-can-change-they-just-need-a-nudge.

15. Bennett J. Tepper, "Consequences of Abusive Supervision," *Academy of Management Journal* 43, no. 2 (April 2000): 178–90, https://www.jstor.org/stable/1556375.

16. Lilia M. Cortina, "Selective Incivility as Modern Discrimination in Organizations: Evidence and Impact," *Journal of Management* 39, no. 6 (September 2013): 1579–1605, https://doi.org/10.1177/0149206311418835.

17. Allison S. Gabriel, Marcus M. Butts, and Michael T. Sliter, "Women Experience More Incivility at Work—Especially from Other Women," *Harvard Business Review*, March 28, 2018, https://hbr.org/2018/03/women-experience-more-incivility-at-work-especially-from-other-women.

18. Anna Steinhage, Dan Cable, and Duncan Wardley, "The Pros and Cons of Competition Among Employees," *Harvard Business Review*, March 20, 2017, https://hbr.org/2017/03/the-pros-and-cons-of-competition-among-employees.

19. Leah D. Sheppard and Karl Aquino, "Sisters at Arms: A Theory of Female Same-Sex Conflict and Its Problematization in Organizations," *Journal of Management* 43, no. 3 (June 2014): 691–715, https://journals.sagepub.com/doi/10.1177/0149206314539348.

20. Isabel Fernandez-Mateo and Sarah Kaplan, "The Immortal—and False—Myth of the Workplace Queen Bee," *The Conversation*, January 9, 2020, https://theconversation.com/the-immortal-and-false-myth-of-the-workplace-queen-bee-129680.

21. Martin Abel, "Do Workers Discriminate Against Female Bosses?," IZA Institute of Labor Economics Discussion Paper no. 12611 (September 2019), https://www.iza.org/publications/dp/12611/do-workers-discriminate-against-female-bosses.

22. Robert W. Livingston, Ashleigh Shelby Rosette, and Ella F. Washington, "Can an Agentic Black Woman Get Ahead? The Impact of Race and Interpersonal Dominance on Perceptions of Female Leaders," *Psychological Science* 23, no. 4 (March 2012): 354–58, https://doi.org/10.1177/0956797611428079.

23. Valerie Purdie Greenaway, "Are There Black 'Queen Bees'?" *The Atlantic*, August 11, 2017, https://www.theatlantic.com/business/archive/2017/08/black-queen-bees-women-khazan/536391/.

24. Alison M. Konrad, Kathleen Cannings, and Caren B. Goldberg, "Asymmetrical Demography Effects on Psychological Climate for Gender Diversity: Differential Effects of Leader Gender and Work Unit Gender Composition among Swedish Doctors," *Human Relations* 63, no. 11 (August 2010): 1661–85, https://doi.org/10.1177/0018726710369397.

25. Marianne Cooper, "Why Women (Sometimes) Don't Help Other Women," *The Atlantic*, June 23, 2016, https://www.theatlantic.com/business/archive/2016/06/queen-bee/488144/; Sharon Foley et al., "The Impact of Gender Similarity, Racial Similarity, and Work Culture on Family-Supportive Supervision," *Group & Organization Management* 31, no. 4 (August 2006): 420–41, https://doi.

org/10.1177/1059601106286884; Lynn Pasquerella and Caroline S. Clauss-Ehlers, "Glass Cliffs, Queen Bees, and the Snow-Woman Effect: Persistent Barriers to Women's Leadership in the Academy," *Liberal Education* 103, no. 2 (Spring 2017), https://www.aacu.org/liberaleducation/2017/spring/pasquerella_clauss-ehlers.

26. Taekjin Shin, "The Gender Gap in Executive Compensation: The Role of Female Directors and Chief Executive Officers," *ANNALS of the American Academy of Political and Social Science* 639, no. 1 (December 2011): 258–78, https://doi.org/10.1177/0002716211421119.

27. Heather M. Rasinski and Alexander M. Czopp, "The Effect of Target Status on Witnesses' Reactions to Confrontations of Bias," *Basic and Applied Social Psychology* 32, no. 1 (February 2010): 8–16, https://doi.org/10.1080/01973530903539754.

28. Amy Gallo, "How to Respond to an Offensive Comment at Work," *Harvard Business Review*, February 8, 2017, https://hbr.org/2017/02/how-to-respond-to-an-offensive-comment-at-work.

29. Gabriel, Butts, and Sliter, "Women Experience More Incivility at Work."

30. Derks, Van Laar, and Ellemers, "The Queen Bee Phenomenon."

31. Shannon G. Taylor et al., "Does Having a Bad Boss Make You More Likely to Be One Yourself?," *Harvard Business Review*, January 23, 2019, https://hbr.org/2019/01/does-having-a-bad-boss-make-you-more-likely-to-be-one-yourself.

32. Robin J. Ely, "The Effects of Organizational Demographics and Social Identity on Relationships among Professional Women," *Administrative Science Quarterly* 39, no. 2 (June 1994): 203–38, https://www.jstor.org/stable/2393234?seq=1.

33. Baker, "10 Signs of Generational Envy."

34. Mary Wawritz et al., "We're All Capable of Being an Abusive Boss," *Harvard Business Review*, October 14, 2016, https://hbr.org/2016/10/were-all-capable-of-being-an-abusive-boss.

35. Christopher M. Barnes et al., "'You Wouldn't Like Me When I'm Sleepy': Leaders' Sleep, Daily Abusive Supervision, and Work Unit Engagement," *Academy of Management Journal* 58, no. 5 (November 2014): 1419–37, https://doi.org/10.5465/amj.2013.1063.

36. Stephen H. Courtright et al., "My Family Made Me Do It: A Cross-Domain, Self-Regulatory Perspective on Antecedents to Abusive Supervision," *Academy of Management Journal* 59, no. 5 (May 2015): 1630–52, https://doi.org/10.5465/amj.2013.1009.

37. Manuela Priesemuth et al., "Abusive Supervision Climate: A Multiple-Mediation Model of Its Impact on Group Outcomes," *Academy of Management Journal* 57, no. 5 (October 2013): 1513–34, https://journals.aom.org/doi/10.5465/amj.2011.0237.

38. Manuela Priesemuth, "Time's Up for Toxic Workplaces," *Harvard Business Review*, June 19, 2020, https://hbr.org/2020/06/times-up-for-toxic-workplaces.

39. Roderick M. Kramer, "The Great Intimidators," *Harvard Business Review*, February 2006, https://hbr.org/2006/02/the-great-intimidators.

40. Author interview with Rosalind Chow, February 18, 2021.

41. "Belle Derks," Utrecht Groups & Identity Lab, https://www.bellederks.com/research-publications; Derks, Van Laar, and Ellemers, "The Queen Bee Phenomenon."

42. Author interview with Belle Derks, February 15, 2021.

43. Hui Liao, Elijah Wee, and Dong Liu, "Research: Shifting the Power Balance with an Abusive Boss," *Harvard Business Review*, October 9, 2017, https://hbr.org/2017/10/research-shifting-the-power-balance-with-an-abusive-boss.html.

44. Liao, Wee, and Liu, "Shifting the Power Balance with an Abusive Boss."

Chapter 9

1. Shankar Vedantam, host, "How They See Us," *Hidden Brain*, podcast, February 8, 2021, https://hiddenbrain.org/podcast/how-they-see-us/.

2. Derald Wing Sue, *Microaggressions in Everyday Life: Race, Gender, and Sexual Orientation* (Hoboken, NJ: 2010); Derald Wing Sue et al., "Racial Microaggressions in Everyday Life: Implications for Clinical Practice," *American Psychologist* 62, no. 4 (May–June 2007): 271–86, https://gim.uw.edu/sites/gim.uw.edu/files/fdp/Microaggressions%20File.pdf.

3. Tiffany Jana and Michael Baran, *Subtle Acts of Exclusion: How to Understand, Identify, and Stop Microaggressions* (Oakland, CA: Berrett-Koehler Publishers, 2020).

4. Molly McDonough, "4 Common Patterns of Bias That Women Face at Work—and How You Can Correct Them," *ABA Journal*, April 1, 2016, https://www.abajournal.com/magazine/article/4_common_patterns_of_bias_that_women_face_at_work_and_how_you_can_correct_t.

5. Ella L. J. Edmondson Bell and Stella M. Nkomo, *Our Separate Ways* (Boston: Harvard Business Review Press, 2003).

6. Lilia M. Cortina, "Unseen Injustice: Incivility as Modern Discrimination in Organizations," *Academy of Management Review* 33, no. 1 (January 2008): 55–75, https://doi.org/10.2307/20159376; Lilia M. Cortina et al., "Selective Incivility as Modern Discrimination in Organizations: Evidence and Impact," *Journal of Management* 39, no. 6 (September 2013): 1579–1605, https://doi.org/10.1177/0149206311418835.

7. John Suler, "The Online Disinhibition Effect," *Cyberpsychology & Behavior: The Impact of the Internet, Multimedia and Virtual Reality on Behavior and Society* 7, no. 3 (June 2004): 321–26, https://pubmed.ncbi.nlm.nih.gov/15257832/.

8. Nellie Bowles, "How to Keep Internet Trolls Out of Remote Workplaces," *New York Times*, January 24, 2021, https://www.nytimes.com/2021/01/24/business/remote-work-culture-online.html.

9. I first heard Kendi share this metaphor on Brené Brown's podcast: Brené Brown, host, "How to Be an Antiracist," *Unlocking Us*, podcast, June 3, 2020, https://brenebrown.com/podcast/brene-with-ibram-x-kendi-on-how-to-be-an-antiracist/.

10. If you aren't yet familiar with the term *privilege*, I like the way Dolly Chugh talks about what she calls "ordinary privilege" as the ability to forget about aspects of who you are because they represent the majority demographics of your country or organization. You can find out more in her book, *The Person You Mean to Be*.

11. Ella F. Washington, Alison Hall Birch, and Laura Morgan Roberts, "When and How to Respond to Microaggressions," *Harvard Business Review*, July 3, 2020, https://hbr.org/2020/07/when-and-how-to-respond-to-microaggressions.

12. Monnica T. Williams, "Microaggressions: Clarification, Evidence, and Impact," *Perspectives on Psychological Science* 15, no. 1 (January 2020): 3–26, https://doi.org/10.1177%2F1745691619827499.

13. Adwoa Bagalini, "5 Ways Racism Is Bad for Business—and What We Can Do About It," *World Economic Forum*, July 14, 2020, https://www.weforum.org/agenda/2020/07/racism-bad-for-business-equality-diversity/.

14. Stephen Ashe and James Nazroo, "Why It's Time to Address Workplace Racism as a Matter of Health and Safety," *Manchester Policy Blogs*, University of Manchester, April 19, 2018, http://blog.policy.manchester.ac.uk/posts/2018/04/why-its-time-to-address-workplace-racism-as-a-matter-of-health-and-safety/.

15. Author interview with Ruchika Tulshyan, February 9, 2021.

16. Kristen P. Jones et al., "Not So Subtle: A Meta-Analytic Investigation of the Correlates of Subtle and Overt Discrimination," *Journal of Management* 42, no. 6 (September 2016): 1588–1613, https://doi.org/10.1177/0149206313506466.

17. Eden King and Kristen Jones, "Why Subtle Bias Is So Often Worse Than Blatant Discrimination," *Harvard Business Review*, July 13, 2016, https://hbr.org/2016/07/why-subtle-bias-is-so-often-worse-than-blatant-discrimination.

18. Bagalini, "5 Ways Racism Is Bad for Business."

19. Author interview with Aneeta Rattan, February 12, 2021.

20. Heather M. Rasinski and Alexander M. Czopp, "The Effect of Target Status on Witnesses' Reactions to Confrontations of Bias," *Basic and Applied Social Psychology* 32, no. 1 (February 2010): 8–16, https://doi.org/10.1080/01973530903539754.

21. Linn Van Dyne and Jeffrey A. LePine, "Helping and Voice Extra-Role Behaviors: Evidence of Construct and Predictive Validity," *Academy of Management Journal* 41, no. 1 (February 1998): 108–19, https://www.jstor.org/stable/256902?seq=1; Janet Swim and Lauri L. Hyers, "Excuse Me—What Did You Just Say?!: Women's Public and Private Responses to Sexist Remarks," *Journal of Experimental Social Psychology* 35, no. 1: 68–88, https://doi.org/10.1006/jesp.1998.1370.

22. A. M. Czopp and Leslie Ashburn-Nardo, "Interpersonal Confrontations of Prejudice," *Psychology of Prejudice: Interdisciplinary Perspectives on Contemporary Issues* (January 2012): 175–202, https://www.researchgate.net/publication/285966720_Interpersonal_confrontations_of_prejudice.

23. Author interview with Ruchika Tulshyan, February 9, 2021.

24. Washington, Birch, and Roberts, "When and How to Respond to Microaggressions."

25. Author interview with Dolly Chugh, April 22, 2021.

26. Author interview with Aneeta Rattan, February 12, 2021.

27. Amy Gallo, "How to Respond to an Offensive Comment at Work," *Harvard Business Review*, February 8, 2017, https://hbr.org/2017/02/how-to-respond-to-an-offensive-comment-at-work.

28. Washington, Birch, and Roberts, "When and How to Respond to Microaggressions."

29. Author interview with Dolly Chugh, April 22, 2021.

30. Juliet Eilperin, "White House Women Want to Be in the Room Where It Happens," *Washington Post*, September 13, 2016, https://www.washingtonpost.com/news/powerpost/wp/2016/09/13/white-house-women-are-now-in-the-room-where-it-happens/.

31. James R. Detert and Ethan Burris, "When It's Tough to Speak Up, Get Help from Your Coworkers," *Harvard Business Review*, March 4, 2016, https://hbr.org/2016/03/when-its-tough-to-speak-up-get-help-from-your-coworkers.

Chapter 10

1. Tomas Chamorro-Premuzic, "The Underlying Psychology of Office Politics," *Harvard Business Review*, December 25, 2014, https://hbr.org/2014/12/the-underlying-psychology-of-office-politics.

2. Rob Cross, Reb Rebele, and Adam Grant, "Collaborative Overload," *Harvard Business Review*, January–February 2016, https://hbr.org/2016/01/collaborative-overload.

3. Robert Half, "Game On! How to Navigate Office Politics to Win," *The Robert Half Blog*, October 12, 2016, https://www.roberthalf.com/blog/salaries-and-skills/game-on-how-to-navigate-office-politics-to-win.

4. Takuma Kimura, "A Review of Political Skill: Current Research Trend and Directions for Future Research," *International Journal of Management Reviews* 17, no. 3 (July 2015): 312–32, https://doi.org/10.1111/ijmr.12041.

5. Pamela L. Perrewé et al., "Political Skill: An Antidote for Workplace Stressors," *Academy of Management Executive* 14, no. 3 (August 2000): 115–23, https://www.jstor .org/stable/4165664?seq=1.

6. Emily Stone, "Why Bad Bosses Sabotage Their Teams," *Kellog Insight* (blog), January 5, 2015, https://insight.kellogg.northwestern.edu/article/why-bad-bosses -sabotage-their-teams.

7. Kathryn Heath, "4 Strategies for Women Navigating Office Politics," *Harvard Business Review*, January 14, 2015, https://hbr.org/2015/01/4-strategies-for-women -navigating-office-politics; Pamela L. Perrewé and Debra L. Nelson, "Gender and Career Success: The Facilitative Role of Political Skill," *Organizational Dynamics* 33, no. 4 (December 2004): 366–78, https://doi.org/10.1016/j.orgdyn.2004.09.004.

8. Michelle King, David Denyer, and Emma Parry, "Is Office Politics a White Man's Game?," *Harvard Business Review*, September 12, 2018, https://hbr.org/2018/09 /is-office-politics-a-white-mans-game.

9. Kathryn Heath, "3 Simple Ways for Women to Rethink Office Politics and Wield More Influence at Work," *Harvard Business Review*, December 18, 2017, https://hbr .org/2017/12/3-simple-ways-for-women-to-rethink-office-politics-and-wield-more -influence-at-work.

10. Author interview with Nancy Halpern, February 16, 2021.

11. Giuseppe "Joe" Labianca, "Defend Your Research: It's Not 'Unprofessional' to Gossip at Work," *Harvard Business Review*, September 2020, https://hbr.org/2010/09 /defend-your-research-its-not-unprofessional-to-gossip-at-work.

12. Nancy B. Kurland and Lisa Hope Pelled, "Passing the Word: Toward a Model of Gossip and Power in the Workplace," *Academy of Management Review* 25, no. 2 (April 2000): 428–39, https://doi.org/10.5465/amr.2000.3312928.

13. Author interview with Nancy Halpern, February 16, 2021.

14. Marc J. Lerchenmueller, Olav Sorenson, and Anupam B. Jena, "Research: How Women Undersell Their Work," *Harvard Business Review*, December 20, 2019, https://hbr.org/2019/12/research-how-women-undersell-their-work; Christine Exley and Judd Kessler, "Why Don't Women Self-Promote as Much as Men?," *Harvard Business Review*, December 19, 2019, https://hbr.org/2019/12/why-dont-women -self-promote-as-much-as-men.

15. Katie Liljenquist and Adam D. Galinsky, "Win Over an Opponent by Asking for Advice," *Harvard Business Review*, June 27, 2014, https://hbr.org/2014/06/win -over-an-opponent-by-asking-for-advice.

Chapter 11

1. Adam Grant, "The Science of Reasoning with Unreasonable People," *New York Times*, January 31, 2021, https://www.nytimes.com/2021/01/31/opinion/change -someones-mind.html.

2. Lee Ross and Andrew Ward, "Naive Realism in Everyday Life: Implications for Social Conflict and Misunderstanding," in *Values and Knowledge*, eds. Edward S. Reed, Elliot Turiel, and Terrance Brown (Mahwah, NJ: Lawrence Erlbaum Associates, 1996), 103–35.

3. Elizabeth Louise Newton, "The Rocky Road from Actions to Intentions," PhD diss., Stanford University, 1990, https://creatorsvancouver.com/wp-content/uploads /2016/06/rocky-road-from-actions-to-intentions.pdf.

4. Katie Shonk, "Principled Negotiation: Focus on Interests to Create Value," *Harvard Law School Program on Negotiation,* blog, September 27, 2021, https://www .pon.harvard.edu/daily/negotiation-skills-daily/principled-negotiation-focus-interests -create-value/.

5. Phyllis Korkki, "Conflict at Work? Empathy Can Smooth Ruffled Feathers," *New York Times,* October 8, 2016, https://www.nytimes.com/2016/10/09/jobs/conflict -at-work-empathy-can-smooth-ruffled-feathers.html.

6. Author interview with Gabrielle Adams, January 12, 2021.

7. Gabrielle S. Adams and M. Ena Inesi, "Impediments to Forgiveness: Victim and Transgressor Attributions of Intent and Guilt," *Journal of Personality and Social Psychology* 111, no. 6 (2016): 866, https://pubmed.ncbi.nlm.nih.gov/27537273/.

8. Mark Murphy, "Neuroscience Explains Why You Need to Write Down Your Goals If You Actually Want to Achieve Them," *Forbes,* April 15, 2018, https://www .forbes.com/sites/markmurphy/2018/04/15/neuroscience-explains-why-you-need-to -write-down-your-goals-if-you-actually-want-to-achieve-them/.

9. Matthew Feinberg, Robb Willer, and Michael Schultz, "Gossip and Ostracism Promote Cooperation in Groups," *Psychological Science* 25, no. 3 (January 2014): 656–64, https://doi.org/10.1177/0956797613510184.

10. Junhui Wu, Daniel Balliet, and Paul A. M. Van Lange, "Gossip Versus Punishment: The Efficiency of Reputation to Promote and Maintain Cooperation," *Scientific Reports* 6, no. 1 (April 2016), https://www.ncbi.nlm.nih.gov/pmc/articles /PMC4819221/.

11. Jennifer Goldman-Wetzler, *Optimal Outcomes: Free Yourself from Conflict at Work, at Home, and in Life* (New York: HarperCollins, 2020).

12. Francesca Gino, "The Business Case for Curiosity," *Harvard Business Review,* September–October 2018, https://hbr.org/2018/09/the-business-case-for-curiosity.

13. Salvador Minuchin, Michael D. Reiter, and Charmaine Borda, *The Craft of Family Therapy: Challenging Certainties* (New York: Routledge, 2013).

Chapter 12

1. Nedra Glover Tawwab, *Set Boundaries, Find Peace: A Guide to Reclaiming Yourself* (New York: TarcherPerigee, 2021).

2. Michelle Gielan, *Broadcasting Happiness: The Science of Igniting and Sustaining Positive Change* (New York: Gildan Media, 2015).

3. Justin M. Berg, Jane E. Dutton, and Amy Wrzesniewski, "What Is Job Crafting and Why Does It Matter?," University of Michigan Stephen M. Ross School of Business Center for Positive Organizational Scholarship, last modified August 1, 2008, https:// positiveorgs.bus.umich.edu/wp-content/uploads/What-is-Job-Crafting-and-Why -Does-it-Matter1.pdf.

4. Jane E. Dutton and Amy Wrzesniewski, "What Job Crafting Looks Like," *Harvard Business Review,* March 12, 2020, https://hbr.org/2020/03/what-job-crafting -looks-like.

5. Author interview with Robert Sutton, January 29, 2021.

6. Christine Porath and Christine Pearson, "The Price of Incivility," *Harvard Business Review,* January–February 2013, https://hbr.org/2013/01/the-price-of -incivility.

7. Boris Groysberg and Robin Abrahams, "Managing Yourself: Five Ways to Bungle a Job Change," *Harvard Business Review*, January–February 2010, https://hbr.org/2010/01/managing-yourself-five-ways-to-bungle-a-job-change.

Chapter 13

1. Susan David, "Manage a Difficult Conversation with Emotional Intelligence," *Harvard Business Review*, June 19, 2014, https://hbr.org/2014/06/manage-a-difficult-conversation-with-emotional-intelligence.

2. David, "Manage a Difficult Conversation."

3. Author interview with Caroline Webb, February 21, 2021.

4. Brett J. Peters, Nickola C. Overall, and Jeremy P. Jamieson, "Physiological and Cognitive Consequences of Suppressing and Expressing Emotion in Dyadic Interactions," *International Journal of Psychophysiology* 94, no. 1 (October 2014): 100–7, http://www.psych.rochester.edu/research/jamiesonlab/wp-content/uploads/2014/01/peters.pdf.

5. Author interview with Robert Sutton, January 29, 2021.

6. Brené Brown, "Shame vs. Guilt," *Brené Brown*, blog, January 15, 2013, https://brenebrown.com/blog/2013/01/14/shame-v-guilt/.

7. Author interview with Caroline Webb, February 21, 2021.

Chapter 14

1. Annie McKee, "Keep Your Company's Toxic Culture from Infecting Your Team," *Harvard Business Review*, April 29, 2019, https://hbr.org/2019/04/keep-your-companys-toxic-culture-from-infecting-your-team.

2. Christine Porath, "An Antidote to Incivility," *Harvard Business Review*, April 2016, https://hbr.org/2016/04/an-antidote-to-incivility.

3. Amy Jen Su, "6 Ways to Weave Self-Care into Your Workday," *Harvard Business Review*, June 19, 2017, https://hbr.org/2017/06/6-ways-to-weave-self-care-into-your-workday.

4. Tony Cassidy, Marian McLaughlin, and Melanie Giles, "Benefit Finding in Response to General Life Stress: Measurement and Correlates," *Health Psychology and Behavioral Medicine* 2, no. 1 (March 2014): 268–82, https://doi.org/10.1080/21642850.2014.889570.

5. Author interview with Kelly Greenwood, March 2, 2021.

6. Rich Fernandez and Steph Stern, "Self-Compassion Will Make You a Better Leader," *Harvard Business Review*, November 9, 2020, https://hbr.org/2020/11/self-compassion-will-make-you-a-better-leader; Serena Chen, "Give Yourself a Break: The Power of Self-Compassion," *Harvard Business Review*, September–October 2018, https://hbr.org/2018/09/give-yourself-a-break-the-power-of-self-compassion.

7. Kristin Neff, "The Three Elements of Self-Compassion," *Self-Compassion*, blog, accessed December 18, 2021, https://self-compassion.org/the-three-elements-of-self-compassion-2/#3elements.

INDEX

Abrahams, Robin, 230
abusive supervisor. *See* tormentor
acceptance, of situation, 249–250
accomplishments, highlighting your,
    193–194
accountability, 111–114
Adams, Gabrielle, 101, 106, 109, 212
advice, asking for, 150, 194–195
affinity bias, 208–209
agency
    increasing sense of, 93–94
    lack of, 69, 89
    pessimistic behavior and,
        69–70, 79
aggression, 52. *See also* microaggressions;
    passive-aggressive peer
allies, 127, 146, 168, 228
Amabile, Teresa, 54–55
ambivalent relationships, 27–28
amplification strategy, 177
amygdala, 34–35, 40–41, 44
antibias strategies, 171–181
appreciation, expressing, 60–61
Aquino, Karl, 144
archetypes, 10–11
    biased coworker, 157–181, 255
    identifying, in coworkers,
        253–256
    insecure boss, 49–65, 254
    know-it-all, 117–135, 255
    passive-aggressive peer, 99–116,
        254–255
    pessimist, 67–85, 254
    political operator, 183–201, 256
    tormentor, 137–156, 255
    victim, 87–98, 254
artificial harmony, 114
assertiveness, 121–122

assumptions
    based on identity, 162, 163
    implicit, 209
    making untrue, 207

Baker, Araya, 141, 147
Baran, Michael, 160
Barrett, Lisa Feldman, 41
belonging, sense of, 39, 167
benefit finding, 246
benevolent bias, 161, 163
biased coworker, 157–181
    background on behavior of, 159–163
    characteristics of, 157–158, 255
    company culture and, 170–171
    costs of working with, 166–167
    defensive reactions by, 176
    microaggressions and, 160–163
    motivations of, 163–165
    phrases to use with, 178–179
    questions to ask yourself about,
        167–171
    tactics to try with, 171–181
    See also microaggressions
bias(es), 8
    about underestimated groups, 124–125
    affinity, 208–209
    antibias strategies, 171–181
    being aware of own, 208–210, 220
    benevolent, 161, 163
    calling out, 167–171, 177
    cognitive, 206–207
    confirmation, 106, 208, 209, 217
    covert, 160–163
    gender, 133–134, 139, 144–146
    harm caused by, 166–167
    negativity, 35–36

bias(es) (*continued*)
    overconfidence, 119–120
    overt, 164–165
    subtle forms of, 159–160, 166–167
Birch, Alison Hall, 166
Black women, 145, 208
boss
    difficult, 1–2, 4, 14
    escalating conflicts to, 227–229
    insecure, 49–65
    taking credit for others' work, 54
    See also leaders
boundary setting, 97, 224–226
Boyes, Alice, 43, 44
brain
    amygdala, 34–35, 40–41, 44
    impact of conflict on, 31–43
    negativity bias of, 35–36
Brown, Brené, 237
Burey, Jodi-Ann, 53
Burris, Ethan, 52

caring less, 248–249
Chamorro-Premuzic, Tomas, 119–120, 123
Chen, Serena, 52
Chicken Little, 69
Chou, Eileen, 72–73, 81
Chow, Rosalind, 143, 150
Chugh, Dolly, 171, 174
coalition building, 176–177
cognitive abilities, stress and, 5–6
cognitive biases, 206–207
cognitive overload, 41
"command and control" approach, 143, 238
competition, 144–145, 151–152
complainers, 67–68, 69. *See also* pessimist
compliments folder, 63, 246, 249
confidence, 119, 120, 124, 125, 153–154
confirmation bias, 106, 208, 209, 217
conflict
    acknowledging own part in, 47–48
    addressing directly, 114
    escalating to higher ups, 227–229
    impact on brain, 31–43
    quitting due to, 229–231
    reactions to, 5–6, 38–39
    self-care and, 241–251
    workplace, 6–9
    See also difficult people
conflict avoidance, 103

control
    focusing on what you can, 204–205, 220
    increasing feeling of, 242–243
    sense of, 61, 62, 72–73
Cooper, Marianne, 146
Cortina, Lilia, 165
covert bias, 160–163
creativity, impact of negative relationships
    on, 24–25
credit-stealing, 54, 196, 197–198, 199
cult of positivity, 76
curiosity, 217–218, 219, 220
cynicism, 77–78, 80. *See also* pessimist

David, Susan, 234–235
"Debbie Downer," 68
decision-making, 61, 78, 81, 121
defensive pessimism, 70
Derks, Belle, 150
devil's advocate, 78, 210
difficult people
    approaches to avoid with, 233–239
    archetypes of (*see* archetypes)
    changing, 13–14
    disengaging from, 223–226
    documenting transgressions
        of, 226–227
    quitting due to, 2, 229–231
direct approach
    to microaggressions, 169, 170, 175–176
    with passive-aggressive peers, 109, 110
    with political operators, 195–196
    with tormentors, 153, 154
disengagement, 223–226, 248–249
double bind, 104, 189
downward envy, 140–141
Duffy, Michelle, 140
Dutton, Jane, 26–27

ego defensiveness, 52
emotional contagion, 74, 91, 97, 235
emotional disengagement, 248–249
emotional leakage, 234–235
emotional pain, 36–37
emotions
    labeling, 107
    suppressing, 234–235
empathy
    inward, 247–248

lack of, 139–140
using, to see differently,
211–213, 220
envy, 140–141
exclusion, subtle acts of, 160–163,
166–167. *See also* microaggressions
experimentation, 216–217, 220

failure, fear of, 102–103
Fast, Nathanael, 52, 55, 60
favoritism threat, 143
fight-or-flight reaction, 35, 39
flattery, 60–61
"flip it to test it," 125, 210
Floyd, George, 165, 170–171
Frankl, Viktor, 38
frenemies, 28
friendships
best friend at work, 14, 23
with coworkers, 3–4, 20, 22–24
remote work and, 22–23
frustration, venting, 233–234
fundamental attribution error,
206–207

gaslighting, 167
gender, 120, 121, 127, 133–134,
142, 150
gender bias, 133–134, 139, 144–146
gender norms, 161
generational differences, 138, 139, 141
generational envy, 140
generosity, modeling, 199–200
Gielan, Michelle, 69, 224, 249
Gino, Francesca, 121–122
goals
focusing on shared, 151, 154
helping boss to achieve, 58–59
identifying your, 213–214, 220
Goldman-Wetzler, Jennifer, 217
Goleman, Daniel, 35
gossip, 111, 190, 197, 199, 214–216,
220, 243
Grant, Adam, 205
Grant, Heidi, 70, 77, 79, 81, 109
gratitude, expressing, 60–61
Greenwood, Kelly, 11, 246–247
Greer, Lindred, 60, 107
group norms, 113–114

growth mindset, 172, 218
Groysberg, Boris, 230

Halpern, Nancy, 189, 191
Harris, Kamala, 128–129
Heaphy, Emily, 21
Hendriksen, Ellen, 51
Higgins, E. Tory, 70, 102
human resources (HR), taking problems
to, 228
humility, 130–131, 133
hypercompetitive colleagues. *See* political
operator

illegitimate tasks, 138
imposter syndrome, 53, 153
incivility, 24–25, 27, 144, 165, 245
incompetence, 52, 53, 55, 122, 187–188
information sharing, 61, 63, 175–176
inner critic, 33–34
insecure boss, 49–65
background on behavior of, 51–54
being nonthreatening to, 59–60
being objective about, 55–56
characteristics of, 49–50, 254
complimenting, 60
costs of having, 54–55
expressing gratitude and appreciation
for, 60–61
helping to achieve goals, 58–59
phrases to use with, 62
pressures on, 57–58
questions to ask yourself about, 55–57
restoring sense of control to, 60, 63
tactics to try with, 57–65
insecurities, 122–123, 124, 151, 187–188
intelligence, ascription of, 160–161, 163
interpersonal conflict. *See* conflict
interpersonal relationships
impact of, 2–4
importance of, 250–251
interpersonal resilience, 9, 204, 245–247
interruptions
preempting, 126–128, 132
tactfully addressing, 128–129, 132

Jana, Tiffany, 160
job changes, 229–231

job crafting, 225–226
journaling, 244

Kendi, Ibram X., 165
Kets de Vries, Manfred F. R., 89, 90
know-it-all, 117–135
    addressing interruption from,
        128–129, 132
    appreciating contributions of, 126
    asking for facts and data from, 130, 133
    background on behavior of, 118–123
    characteristics of, 117–118, 255
    costs of working with, 123–124
    modeling humility for, 130–131, 133
    phrases to use with, 132–133
    preempting interruptions from,
        126–128, 132
    questions to ask yourself about,
        124–126
    tactics to try with, 126–135

leaders
    preconceptions about, 124–125
    self-doubt in, 52–54
    tormentors, 137–156
    women, 142–146, 150
    See also boss
Lencioni, Patrick, 114
liars, confronting, 196–197, 198

Maner, Jon, 188
mansplaining, 120–121, 127, 132, 133–134
mantras, 241, 250
McKee, Annie, 244
"me against them" mentality,
    210–211, 220
mental health, maintaining your, 241–251
mental space, 38–43
mentors, 138, 150, 154
Merchant, Nilofer, 78
microaggressions, 92, 160–165
    addressing directly, 169, 175–176, 179
    calling out, 167–171, 177
    coalition building to address, 176–177
    costs of, 166–167
    defensiveness about, 176
    emotional response to, 173
    labeling, 174–175

questions to ask yourself about,
    167–171
reporting, 171
responding with question to,
    173–174, 178
sharing information about, 175–176
See also biased coworker
microculture, 244–245
micromanaging, 51, 52, 61
Minuchin, Salvador, 219
motivational focus, 70–71
Murthy, Vivek, 22

naive realism, 206
narcissism, 101, 118–119
Neff, Kristen, 247–248
negative outlook, 69–70, 74, 89. See also
    pessimist
negativity, 67, 68, 76, 81, 83, 91. See also
    pessimist
negativity bias, 35–36
Nelson, Shasta, 3
Nkomo, Stella, 162

office politics, 184–190
    avoiding getting dragged into, 192–193
    corporate culture and, 191
    engaging in, 191–192
    good versus bad, 186–187
    gossip and, 190
    underrepresented groups and, 188–189
    in virtual work environments, 189
    See also political operator
online disinhibition effect, 165
Opie, Tina, 173
optimists, 74, 81, 83
organizational culture, 103, 148–149, 170,
    191, 238
overconfidence bias, 119–120
overfamiliarity, 162, 163
overt bias, 164–165

passive-aggressive peer, 99–116
    avoiding labeling, 107
    background on behavior of, 101–104
    characteristics of, 99–101, 254–255
    conflict avoidance and, 103
    costs of working with, 104–105

fear of failure or rejection and, 102–103
phrases to use with, 112–113
questions to ask yourself about, 105–107
tactics to try with, 107–116
peer pressure, 80–81, 111
people of color
promotions and, 73
self-doubt and, 53
social identity threat and, 142
See also underrepresented groups
Perel, Esther, 3
performance, impact of negative relation-ships on, 24–25
performance reviews, 23, 36, 54–55, 158, 246
perspectives
respecting others', 205–207, 220
viewing from another's, 211–213
pessimist, 67–85
background on behavior of, 69–74
behaviors of, 68, 69, 77
boundary setting with, 224–225
challenging assumptions of, 79–80
characteristics of, 67–68, 254
costs of working with, 74–75
legitimate concerns of, 76
looking at in positive light, 77–78
motivational focus of, 70–71
phrases to use with, 82
power and, 72–73
questions to ask yourself about, 75–77
tactics to try with, 77–85
underlying reasons of, 75–76
See also victim
political operator, 183–201
addressing directly, 195–196
asking for advice, 194–195
background on behavior of, 185–190
characteristics of, 183–185, 256
offering help to, 194, 198
phrases to use with, 198–199
questions to ask yourself about, 190–192
strategies used by, 196–200
tactics to try with, 192–201
Porath, Christine, 24–25, 27, 34, 245
positivity, 83
cult of, 76
leaning into, 80–81

power
changing balance of, 152–153
desire for, 72–73, 188
prejudice, 159, 165, 208. *See also* bias
premature cognitive commitment, 37–38
Pressner, Kristen, 125
prevention-focused people, 70–71
Priesemuth, Manuela, 148–149
principles for getting along
avoiding gossip, 214–216, 220
avoiding "me against them" mentality, 210–211, 220
awareness of own biases, 208–210, 220
being curious, 217–218, 220
experimenting with tactics, 216–217, 220
focusing on what you can control, 204–205, 220
identifying goals, 213–214, 220
respecting others' perspectives, 205–207, 220
using empathy, 211–213, 220
problem-solving pondering, 44
promotion-focused people, 70–71
psychological safety, 106, 167
psychopaths, 52
public accountability, 111–114

"queen bee" trope, 144–146, 150
quitting, 2, 229–231, 237–238

racism, 91, 127, 139, 160, 164, 165
Rattan, Aneeta, 168, 172
reactions, observing your, 38–39
rejection, fear of, 102–103
relationships
ambivalent, 27–28
interpersonal (*see* interpersonal relationships)
negative, 24–28
remote work
biased behavior and, 165
disconnection and, 4
friendships and, 22–23
office politics in, 189
resilience, 9, 22, 23, 204, 245–247
retaliation, 235–236
Roberts, Laura Morgan, 166
ruminations, 33–34, 44
rumors, 216. *See also* gossip

sacrifices, 138, 140, 150, 154, 155
self-care, 241–251
self-compassion, 213, 247–248
self-doubt, 51–54, 56, 63
self-promotion, 193–194, 226–227
sexism, 91, 127, 146
shame, 236–-237
Sheppard, Leah, 144
situation-behavior-impact feedback
    model, 175
Smith, Ella Bell, 162
social identity threat, 142–143
Steele, Claude, 159–160
stress
    brain and, 42
    health impacts of, 26
    impact on cognitive abilities, 5–6
    microaggressions and, 166
    monitoring your, 40–42
    from negative interactions, 9, 20
Su, Amy Jen, 244, 245
Sue, Derald Wing, 160
Sutton, Bob, 228, 229–230, 237, 238

Tawwab, Nedra Glover, 224
tendency for interpersonal victimhood
    (TIV), 89
text-based communication
    misunderstandings with, 4
    not taking bait in, 109–110
therapy, 246–247
tormentor, 137–156
    addressing directly, 153, 154
    avoiding unhealthy competition with,
        151–152
    background on behavior of, 139–143
    changing balance of power with,
        152–153
    characteristics of, 137–139, 255
    costs of working with, 143, 147
    organizational culture and, 148–149
    phrases to use with, 154
    questions to ask yourself about, 147–149
    tactics to try with, 150–156
transgressions, documenting, 226–227
Tulshyan, Ruchika, 53, 166
"two-minute drill," 224

underrepresented groups, 142
    biased coworkers and, 157–181
    microaggressions and, 160–163
    office politics and, 188–189
unhealthy relationships, consequences of,
    24–28
universal values, 236
unproductive approaches, 233–239

values, universal, 236
venting, 243–244
victim, 87–98
    background on behavior of, 89–90
    characteristics of, 87–88, 254
    costs of working with, 90–91
    encouraging to take responsibility,
        94–95
    increasing agency of, 93–94
    offering validation to, 93, 96
    phrases to use with, 96
    questions to ask yourself about, 91–92
    tactics to try with, 92–98
    validity of complaints of, 91–92
victim mentality, 70, 89–90, 97
victim syndrome, 89, 90
virtual work environments. *See* remote
    work

Washington, Ella, 166
Wasserman, Noam, 27
Webb, Caroline, 235
well-being, as priority, 241–251
Williams, Joan, 146, 161
women
    know-it-alls and, 133–134
    mistreatment of, by other women,
        144–146
    office politics and, 188–189
    overconfidence bias and, 120
    "queen bee" trope, 144–146, 150
    social identity threat and, 142
work friends, benefits of, 22–24
work from home. *See* remote work
workplace gossip, 111, 190, 197, 199,
    214–216
work-related stress, 21. *See also* stress

ACKNOWLEDGMENTS

I have a confession. I *love* reading the acknowledgments in a book. Sometimes I'll even turn to them first when I pick up a new book. This minor obsession of mine is in part because I know that the notion of an author sitting in a room alone, writing a book, is rarely a reality. Yes, there are lots of hours staring at a screen by yourself, but there are also endless conversations and check-ins and drafts weighed in on and back-and-forth texts, all of which make the book what it is. There are so many people who influence the end product—often too many to name and several of whom the author probably forgot were even involved.

So, welcome to my favorite part of the book!

First off, thank you to everyone who wrote to me, answered my calls, or filled out surveys sharing their often-painful experiences with their difficult colleagues. These stories, and the vulnerability with which they were shared, pushed my thinking in ways I couldn't conceive of when I first started working on this book.

Even editors need editors! And several of my fellow editors were integral to this process. Kate Adams breathed life into these pages with her sharp editing eye and incredible way with words. Writing a book is a series of tough calls about what to include, what to cut, how to frame something, and Kate was there every step of the way. Nicole Torres supported me in the research on archetypes and provided some well-timed cheerleading early in the process when I had the confidence wobbles. Amanda Kersey asked smart, insightful questions (her superpower) on a very early outline of the archetypes. Holly Forsyth wrestled the mess of endnotes into shape.

Jeff Kehoe, from the first moment I described the book concept to him, believed in it and in me. His calm demeanor and assured guidance saw me through the various "valleys of despair" that many writers experience in the book-writing process.

Thank you to my agent, Giles Anderson, for having my back throughout the (long) book process. When I called to tell him I needed an extension on the manuscript, he told me that I wasn't alone—several of his authors had made similar requests that week! He was patient and kind, and his counsel was just what I needed at critical moments. I feel fortunate to have him on my side.

A huge thank you to Erica Truxler, Alison Beard, Holly Forsyth, Maureen Hoch, Sarah Moughty, and Dagny Dukach for stepping up at crucial moments to give me the space I needed to work on this book. Amy Bernstein gave me some brief and incisive compliments (*her* superpower) when I needed them most. And the entire web team at HBR was understanding and flexible with my schedule as I worked on this book over the last two years. You are the best colleagues I could ask for, and none of the archetypes are based on you, I promise.

I was lucky to already know the Harvard Business Review Press team before I started working on this particular book, and I continue to be impressed with their professionalism, enthusiasm, and dedication: Adi, Alex, Alicyn, Allison, Anne, Brian, Courtney, Dave, Emma, Erika, Felicia, Jen, Jon, Jordan, Julie, Kevin, Lindsey, Melinda, Rick, Sal, Scott, Stephani, Susan, and Victoria.

I'm grateful to all my friends who answered panicked calls, reviewed chapters, gave me invaluable advice, and cheered me along the way: Amy Genser, Amy Jen Su, Ellie Feinglass, Gretchen Anderson, Katherine Bell (who talked me off a metaphorical ledge multiple times), Lisa Freitag (who wrote the tag lines for each of the archetypes), Mark Moskovitz, Megan Poe, Muriel Wilkins, and Ruchika Tulshyan (who was a few months ahead of me in the book process and was always generous with her hard-earned wisdom).

Kelley Boyd (aka "Pants") is not only a lifelong friend and fantastic travel companion but an incredible coworker, and the sole member (besides me!) of the Amy E. Gallo team. Thank you for everything, big and small, that you do for me, our business, and this book.

Last but not least, I am indebted to the people who I consider my family, either because we share genes or because we are close enough that it feels like we do. You all have shown me over and over that we can choose what we want our relationships to be. My mom, Betty Gallo, curated this amazing family for me and my brother, Chris. She showed us that caring about your work is crucial, but caring about people matters even more.

Damion, you never once doubted I could do this, even when *I* did. Harper, you teach me every day what it means to be a thoughtful, kind human being.

I miss you, Dante.

ABOUT THE AUTHOR

AMY GALLO is a workplace expert who frequently writes and speaks about gender, interpersonal dynamics, difficult conversations, feedback, and effective communication. She works with individuals, teams, and organizations in the United States and abroad to help them collaborate, improve how they communicate, and transform their organizational culture to one that supports dissent and debate.

Gallo is the author of the *HBR Guide to Dealing with Conflict,* a how-to book about handling conflict professionally and productively. She has written hundreds of articles for *Harvard Business Review,* where she is a contributing editor. Her writing has been collected in numerous books on a range of topics, from feedback to emotional intelligence to managing others.

For the past three years, Gallo has cohosted HBR's popular *Women at Work* podcast, which examines the struggles and successes of women in the workplace.

Gallo is a sought-after speaker who has delivered keynotes and workshops at hundreds of companies and conferences, including SXSW, the Conferences for Women, the World Economic Forum, the Bill & Melinda Gates Foundation, Google, Deutsche Bank, MetLife, Adobe, and the American Chambers of Commerce in Finland and Sweden. In 2019 she delivered a talk at TEDxBroadway about the positive benefits of conflict.

Gallo is frequently sought out by media outlets for her perspective on workplace dynamics, conflict, and difficult conversations. Her advice has been featured in the *New York Times,* the *Washington Post (The Lily), Fast Company, Marketplace,* and the *Austin American-Statesman.*

She has been a guest on numerous podcasts and radio shows, including HBR's *IdeaCast* and *The Anxious Achiever*, WNYC, the BBC, and ABC (Australian Broadcasting Corporation).

Before working with *Harvard Business Review*, she was a management consultant at Katzenbach Partners, a strategy and organization firm based in New York. She contributed to the firm's research on the "informal organization"—the unofficial networks and communities that govern how people work together in practice.

Gallo is on the faculty of the Emotional Intelligence Coaching Certification program, launched by Daniel Goleman. She has taught at Brown University and the University of Pennsylvania and is a graduate of both Brown and Yale University.

She lives in Providence, Rhode Island, with her husband, daughter, and their dog, Emmet.